THE BEST OF TREASURE HUNT

THE BEST OF TREASURE HUNT

Jean Ashton and Liz Pooley

Based on the Treasure Hunt series.
A Chatsworth Television production for Channel Four.

First published in 1988 by Boxtree Limited

Mapping drawn and produced by the Automobile Association
based on Ordnance Survey maps, with the permission of the
Controller of Her Majesty's Stationery Office. Crown copyright
reserved.
Maps © copyright The Automobile Association.

The publishers wish to thank the English Tourist Board for their
collaboration, and the following sources for the use of
photographs: The British Tourist Authority © Britain on View:
pp 10, 11, 15, 17, 19, 31, 35, 37, 49, 58, 59, 65, 74, 75, 79, 82,
85, 101, 115. The Welsh Tourist Board: pp 8, 12, 17, 18, 21, 22.
Heart of England Tourist Board: pp 23, 26, 66, 68, 69. West
Country Tourist Board: pp 27, 33. South East England Tourist
Board: pp 48, 52. East Anglia Tourist Board: pp 53, 55, 56, 63.
Thames and Chilterns Tourist Board: p 62. East Midlands Tourist
Board: p 72. Yorkshire and Humberside Tourist Board: p 86.
Cumbria Tourist Board: pp 96, 94, 97 (Martin Gallagher); 95, 98
(Ronnie Mullin). Northumbria Tourist Board: pp 105, 107, 109.
Scottish Tourist Board: pp 112, 114, 115, 117, 118, 119, 121,
122, 124, 125. Simon Farrell/Chatsworth Television: pp 14, 29,
30, 34, 38, 40, 41, 46, 50, 60, 77, 78, 81, 84, 99, 102, 104, 108.
Ray Robinson/Chatsworth Television: pp 42, 44, 45, 111. Tim
Laming/Chatsworth Television: pp 89, 90, 91. Sven Arnstein/
Chatsworth Television: p 70.

Front cover photograph: Sven Arnstein.

Designed by Groom and Pickerill
Typeset by Bookworm Typesetting, Manchester
Printed in Italy by Amadeus Spa, Rome,
for Boxtree Limited, 36, Tavistock Street, London WC2E 7PB

British Library Cataloguing in Publication Data

Ashton, Jean
    The best of Treasure Hunt – (A Channel Four book)
    1. Great Britain. Television programmes
    Quiz programmes: Treasure Hunt.
    I. Title II. Pooley, Liz
    791.45'72

ISBN 1–85283–240–1

CONTENTS

Key to Maps

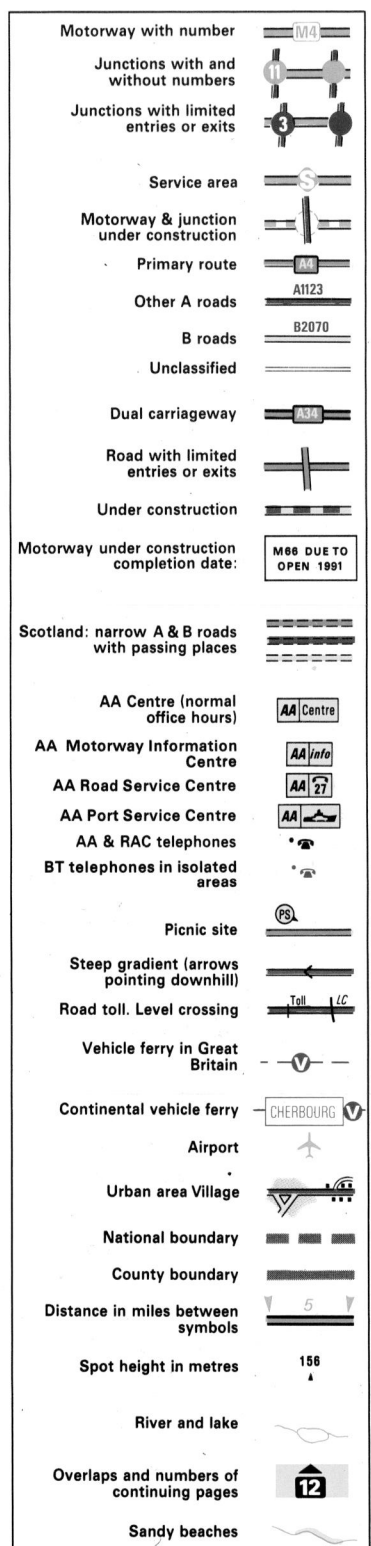

Motorway with number	M4
Junctions with and without numbers	11
Junctions with limited entries or exits	3
Service area	S
Motorway & junction under construction	
Primary route	A4
Other A roads	A1123
B roads	B2070
Unclassified	
Dual carriageway	A34
Road with limited entries or exits	
Under construction	
Motorway under construction completion date:	M66 DUE TO OPEN 1991
Scotland: narrow A & B roads with passing places	
AA Centre (normal office hours)	AA Centre
AA Motorway Information Centre	AA info
AA Road Service Centre	AA 27
AA Port Service Centre	AA
AA & RAC telephones	☎
BT telephones in isolated areas	☎
Picnic site	PS
Steep gradient (arrows pointing downhill)	
Road toll. Level crossing	Toll LC
Vehicle ferry in Great Britain	V
Continental vehicle ferry	CHERBOURG V
Airport	
Urban area Village	
National boundary	
County boundary	
Distance in miles between symbols	5
Spot height in metres	156
River and lake	
Overlaps and numbers of continuing pages	12
Sandy beaches	

⛪	Abbey or Cathedral
	Ruined Abbey or Cathedral
	Castle
	House and Garden
	House
☀	Garden
	Industrial Interest
	Museum or Collection
	Prehistoric Monument
✕	Famous Battle Site
	Preserved Railway or Steam Centre
	Windmill
	Sea Angling
	Coastal Launching Site
	Surfing
	Climbing School
	County Cricket Ground
	Gliding Centre
	Artificial Ski Slope
	Golf Course
	Horse Racing
	Show Jumping/Equestrian Centre
	Motor Racing Circuit
	Cave
	Country Park
	Dolphinarium or Aquarium
	Nature Trail
	Wildlife Park (mammals)
	Wildlife Park (birds)
	Zoo
	Forest Drive
	Lighthouse
i	Tourist Information Centre
i	Tourist Information Centre (summer only)
	Long Distance Footpath
	AA Viewpoint
•	Other Place of Interest
	Boxed symbols indicate tourist attractions in towns

The abbreviation NT used in the text stands for the National Trust. This is a charity, independent of Government. Since 1885 it has worked for the preservation of places of historic interest and natural beauty in England, Wales and Northern Ireland. Send s.a.e. to The National Trust, PO Box 39, Bromley, Kent, BR1 1NH, (Tel:01-464 1111), for membership details.

The abbreviation EH used in the text stands for English Heritage. The English Heritage is a government-sponsored organisation which manages about 400 different historic places in the nation's care. Free admission to all of these is gained through annual membership of the English Heritage. For membership details contact the Memberships Department, Freepost, Bromley, Kent BR1 1BR.

English ✠ Heritage

Introduction

Since 1983, when *Treasure Hunt* first arrived on Channel Four, millions of viewers have become dedicated fans of the show's unique blend of adventure, entertainment and scenic beauty. The only British television series to use helicopters as an integral part of the action, *Treasure Hunt* has taken its audience to some spectacular, and often little known, locations in the UK.

Many viewers watch *Treasure Hunt* for the beauty of the British landscape, shown from the air in all its richness and variety. Other viewers enjoy watching the discovery of the surprises, which are often hidden in elegant stately homes, historic churches and other fascinating places of interest. Some people watch *Treasure Hunt* because they enjoy the challenge of the game and like to test their skill by solving the cryptic clues and 'beating the clock'.

The Best of Treasure Hunt combines all these elements. Cryptic clue enthusiasts will enjoy the first part of each hunt which features the screen clues and their solutions (originally written for the programmes by Anne Evans, the *Treasure Hunt* creative consultant) and two competition clues. We hope that readers will want to pit their wits against the latter and compete for the £1000 prize. In each hunt, this section is followed by descriptions of places of interest around which the original screen hunt was centred. Useful tourist tips and fascinating background information enable this section to be used as a holiday planner and guide book.

The 34 Treasure Hunt routes featured here have been selected for their general interest, scenic value and geographic location. As much of the country as possible has been covered, although limitations on space mean that some areas are under-represented. Still, there is a wealth of material here which can be used to plan exciting holidays throughout Britain.

CHATSWORTH TELEVISION

Enjoying your own treasure hunt or a simple afternoon jaunt into the countryside could not be easier – especially if you know where to go.

There are over 700 Tourist Information Centres (TICs) around the country staffed by experts who are on hand to help you enjoy your visit to the full. Most centres book accommodation and many offer the 'Book a Bed Ahead' (BABA) scheme which enables you to plan your journey as you go. All TICs give local information on attractions, events, entertainment and things to see and do. Many of the larger centres give information on the whole country and offer a holiday planning service. To help find a Tourist Information Centre the English Tourist Board provides a free guide available from Debbie Knight, ETB, Thames Tower, Black's Road, Hammersmith, London, W6 9EL.

If you are entering the *Treasure Hunt* competition (the first prize for which is £1000 cash offered by the Heart of England and English Tourist Board) the local Tourist Information Centres are a good place to start. They won't give you the answers but they might sell you a map! Good luck and happy hunting.

Cumbria Tourist Board	(096 62) 4444
Northumbria Tourist Board	091–384 6905
North West Tourist Board	(0204) 591511
Yorkshire and Humberside Tourist Board	(0904) 707961
Heart of England Tourist Board	(0905) 613132
East Midlands Tourist Board	(0522) 531521/3
Thames and Chilterns Tourist Board	(0993) 778800
East Anglia Tourist Board	(0473) 822922
London Tourist Board	01–730 3450
West Country Tourist Board	(0392) 76351
Southern Tourist Board	(0703) 616027
South East England Tourist Board	(0892) 40766

TREASURE HUNT 1 & 2

North Wales

HUNT 1

START POSITION MYNYDD CILGWYN

CLUE ONE **Towards an ancient fort, use Wynning ways to make hay with the young farmers – and then bale out!**

Leads to GLYNLIFFON COLLEGE   Students are making hay at this agricultural college, a former home of the Wynn family, which is situated by an ancient fort. The clue is on the top of a cart loaded with hay bales.

CLUE TWO **By Segontium to the place where they spin tales of a Constantinople look-alike; peep behind the curtain to find someone who spins a yarn.**

Leads to CAERNARFON CASTLE   Beyond Segontium, the Roman fort, is Caernarfon Castle, whose walls resemble those of Constantinople. The curtain wall encloses the courtyard where a lady sits spinning.

CLUE THREE **Make for Mona's Isle, the seat of a Waterloo hero, and a decorative dining room. Look where the artist is sweeping leaves.**

Leads to PLAS NEWYDD, ANGLESEY   Lord Paget, whose home this was, was second in command at Waterloo. In the Long Dining Room is a *trompe l'oeil* by Whistler in which he himself appears, sweeping leaves. Mona's Isle is, of course, Anglesey.

CLUE FOUR **Keep on the strait and narrow to where Hansom left his cab for jail. But silence in court! Rice is up for sentence.**

Leads to BEAUMARIS COURT HOUSE   Hansom designed the Court House at Beaumaris, on the Menai Strait. A mock trial is taking place, and Anneka is put in the dock.

CLUE FIVE **Bible flowers bloom for the Bishop; but off the pier there's a sporting chance of reaching the stem of Plas Menai's French Daisy.**

Leads to BANGOR PIER   Near Bangor cathedral is the Bible Garden, noted for its collection of every plant mentioned in the Bible. The treasure, a cap, is aboard the yacht 'Marguerite' (a French Daisy) cruising off the pier.

CLUE SIX Down, now, to find a lakeside window. Look in and you will see an interpretation of your surroundings and an illustration of the relationship they have with you. What is the name of this centre?

CLUE SEVEN Arrange a trip for Nordic W.I. to visit the workshop in which elevated ladies, such as princesses and duchesses, were once cut down to size. In which village are you?

The Menai Bridge.

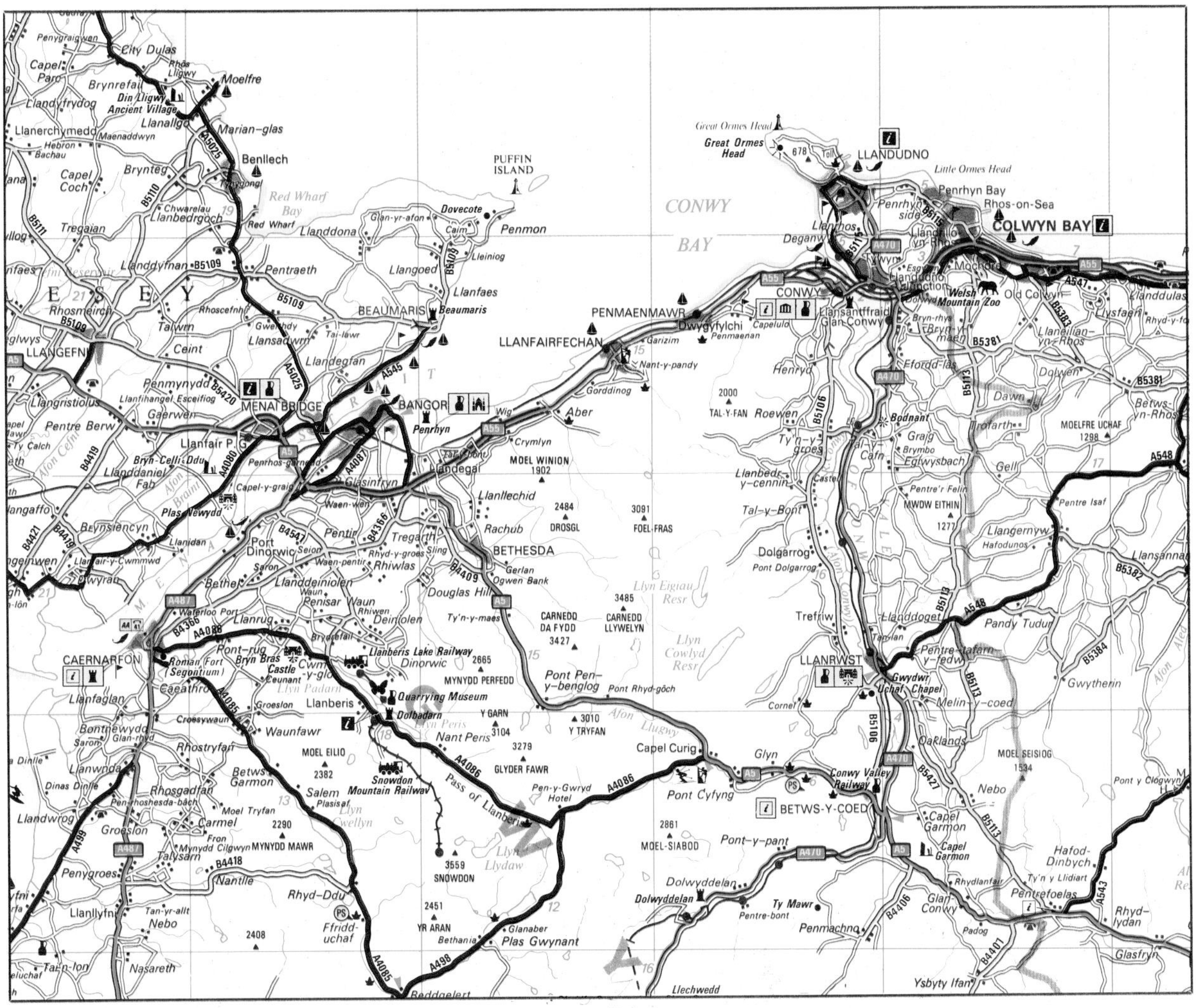

[Map of North Wales region]

Caernarfon Castle

Caernarfon, Gwynedd

Constructed between 1283 and 1330, Caernarfon is one of the noblest examples of medieval military architecture in Britain. Together with Harlech and Conway, it was built by Edward I to hold the rebellious heart of Northern Wales, and to provide a safe residence for government officials and their activities. From the beginning, the castle and the town with its walls and gates were planned and built together under the directions of the Master of the King's Works in Wales, James of St George. By 1285 the building was substantially complete.

Already Caernarfon's historic role had been assured, for the 25 April 1284 had seen the birth here of the baby whom Edward I is said to have presented to local people as the prince 'that was born in Wales, and could speak never a word of English'. The young Edward was formally created Prince of Wales in 1301 and endowed with the rule and revenues of all the Crown's Welsh lands, and in 1969 the castle provided the setting for the Investiture of HRH Prince Charles as the present Prince of Wales. In its early days, Caernarfon was subjected to many attacks, notably by the forces of Madoc ap Llywelyn, a cousin of the last Welsh prince, and Owain Glyndwr, but the accession of the Tudors softened old hostilities and diminished the need for English castles in Wales.

From the sixteenth century onwards the castles were largely neglected, but, despite this, Caernarfon's strength and external appearance remained very much as it was, and the castle was garrisoned for the King and thrice beseiged in the Civil War. In the late nineteenth century extensive repairs were carried out, and today's visitors can admire Caernarfon's mighty walls and towers very much in their original form. The great Eagle Tower houses an exhibition and audio-visual programme entitled 'Heritage of a Nation', the Chamberlain Tower has an arms exhibition, and the North East Tower houses the Prince of Wales Exhibition. The Queen's Tower is the home of the Royal Welsh Fusiliers Regimental Museum.

Guide to opening: all the year. [T] Caernarfon (0286) 3094 for details.

Plas Newydd

Llanfairpwll, Anglesey

Set in parkland and gardens bright with rhododendrons, hydrangeas and a range of exotic shrubs, Plas Newydd enjoys spectacular views of Snowdonia across the waters of the Menai Strait. The house was built mainly in the eighteenth century by

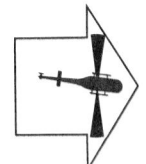

Caernarfon Castle by night.

James Wyatt in the 'Gothick' style, and Humphry Repton designed the layout of the parks and gardens in 1799. The owner at that time was the Earl of Uxbridge, and he was succeeded by his son who was created first Marquess of Anglesey for his heroism at Waterloo, where he lost a leg. Plas Newydd now contains a Cavalry Museum devoted to the relics of his campaigns, including the remains of the trousers he wore at Waterloo together with one of his articulated artificial limbs, the model for other such members sold commercially as 'the Anglesey leg'. Displays also include medals awarded to his son, whose coolness under fire was such that he smoked a cigar throughout the Charge of the Light Brigade.

The rest of the house boasts very fine pictures and pieces of furniture, but the grandest rooms are the Gothick Hall, and the Music Room, which is the largest and most splendid room in the house. The Gothick Hall rises through two storeys with a gallery at one end; its arches and elaborate fan vaulting make it one of the finest late-eighteenth-century interiors to survive in Wyatt's 'Gothick' style. The Rex Whistler Room is, perhaps, more memorable still. The artist was a friend of the family who, in 1937, commis-

sioned him to decorate the dining room in *trompe l'oeil*. For this Whistler produced the most extensive of his murals, which he painted in London on a 58-foot canvas which was then fitted on the main wall, continuing onto the two return walls as far as the fireplaces. The subject was inspired by the room's own view of the Strait, but the artist replaced Welsh woods and farms with Renaissance cities where buildings of every period and style jostle together at the quaysides. What was formally the Billiard Room is now also devoted to Rex Whistler's art, containing a number of portraits together with a selection of his work as a book illustrator, stage designer and decorative artist.

Guide to opening: April to October. [T] Beaumaris (0248) 714795. NT

Beaumaris

Anglesey

Beaumaris derives its name from the Norman *beau marais* meaning beautiful marsh and, with its early

Victorian terraces, half-timbered houses and medieval castle, it is certainly very attractive still.

The castle was the last and largest of those built by Edward I to contain the Welsh, and when it was begun in 1295 no fewer than 400 masons and 2,000 labourers were allocated to the task. Like other Welsh castles it was designed by James of St George, who in this case produced a symmetrical, geometric plan with rings of defences one within the other. Though never completed, its remains are impressive, and visitors can still cross the moat, climb its turrets and explore the passageways within its stone walls. The parish church nearby (containing the coffin of Princess Joan, Llywelyn's wife) was founded soon after the castle, and the town gradually grew up around them both. The oldest surviving domestic building is the Tudor House, built around 1400, followed by the 'Bull's Head' hotel, the headquarters of Cromwell's men when they beseiged the castle in the Civil War. The Courthouse – hiding place for Clue 4 – dates from the early seventeenth century, and is reputed to have been used for one of Judge Jeffrys' famous assizes. Its court is the oldest in Britain still to hear cases, and is open to the public when not in session. The courtroom was renovated in Victorian times, and sentenced prisoners were taken from here to the Gaol, opened in 1829. Now visitors themselves may go 'inside', where the old treadwheel and grim entrance to the scaffold are still on view.

TOURIST INFORMATION

Tourist Information centres: Oriel Pendeitsh, **Caernarfon** [T] (0286) 2232. Oriel Eryri, **Llanberis** [T] (0286) 870765. Station Site, **Llanfair P.G.** [T] (0248) 713177. Coed Cyrnol, **Menai Bridge** [T] (0248) 712626.

- **Bryn Bras Castle, Llanrug.**
- **Dinorwig Power Station & Information Centre, nr Llanberis.**
- **Dolbadarn Castle, nr Llanberis.**
- **Llanberis Lake Railway.**
- **National Museum of Wales Environment Exhibition Centre, Llanberis.**
- **Segontium Roman Fort Museum, Caernarfon.**
- **Seiont 11 Maritime Museum, Caernarfon.**
- **Snowdon Mountain Railway, Llanberis.**
- **Snowdon Pleasure Flights, Dinas Dinlle, Caernarfon.**
- **Sygun Copper Mine, Beddgelert.**
- **Welsh Slate Museum, Llanberis.**
- **Angelsey: Butterfly Palace, Menai Bridge; James Pringle Mill Shop, Llanfairpwll; Museum of Childhood, Beaumaris; Sea Zoo, Brynsiencyn.**

Plas Newydd – Rex Whistler's dining room mural.

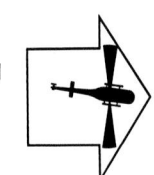

11

HUNT 2

START POSITION WATERFALL NEAR DOLGARROG

CLUE ONE Seawards to the mountain ash alternative and a place where Eliot took young Cyril, to hear a snatch of *bel canto*.

Leads to **ROEWEN CHAPEL** 'Young Cyril' was taken to a chapel by poet T.S. Eliot. Towards the sea is Roewen, which has a chapel. The next clue is sung by the choir.

CLUE TWO They'll keep a welcome for you, Annie,
    At Aberconway's on the hill.
    Look at the lantern bushes glowing
    On a Terrace above a mill.

Leads to **BODNANT GARDENS** The hilly site of Lord Aberconway's garden shows off to perfection many plants, including the *Crinodendron hookerianum* which is likened to Chinese lanterns. The bush which conceals the clue is on a terrace above the pin mill.

CLUE THREE Take to the hills above Pwyllycrochan, make for the anthropoids, wait till the Penny drops.

Leads to **WELSH MOUNTAIN ZOO** The zoo is situated on a hillside above Colwyn Bay. One of its inmates, Penny, the chimp (anthropoid), has the clue. Will she had it over when given a grape?

CLUE FOUR The White Rabbit tells the West Side story; but on the north side Codman's woodentops will deliver the punchline.

Leads to **PUNCH & JUDY SHOW, LLANDUDNO** On the West Shore is a statue of Alice Liddell for whom *Alice in Wonderland* was written. On the north promenade, Mrs Codman's Punch & Judy Show is under way and her puppets have the clue.

CLUE FIVE With one eye to Master James's designs, keep another on the suspenders – there's a golden opportunity there!

Leads to **CONWY SUSPENSION BRIDGE** James of St George, a master mason and military engineer, designed the castle, but there is only one place the suspenders can lead – to the bridge where the treasure, a bunch of golden daffodils, hangs from one of the supports.

CLUE SIX Head back through familiar territory to be drawn by Inigo's three arches to the home of a trail-blazing O.T. translator. Who was he?

CLUE SEVEN Although it sounds like a childrens' crossing, there's not a lollipop lady in sight – just an avian cascade. What is the name of the crossing?

Bodnant Garden.

Bodnant Garden

Tal-y-Cafn, near Colwyn Bay, Clwyd

Situated above the River Conwy with wonderful views across the valley to the Snowdonia range, Bodnant is one of the loveliest and finest gardens in the world. Its development began under Mr Henry Pochin in the late nineteenth century, but it became what it is today under the guiding hand of his grandson (the second Lord Aberconway) who, like his son after him, was President of the Royal Horticultural Society for many years. The garden is everything its pedigree would suggest. Its 70 acres are divided mainly into two parts, the upper part around the house consisting of informal lawns shaded by trees, and a series of superb Terrace Gardens. These include the Rose Terrace, the Lily Terrace, the Canal Terrace which features an open-air stage with wings and background of clipped yew, and an early-eighteenth-century garden house known as the Pin Mill. The lower part of the garden, known as The Dell, is formed by the valley of a tributary of the Conwy and contains the Pinetum and Wild Garden. Reached via the Rock Garden, The Dell is an idyllic place of colourful shrubs and noble trees reaching down to a pretty little river with attendant bridges, waterfalls and ponds, all focusing on a lovely Old Mill.

Together, these formal and informal gardens contain a vast collection of plants which ensure colour and interest all the year round. March and April bring a mass of daffodils and other bulbs; Rhododendrons, Magnolias, Camellias and other shrubs are in bloom from March until the end of June; the famous Laburnum Arch, near the Visitors' Entrance, is at its best at the end of May; and azaleas provide a mass of colour in May and June. The Terrace Gardens are at *their* best in the summer months, and August and September bring a blaze of Autumn glory.

Guide to opening: March to October; Bodnant Garden Nursery, all the year round. [T] Colwyn Bay (0492) 650460. NT

Welsh Mountain Zoo and Gardens

Colwyn Bay, Clwyd

The zoo is set in informal gardens originally designed by Sir Thomas Mawson, the eminent Victorian landscape architect, and occupies a 37-acre site which affords panoramic views of Snowdonia, the Conwy Valley, Anglesey and the North Wales coast. As far as possible the animals are housed in attractive natural settings among the gardens and woodlands, where residents include elephants, lions, leopards, bears, monkeys, chimpanzees, deer, ostriches, flamingoes, penguins and many other species. In addition there is a Reptile House and Crocodile Beach, Tropical Houses and a Children's Zoo. The woodlands here are laid out with nature trails as well as a brand new Jungle Adventure Trail and Tarzan Trail. This superb complex of play and activity equipment is the biggest of its kind in Wales, and provides enormous fun for all ages. Next door to it is a picnic and viewing area, restaurant, bar and café. The zoo also stages its own 'special events' in the form of popular displays: colourful macaws and parrots put on a special show; Sealion Feeding and Training Displays take place four times a day; and, weather permitting, eagles are released to fly completely free. Swooping and soaring against the mountain scenery, the eagles make a particularly spectacular sight.

Guide to opening: all the year. [T] Colwyn Bay (0429) 532938.

Llandudno

Gwynedd

The largest resort in Wales occupies one of the loveliest settings of any seaside town in the country. It lies on a sweeping bay of safe, sandy beaches flanked by the giant limestone headlands of the Great and Little Orme and backed by the towering mountains of Snowdonia. The resort was purpose-built by the Mostyn family in the mid-nineteenth century and has elegant, Victorian buildings to prove it. Though uncommercialised, its 3-mile promenade is busy with holiday pastimes and attractions such as a children's funland, paddling and boating pools, boat trips, pony rides and donkeys on the beach. As shown on *Treasure Hunt*, Punch and Judy stage their knock-about act opposite the Victorian pier, one of the very finest in Britain. Llandudno's sheltered bay offers ideal conditions for watersports and facilities on dry land provide for tennis, bowling, riding and golf, together with dry-skiing and tobogganing on the slopes of the Great Orme. At 679 feet high, this is one of the resort's largest attractions in every sense of the word.

Holidaymakers can follow the 4½-mile Marine Drive around the foot of the Great Orme, walk to the top through the gardens of Happy Valley, ride up on a tram, or take the Cabin Lift which provides the longest aerial cable car ride in Britain. This local landmark is now protected as a Country Park and Nature Reserve and there is a new interpretive centre on its summit, devoted to the history, wildlife and vegetation of the area. Back in town, places of interest include the Mostyn Art Gallery, the Doll Museum and Model Railway, the Dungeon horror waxworks and the Rabbit Hole, a grotto-style 'Alice in Wonderland' exhibition which pays tribute to the fact that Lewis Carroll stayed here with the Liddells, whose daughter Alice inspired the classic stories.

Conwy

Gwynedd

As at Caernarfon, Conwy's castle and town walls were built together and designed by James St George. When they were completed in 1289, the castle could

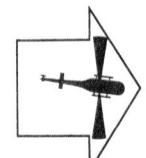

13

claim to be one of the finest in Wales, with barbicans at either end, and eight almost identical towers. Like most Welsh castles, it is the scene of many historic events: Edward I was beseiged here in 1290, and it was at Conwy that Richard II surrendered to Henry Bolingbroke in 1399; in 1646 the castle held out for three months against Cromwell's army, but at the restoration it was given to the Earl of Conwy who dismantled it for its iron, timber and lead. This destruction gained him nothing, for the ship carrying the spoils was wrecked at sea.

Like the external appearance of the castle, the walls have changed little since they were built; over ¾ mile in length, with 21 towers and 3 gateways, they are now the finest of their kind in Britain. Places of interest within their circuit include sixteenth-century Plas Mawr, home of the Royal Cambrian Academy of Art, the medieval house Aberconwy built

in 1500 and now owned by the National Trust, and the Conwy Visitor centre, a good place to start any exploration of the town.

Outside the walls, on the old quay, is a house reputed to be the smallest in Britain, furnished as a mid-Victorian Welsh cottage. Pedestrians still approach the castle across Thomas Telford's elegant suspension bridge. Built between 1822 and 1826, it has a span of 327 feet, and its supporting towers, designed like medieval battlements, are in perfect keeping with its setting. The bridge retains its original iron chains, thought to have escaped corrosion by having been dipped in linseed oil during manufacture. Thomas Telford's best-known engineering feat is also here in Wales: the Menai Suspension Bridge which links Anglesey with the mainland was the first big iron suspension bridge in the world, and one of the great monuments of the Industrial Revolution.

TOURIST INFORMATION

Tourist Information Centres: Theatr Gwynedd, **Bangor** [T] (0248) 352786. Royal Oak Stables, **Betws-y-Coed** [T] (06902) 426/665. 77 Conwy Road, **Colwyn Bay** [T] (0492) 531731. Castle Street, **Conwy** [T] (0492) 592248. Chapel Street, **Llandudno** [T] (0492) 76413.

- **Bangor Cathedral.**
- **Conwy Valley Railway Museum, nr Betws-y-Coed.**

- **Gwydir Uchaf seventeenth-century chapel, nr Llanrwst.**
- **Llandudno Doll Museum & Model Railway.**
- **Motor Museum, Betws-y-Coed.**
- **Museum of Welsh Antiquities, Bangor.**
- **Penmachno Woollen Mill, nr Betws-y-Coed.**
- **Penrhyn Castle, nr Bangor.**
- **Treborth Botanical Gardens, Bangor.**
- **Trefriw Woollen Mill.**

Skyrunner beside Conwy bridge and castle.

TREASURE HUNT 3

Mid Wales

START POSITION DOVEY ESTUARY

CLUE *ONE* Cross the Bells of Aberdovey to where they survive on burgees and notepaper. Your clue is on the notice board.

Leads to **THE YACHT CLUB AT ABERDOVEY**   Legend has it that the Bells can be heard ringing under the sea; their picture is incorporated in the Yacht Club's emblem which appears on its burgee (flag) and notepaper. The clue is on the Club notice board.

CLUE *TWO* If you can catch the little puffer the driver will give you a danger signal.

Leads to **DOLGOCH STATION**   On the Talyllyn Railway, the little puffer is on its way from Brynglass to Dolgoch. After a helicopter chase to the station, Annie gets a red flag (the danger signal) and the clue from the train driver.

CLUE *THREE* No sea for the cormorants at this rock nowadays; but they don't seem to have noticed! When you find them, the clue is in the wall that stops access to the road and the scree.

Leads to **BIRD ROCK**   This inland 'island' once stood at the head of the sea inlet; it is still home for a colony of cormorants. The clue is hidden in a crevice in the wall.

CLUE *FOUR* Lower than 2927 feet, there is a reputedly bottomless lake. On its rim, a boulder with a patch of white quartz enables you to fish up the treasure that might have been mined in Wales, but wasn't.

Leads to **CADER IDRIS**   South of Cader Idris (height 2927 feet) is Llyn Cau. On its bank is a boulder containing veins of white quartz, and a golden nugget gleams in the water below. Gold was once mined in Wales.

CLUE *FIVE* Among the windmills and solar panels, wash your hands in the pink basin before milking a goat in the smallholding. Half a glass will do!

Leads to **CENTRE FOR ALTERNATIVE TECHNOLOGY**   Windmills and solar panels provide the power at this Centre at Llwyngwern Quarry. Having washed her hands, as instructed, in the pink basin, Annie has to find a goat in the smallholding and collect half a glass of milk – some treasure!

CLUE *SIX* Near the clock tower in Owen's capital place, a link with the future Henry VII will take you to the oldest house in town. What is it called?

CLUE *SEVEN* It's a fair way to Mr McDougall's old estate. When you arrive, you have a choice to make. You say 'no' to steam, so what flighty trip do you take?

Cader Idris – view from Afon Mawddach.

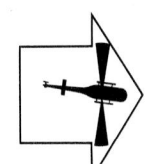

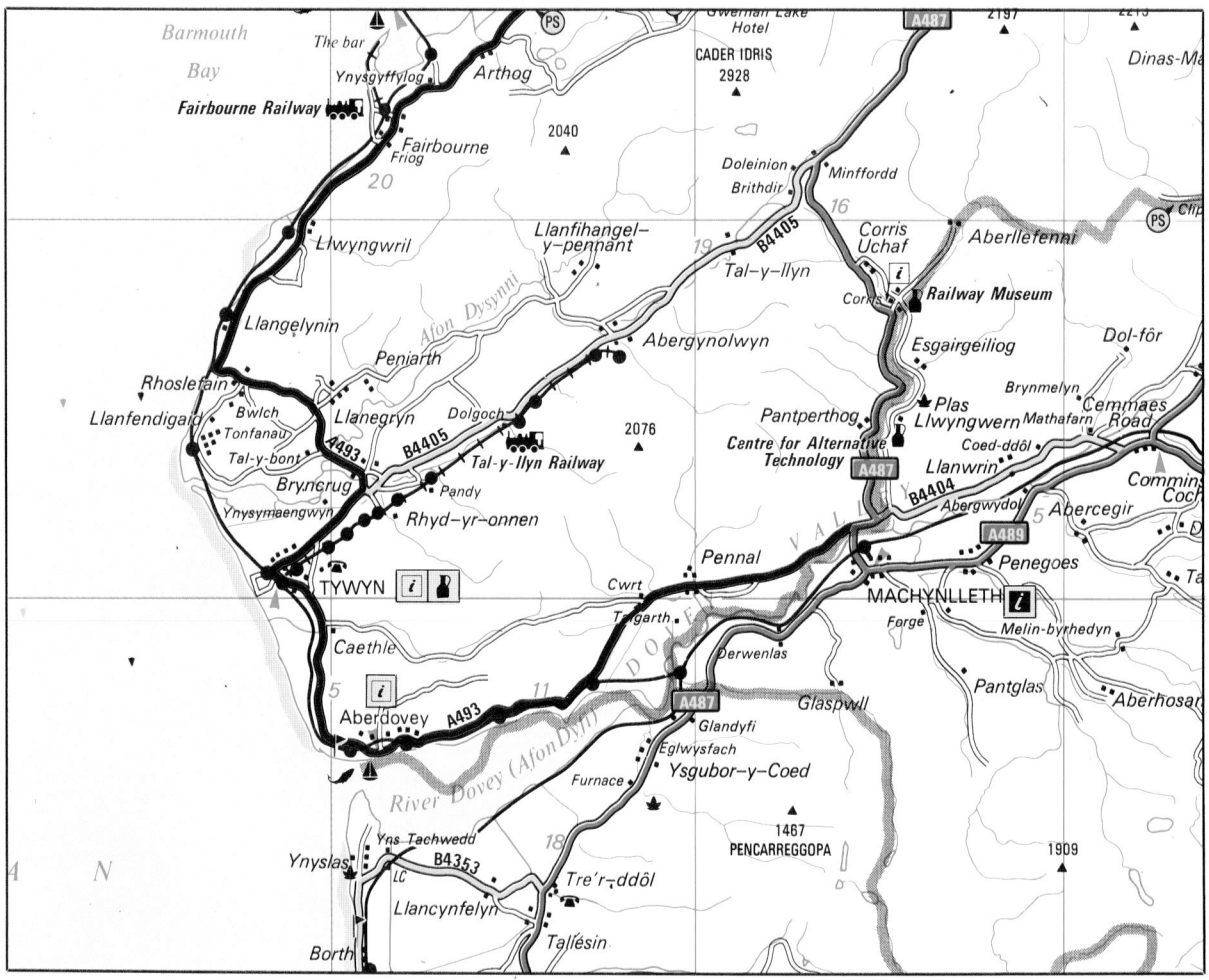

Aberdovey

Gwynedd

This picturesque harbour village lies on the edge of the Snowdonia National Park and the estuary of the River Dovey. The sheltered waters of the estuary are a haven for yachting, canoeing, waterskiing and windsurfing and, as Treasure Hunters discovered, the Yacht Club is one of the main centres of activity here. Holidaymakers can take to the water too; boats are available for hire together with any tuition required, and scheduled trips operate on the River Dovey, which is also famous for its salmon and trout fishing. Facing south and sheltered by a horseshoe of hills, Aberdovey's sandy beaches and dunes are a popular children's playground, and facilities for tennis and bowling, and an 18-hole golf course provide recreation for adults too. There is also a pony trekking centre here, and an Outward Bound Centre offering residential courses in canoeing, sailing, mountain craft, rock climbing and camping.

The village is a great walking centre; many visitors head for Cader Idris via Cwm Meathlon in Happy Valley, where the hoof prints of King Arthur's horse are still visible, marking the point from which he leapt – and cleared – the Dovey Estuary! But 'The Bells of Aberdovey' make the best known legend here. Although the famous song first appeared in an eighteenth-century Drury Lane show called 'Liberty Hall', the legend itself is considerably older than that; tradition insists that a lonely kingdom which stood in Cardigan Bay was engulfed by the sea 1500 years ago, and that on summer evenings the bells of the town still chime faintly from the deep.

Talyllyn Railway

Twywn, Gwynedd

One of the 'Great Little Trains of Wales', the Talyllyn Railway begins 4 miles from Aberdovey at the coastal resort of Twywn. It was built in 1866 to bring slate down the mountain from the Bryn Eglwys quarry and to take quarrymen to and from work, and it was soon carrying passengers for pleasure too. The quarry closed in 1946, but demand by holidaymakers kept the line open, and in 1951 it was taken over by the Talyllyn Railway Preservation Society and became the first railway in the world to be run by volunteers. Now steam engines and carriages, about half the size of those on the main line, run on this 7¼-mile narrow-gauge track which takes is passengers close to the foot of the Cader Idris range.

Train times usually tie in with the British Rail service to Tywyn, and although the complete round trip takes nearly two hours many people break the journey to enjoy the countryside along the way. Pendre, the first station on the line, serves the workshops and sheds where the rolling stock is rebuilt and repaired; Cynfal Halt lets passengers off to explore the ancient earthworks at Bryn-y-Castell; mountain walks lead from Brynglas to the summit of Trum-Gelli (1743 feet), and beyond Abergynolwyn, the train skirts a wooded gorge to reach the Nant Gwernol terminus, the start of several award-winning, waymarked forest walks. Dolgoch, featured in *Treasure Hunt*, is one of the highlights of the trip. The train approaches the station across a 51-foot viaduct spanning the gorge and Dolgoch stream, and passengers alight to explore the Lower, Middle and Upper Falls, which produce a particularly impressive display after heavy rain.

The Narrow Gauge Railway Museum at Tywyn provides an interesting introduction to the line; exhibits include a display of narrow gauge locomotives, wagons and signals and a host of other items rescued from the breaker's torch.

Guide to opening: trains run from Easter to the end of October, and at Christmas. [T] Tywyn (0654) 711297 for details.

Talyllyn Narrow Gauge Railway.

Bird Rock

Near Twywn, Gwynedd

The huge buttress of Craig yr Aderyn (Bird Rock) lies just inland from Twny, on the River Dysynni. It once stood at the head of a sea inlet, but that has long since silted up, and the great rock now looks down on hay meadows instead. However, old habits die hard, and this craggy pinnacle is still a nesting place for seabirds; a colony of cormorants share the rock with chough, jackdaw, kestrel, stock dove – and a flock of feral goats! The rock can be reached easily from the road, and also provides a goal for walkers leaving the Talyllyn Railway at Dolgoch Falls station.

Cader Idris

Gwynedd

Cader Idris is a walkers' mountain in the southern part of the Snowdonia National Park. Its name means Idris's Chair for according to legend, Idris the giant would sit on its summit to study the stars. That summit, 2,927 feet high, now acts as a magnet to walkers who approach it by three main routes. The north approach from Ty Nant is known as the Pony Path; walkers join the western path at Llanfihangel-y-Pennat; while the Minffordd Path starts its 2,700 foot climb at Talyllyn – it is this approach which skirts Llyn Cau, a 'bottomless' glaciated lake in a dramatic amphitheatre setting. A large part of Cader Idris is now a National Nature Reserve of particular geological importance, and its summit also rewards walkers and climbers with extensive views along the coast of Cardigan Bay to Snowdon and Plynlimon. Yet no-one should linger here too long; local folklore warns that anyone who spends the night at the top of Cader Idris risks waking up as a lunatic or a poet – if they wake up at all!

Centre for Alternative Technology

Machynlleth, Powys

This award-winning 'village of the future' is sited in an old slate quarry overlooking the Snowdonia National Park. It is not a museum, but rather a living and working community practising technologies which offer an alternative to those currently destroying man's environment. Its aim is to demonstrate the possibilities of renewable technologies which save resources and cut waste and pollution. One of the chief among them is solar energy, and exhibits here include a solar-heated cottage and exhibition hall, together with numerous types of DIY solar panels available commercially for domestic use. Every 'alternative' means of producing power is explored: there are working windmills and aerogenerators, water turbines and a DIY watermill, and a woodgas generator and steam engine demonstrate the energy available from plants and trees.

Organic food is another major theme here; the Organic Vegetable Garden produces healthy food

Centre for Alternative Technology, Machynlleth.

free of artificial additives, and there are a number of special displays on such subjects as composting, rotation and life in the soil. The Ecological Gardening Display shows how to make a garden attractive to wildlife, and the woodlands illustrate treeplanting and coppice crafts. There is also a 10-acre small-holding supporting ducks, goats and chickens and demonstrating nutrient recycling with composts.

The Centre caters for young visitors too, with a maze, adventure playground and play area. The bookshop sells over 1,000 publications including many DIY plans, and short residential courses are available on many practical themes. The Restaurant serves vegetarian and organic food, and the Centre also has a wholefood shop and café in Machynlleth itself.

Guide to opening: all the year. [T] Machynlleth (0654) 2400 for details.

TOURIST INFORMATION

Tourist Information Centres: The Wharf, **Aberdovey** [T] (0654 72) 321. Craft Centre, **Corris** [T] (0654 73) 343. Canolfan Owain Glyndwr, **Machynlleth** [T] (0654) 2401. High Street, **Tywyn** [T] (0654) 710070.

- **Borth Livestock Centre.**
- **Castell y Bere, nr Abergynolwyn.**
- **Corris Craft Centre.**
- **Dyfi Furnace Restored Oil Smelter, nr Borth.**
- **Fairbourne & Barmouth Railway & Butterfly Safari.**
- **Felin Crewi seventeenth-century Watermill, Penegoes.**
- **Holgates Honey Farm, Tywyn.**
- **Religious Life Museum, Tre'rddol, nr Borth.**
- **Royal Society for the Protection of Birds Interpretation Centre, Ynys-Hir, nr Borth.**

TREASURE HUNT 4

Pembrokeshire

START POSITION Elegug Stack

CLUE ONE Ahead, where the courteous knight of the Round Table changed his name, get a rundown on his hermitage.

Leads to **ST GOVAN'S CHAPEL** Set into the cliff at St Govan's (Sir Gawain) Head is this tiny chapel, reached by a long flight of stone steps. The clue hangs from a window.

CLUE TWO Where Strongbow held sway over Wogan, use Harry's place to reach Jack.

Leads to **PEMBROKE CASTLE** Richard Strongbow was Earl of Pembroke, and Wogan Cavern is entered from inside Pembroke Castle. Henry VII was born here, and it is through his tower that Annie has to run to reach the clue, which is attached to the Union Jack on the gate house.

CLUE THREE From the quay between a Nesting-place and the big cat's port, barge ahead to raise the 5-ton sinker.

Leads to **LAWRENNY QUAY** Between Port Lion and Carew Castle, one-time home of Princess Nest, is Lawrenny Quay. In the river, men are operating the sinker, which is hanging from twin barges. Annie takes a boat trip to reach the clue.

CLUE FOUR Nurse points the way to the park where an aquiline sweetheart got the message at a jess rehearsal.

Leads to **MANOR HOUSE LEISURE PARK** North east of St Florence (Nightingale) is this Leisure Park, home of Sweetheart, an eagle. When called, he lands on Annie's arm and she detaches the clue from his jesses.

CLUE FIVE This place had no equals before Recorded time. Perseverance by the jetty should bring in a net profit.

Leads to **TENBY HARBOUR** Mathematician Robert Record, inventor of the '=' sign, is commemorated in a medallion portrait in St Mary's Church. In the harbour is the fishing boat, 'Perseverance', and in one of its nets, the treasure, a gold fish.

CLUE SIX Could it be the heady perfume of gorse and lavender, or maybe the aroma from the chocolate factory, that has caused the stone spire of this church to lean so far from the perpendicular? After which saint is the church named?

CLUE SEVEN Probably Wales' most celebrated tourist, this distinguished son of Pembrokeshire set foot in many places. Where, though, would he have taken his first, hesitant steps?

The harbour, Tenby.

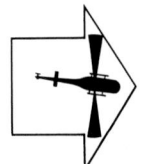

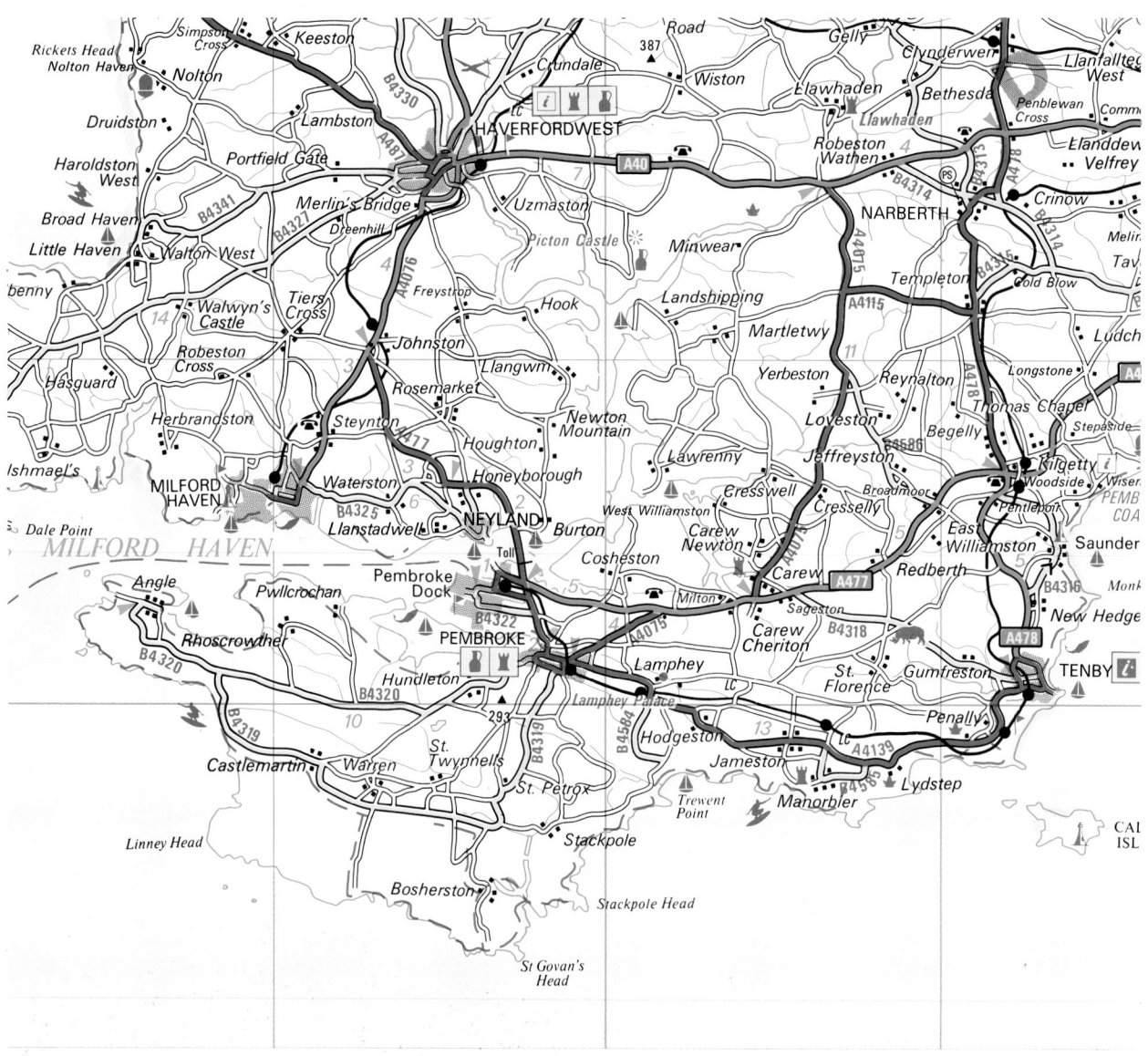

St Govan's Chapel

Near Bosherston, Dyfed

Reached by steep and narrow steps, this simple stone building huddles against the rocks, half way down the cliff at St Govan's Head. The tiny chapel is thought to date from the thirteenth century, but some evidence suggests that its altar was cut into the stone much earlier. Tradition maintains that Sir Gawain of the Round Table came here as a hermit after King Arthur's death, and certainly the spell cast by this romantic site does little to spoil the story. Another claim is more easily put to the test: it is supposedly impossible to count the steps in both directions and arrive at the same total.

Half a mile west of St Govan's head is the 130-foot cleft in the cliffs known as Huntsman's Leap; it is said that a horseman once cleared the gap at full gallop, only to die of shock when he realised his feat. A spectacular cliff-top walk leads to Elegug Stack, the starting point for this Hunt, which is a massive limestone pillar and breeding ground for seabirds.

Pembroke Castle

Dyfed,

Pembroke's massive castle dominates the river approach to the town. In its day it was one of the largest and strongest fortresses in the kingdom, and it is very impressive still. The site was fortified by the Normans against the Welsh in 1093, and one of its earliest custodians was Gerald de Windsor who married the beautiful Welsh Princess Nest, the 'Helen of Wales'. In 1138 the king created the Earldom of Pembroke, and until the time of Henry VIII successive Earls were all-powerful throughout the county. One of the greatest of them was Richard Strongbow, who used Pembroke as a base from which to conquer Ireland, and it was his successors, the Marshalls, who gave the castle much of its present form.

The Great Keep came first, 100 feet high, the walls 19 feet thick at the base and capped with a great stone dome; the Norman Hall was built between 1189 and 1219, and the Northern Hall followed between 1245 and 1265. Both are built over the

Wogan Cavern, an enormous limestone cave unparalleled in other British castles. From 1272–96 the town walls were begun, and the castle gained its Outer Ward with its mighty towers and gatehouse.

In 1453 Henry VI made his half-brother Jasper Tudor (son of Welshman Owain Tudor) Earl of Pembroke, and Jasper's elder brother, Edmund, became Earl of Richmond. Edmund's wife came to Pembroke during the Wars of the Roses, and it was here that she gave birth to the first Tudor King, Henry VII, in the room still on show in the Henry VII Tower. In the Civil War of 1642 Pembroke was the only Welsh town to declare for parliament, and the Mayor, John Poyer held the castle against the royalists, but in 1648 he declared for the King, and a bitter seige began. When the castle finally surrendered to Cromwell, Poyer and his two main associates were tried in London and condemned to be shot, but by some curious freak the prisoners were told they should draw lots to decide their fate. Death fell to the lot of Poyer, who was duly shot. Pembroke Castle suffered too; in 1649 Cromwell ordered it to be destroyed, and it remained derelict until 1880, when it was largely restored.

Guide to opening: all the year. [T] Pembroke (0646) 684585 for details.

St Govan's Chapel.

Pembroke Castle.

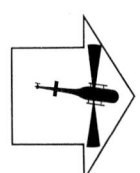

Manor House Wildlife and Leisure Park

St Florence, Tenby, Dyfed

This eighteenth-century manor house and its 12 acres of well-kept grounds provide very pleasant surroundings for the wildlife and other attractions here. Trees and wild flowers form a contrast to the award-winning ornamental displays in more formal gardens, and from spring to autumn there is a rich variety of colour throughout the grounds. Lawns provide the setting for the Falconry Displays which are particularly popular here, and other birds of prey such as buzzards, kites, kestrels, hawks and eagles are also on view together with rare and beautiful snowy owls. More birds have made themselves at home in the original Walled Gardens of the manor; these include penguins, parrots and pheasants, who share the garden with otters, porcupines, mongooses, an aquarium of tropical fish plus rare and exotic snakes and reptiles from all over the world.

Larger creatures needing larger paddocks find themselves in the woodlands; inmates here include emus, deer, wallabies, llamas, Shetland ponies, donkeys and Pigmy goats. Not all the attractions here are animal; the Children's Play Area offers radio-controlled boats and go-karts, a giant Astraglide slide, swings, roundabouts and a motorised go-kart track suitable for children aged 8 to 80. The same could be said of the indoor Model Railway which presents a large display of British and Continental passenger and goods trains, each operating against a suitable scenic background. The manor house itself is now open as a restaurant/snack bar and bar.

Guide to opening: Easter to September. [T] Carew (064 67) 201.

Tenby

Dyfed

An ancient town of character, Tenby is so much more than a popular seaside resort. Much of the town stands within sturdy limestone walls built in the thirteenth century and increased in height against the coming of the Armada; the great 'Five Arches' (the original west gate) is still a famous Tenby landmark. Another notable landmark is St Mary's church, rebuilt and extended in 1245 to become the largest parish church in Wales; this is the heart of the old town where narrow streets and alleyways offer a wide choice of restaurants and interesting shops.

Sooner or later all paths lead to the sea and to the two stunning, sandy beaches. These are backed by cliffs topped with Georgian terraces dating from the early nineteenth century when Tenby was first 'discovered' as a resort, and with fine hotels which were once the homes of the Victorian gentry; one of these (the Belgrade Hotel) incorporates the house where the artist Augustus John was born. The great beaches themselves almost meet at the high grassy headland of Castle Hill. Thrust out into the sea, this panoramic spot bears the remains of Tenby Castle

The flamingoes at Manor House Park.

together with the old watch tower, the excellent Town Museum and a very grand statue of Prince Albert.

Just off the headland is St Catherine's island, with one of the many forts built to protect Milford Haven from an attack by Napolean III which never came. The other side of the hill shelters Tenby's picturesque harbour, now used mainly by pleasure boats. With its tiny 'fishermen's chapel' right on the edge of the sand and its colourwashed Georgian houses, this is a most delightful part of the town. A narrow passageway leads up the side of a yellow house, past the historic Tudor Merchant's House, and emerges at the shop selling perfume and chocolate made by the monks on nearby Caldey Island; the monastery is open to the public (men only), and in the summer boats leave regularly from the harbour below.

TOURIST INFORMATION

Tourist Information Centre: 40 High Street, **Haverfordwest** [T] (0837) 3110. The Croft, **Tenby** [T] (0834) 2402.

- **Caldey Island & Monastery, from Tenby.**
- **Haverfordwest Priory.**
- **Llamphey Palace.**
- **Llawhaden Castle, nr Narberth.**
- **Manorbier Castle.**
- **Narberth Castle.**
- **Oakwood Adventure & Leisure Park, nr Narberth.**
- **Tenby Museum.**
- **Tudor Merchant's House, Tenby.**

THEASUME HUNT 5

Forest of Dean

START POSITION CLEARING IN FOREST OF DEAN

CLUE ONE North east of Simonds Yat is a castle that tried to defy Cromwell in 1646, with a clue in the keep.

Leads to **GOODRICH CASTLE**   The clue is in the entrance to the keep of this castle, which was destroyed by Cromwell's troops.

CLUE TWO Where ironmongers dug till 1946, a goblin left his green beads in a fissure in a cavern.

Leads to **CLEARWELL CAVES**   Near the entrance to the grotto, in this former iron mine, a string of green beads has been tucked away.

CLUE THREE Can it have been Mr Kyrle who said of Ross: 'Every Prospect pleases and only man is vile . . .' and left a clue behind the war memorial?

Leads to **PROSPECT GARDENS, ROSS-ON-WYE**   The Prospect, a public garden, was laid out by John Kyrle. The clue is in the grass behind the war memorial.

CLUE FOUR In the garden behind my birthplace is an odd bird in a summerhouse where the chick in an egg is your treasure.

Leads to **MAN OF ROSS HOUSE**   In the garden of this house, where Kyrle was born, is a swan design, made of horses' teeth. Inside the summerhouse an egg is hidden.

CLUE FIVE Blaize Bailey overlooks vast loops of river. From the viewpoint, up the steps, through the trees, and behind the plan there's an improved view.

Leads to **BLAIZE BAILEY**   Hanging from the map provided at this viewpoint and picnic area on the Forest Drive is the treasure, a telescope.

CLUE SIX Between the Broads, above Saxon remains stands England's oldest known house. At one time the home of the Lords of Dene, where is the forest's 'most haunted house'?

CLUE SEVEN Any eagle-eyed hunter who went to the north east would be lured to this clue. Near which town would he be?

Kyrle's House, Ross-on-Wye.

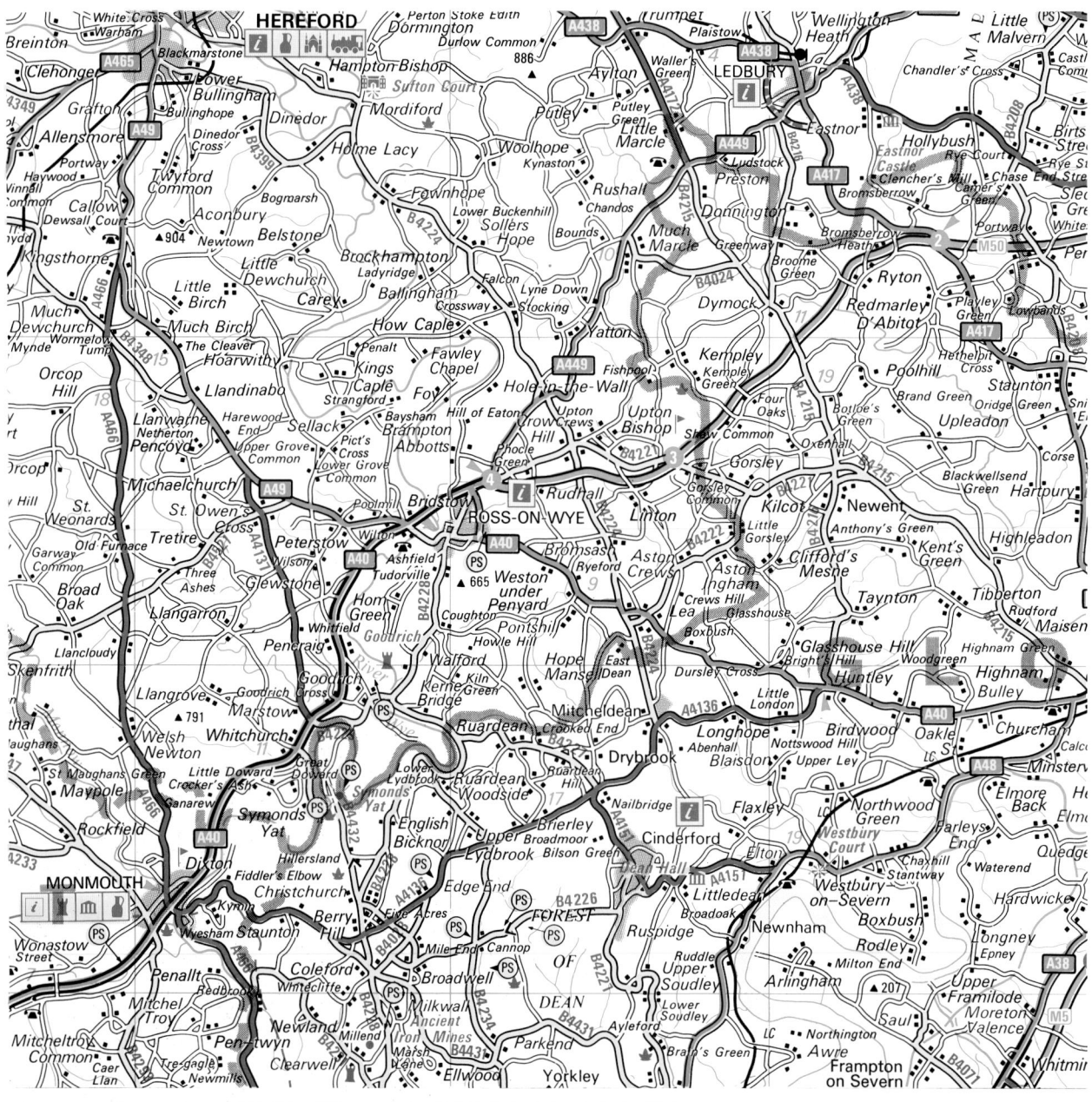

Goodrich Castle

Hereford & Worcester

The ruins of this great sandstone fortress sit high on a spur dominating an important crossing of the River Wye. Records show that a castle existed here as early as 1102, but the magnificent structure seen today was built largely by the Earl of Pembroke in the late thirteenth century as a border stronghold. In the fourteenth century it passed to the Talbots, Earls of Shrewsbury, who owned it for 200 years, but its downfall came in the Civil War, when it held out for the Royalists. Under siege, its south walls were breached by 200-lb cannon balls fired by a locally-made cannon, Roaring Meg (now on show by Hereford cathedral), and when the castle water supply was cut off, the garrison finally surrendered. The castle was then slighted, and has never been restored since. Stern as they are, its ruins have always appealed to romantics; Wordsworth was a frequent visitor, and it was here he met the little girl who inspired his poem 'We are Seven'.

Set behind a deep moat (now dry) and approached via a massive gatehouse tower, it is clear even now that Goodrich must have been one of the most powerful of the non-royal castles. Opposite the gatehouse is the oldest part of the castle, a three-storey Norman keep where high arched windows with stone seats give wonderful views over the valley 100 feet below; also safe inside the courtyard is the 65-foot great hall with an early example of a walled fireplace, and separated from the dais end of the hall by a small vestibule is the solar, with a private chapel above. Adjoining the great hall is the south west tower which housed the buttery and pantry. Between the gatehouse and the south west tower a garderobe block projects from the wall, where three toilets known as 'jakes' drained into the moat. Lime thrown

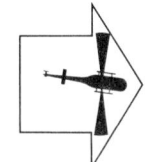

Goodrich Castle.

down toilets was efficient at killing germs and bugs, so people hung their clothes here too – hence the name 'garderobe'.

Guide to opening: all year. [T] Goodrich (0600) 890538 for details. EH

Clearwell Caves

Near Coleford, Gloucestershire

Clearwell Caves are part of a natural cave system which lies beneath the Forest of Dean. The caves partially filled with iron ore, and this was mined extensively for over 2,000 years, creating a vast underground complex with miles of passages and thousands of caves. Eight of the largest caverns are open to the public today. Miners once worked down here by the light of a candle pushed into a ball of clay, which was then attached to a stick called a 'Nelly', held in the mouth to keep both hands free. Prior to 1842, when a law was passed preventing children from working in the mines, the ore was carried up to the surface in boxes known as 'Billies' strapped to the backs of 'Billy boys'. Some of the mines were a formidable 50 feet deep, and sometimes the Billy boys had to make the haul with loads weighing 60 or 70 lb.

Now the caves are lit with electric light, revealing details like the marks of pick axes, pools hollowed out to collect drinking water, and the soot from gunpowder, introduced to the mines in the fifteenth century. Although the skeleton in the Pillar Chamber appeared after a Hallowe'en barbecue held here by students many years ago, visitors may yet meet something spooky in the ghost of an old man dressed in fourteenth-century mining costume, and in the shadowy residents of the Bat Chamber. Back above

Clearwell Caves – ancient iron mine.

It is tucked away on the edge of the Scenic Drive, a signposted circular route which guides motorist through the heart of the Forest. The drive encompasses many superb walks winding amongst new plantations and ancient woodlands that are splendid in their autumn colours and carpeted with bluebells in the spring.

The Scenic Drive also touches on many other attractions. The Dean Heritage Centre is a sensible place to start, for it illustrates the story of the Forest with a reconstructed cottage and mine, working smallholding, a Living Forest exhibition, demonstrations of charcoal burning and other specialist displays. Littledean Hall, with its Saxon cellars, claims to be England's oldest continuously inhabited house, and its 50-acre grounds offer a water garden, Panoramic Walk and Roman remains. The Speech House Arboretum has over 200 fine specimens of trees and shrubs while the Great Western Railway Museum at Coleford is a restored GWR goods station with ticket office, station master's office and a display of model steam locomotives and various railway memorabilia. Nearby Puzzlewood features a 'puzzle path', created out of open-cast iron workings which are now a maze of weather rocks, covered with moss and ferns.

ground, in the Engine House, a variety of vintage engines and mining equipment are on display, including the compressor used to drive the early pneumatic drills. There is also a Miners' Store, and a Miners' Canteen which provided visitors with an added insight to mining life.

Guide to opening: March to October. [T] Dean (0594) 32535 for details.

Ross-on-Wye

Herefordshire

The main touring centre for the Wye valley, Ross-on-Wye stands above a bend in the river looking towards the Welsh hills. Tourists exploring its steep streets of Georgian houses, or the Market Square with its seventeenth-century market hall will sooner or later come across some legacy of local philanthropist, John Kyrle, immortalised by Alexander Pope as 'The Man of Ross'. Born in 1637 he spent most of his long life here, during which he paid for many good works in the town. He introduced a public water supply, built the causeway to Wilton Bridge and restored the church spire, adding its pinnacles. He also laid out The Prospect public gardens (so named because of their wide views) for which the gateway and a special walk in the gardens are dedicated to him. A plaque marks his house (now two shops) in the High Street and in the garden at the back is the design of a swan, laid out in horses' teeth. Both The Prospect and the swan were featured in *Treasure Hunt*.

Blaize Bailey

Near Littledean, Gloucestershire

Blaize Bailey is a picnic site and viewpoint looking down over the River Severn from the Forest of Dean.

TOURIST INFORMATION

Tourist Information Centres: The Library, Belle Vue Road, *Cinderford* [T] (0594) 23184. Market Place, **Coleford** [T] (0594) 36307. Town Hall Annex, St Owen Street, *Hereford* [T] (0432) 268430. St Katherines, High Street, **Ledbury** [T] (0531) 2461. Church Street, **Monmouth** [T] (0600) 3899. 20 Broad Street, **Ross-on-Wye** [T] (0989) 62768.

- **Abbey Dore Court Gardens, Hereford.**
- **Bosbury Vineyards & Gardens, Ledbury.**
- **Eastnor Castle, nr Ledbury.**
- **Frampton Court, Frampton-on-Severn.**
- **Hellen's House, Much Marcle.**
- **Hereford Cathedral, Hereford.**
- **Hereford City Museum & Art Gallery.**
- **Herefordshire Rural Heritage Museum, Hereford.**
- **Herefordshire Waterworks Museum, Hereford.**
- **Hill Court Gardens, Ross-on-Wye.**
- **How Capel Court Gardens, Ross-on-Wye.**
- **Jubilee Maze and Museum of Mazes, Symonds Yat.**
- **Little Malvern Court, Little Malvern.**
- **Museum of Cider, Hereford.**
- **Newent Falconry Centre, Newent.**
- **Newent Butterfly Centre, Newent.**
- **Ryelands House, Taynton.**
- **Sutton Court, nr Hereford.**
- **Three Choirs Vineyard, Newent.**

TREASURE HUNT 6

Cornwall

START POSITION CAPE CORNWALL

CLUE ONE **Use the Elder Brethren's Viking transport to reach Juliet's goodnight setting and a billet-doux by the lantern.**

Leads to **LONGSHIPS LIGHTHOUSE** The Corporation of Trinity House, which maintains the Longships (Viking transport) Lighthouse is run by the Elder Brethren. A balcony (Juliet's goodnight setting) gives access to the lantern (or light) on which the clue (billet-doux) is hidden.

CLUE TWO **Where an Italian masterminded an aerial message, seek out a Greek setting and an Austrian who knows the score.**

Leads to **MINACK THEATRE** Marconi, the Italian physicist and developer of wireless technology, worked at Porthcurno, location of the Greek-style Minack Theatre. A preview of 'Amadeus' is in progress and Mozart has the clue.

CLUE THREE **Where Tom lost Jerry, look in the biggest pot for a dancer in the Mock Turtle's quadrille.**

Leads to **MOUSEHOLE** Tom, the infamous cartoon cat, lost Jerry in a mousehole. Dancers in the Mock Turtle's quadrille (from *Alice in Wonderland*) include a lobster, a pointer to the Lobster Pot restaurant, where the clue is hidden in a display of seafood.

CLUE FOUR **At the lofty link between September 29th and a High Street store, join the chase for a letter-writing duke.**

Leads to **ST MICHAEL'S MOUNT** Michaelmas Day and the Marks & Spencer brand name lead to St Michael's Mount. In the priory's Chevvy Chase room, the clue is hidden behind a portrait of the letter-writing Duke of Albemarle.

CLUE FIVE **A Barbara harbourer, a beach or Leach, and turf by the surf. Get on board for the hoard.**

Leads to **ST IVES** Sculptress Dame Barbara Hepworth and Bernard Leach, the potter, both had studios here. Beyond a golf course is Porthmeor surf beach, from where the treasure (a Jolly Roger) can be reached by surf board.

CLUE SIX A siren call from an eponym's place will lead you to a decorative conclusion. What is its subject?

CLUE SEVEN They're some of the rougher roundures of their year, so would'st thou use thy saucers when supping here?

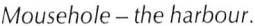

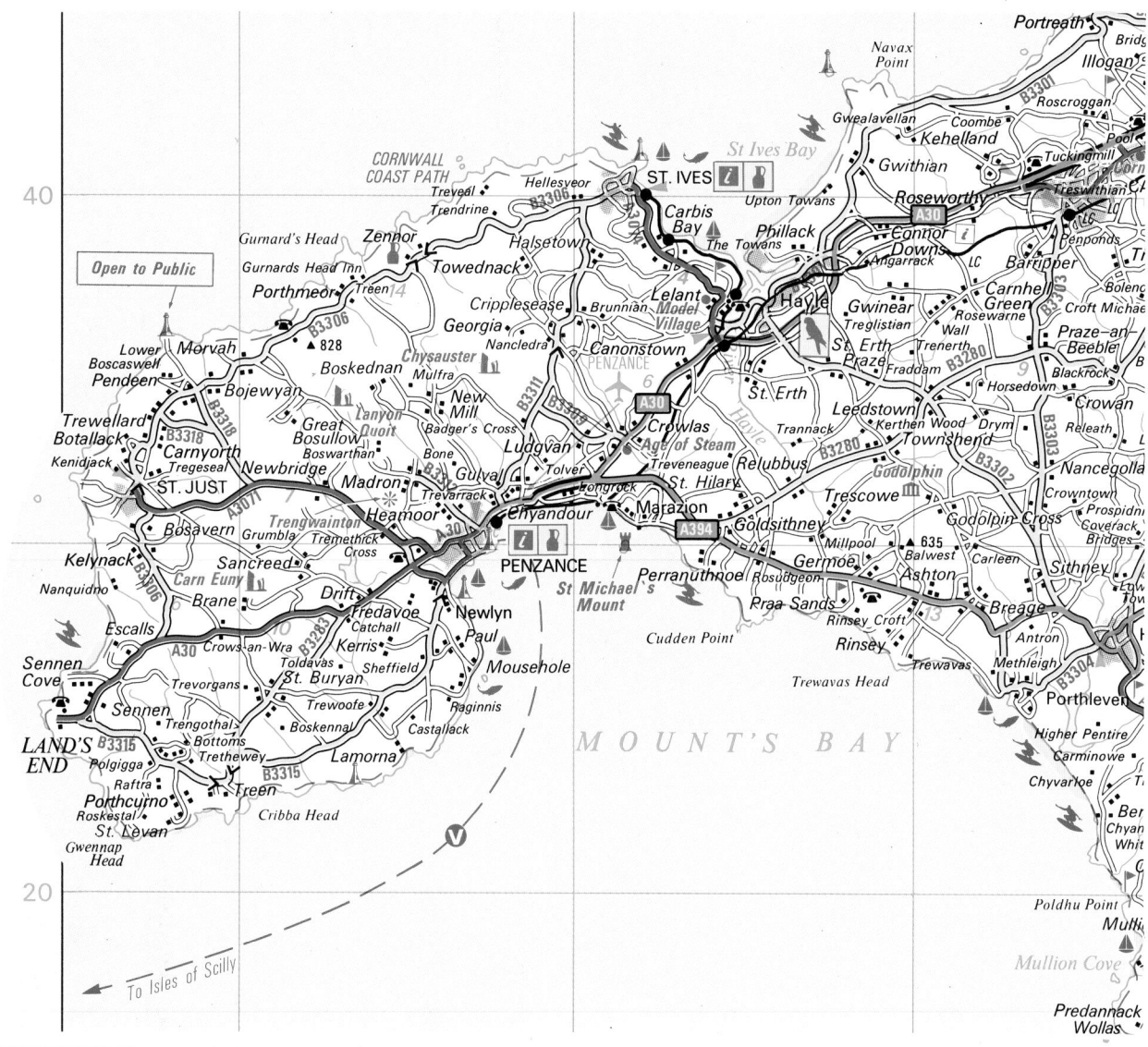

The Land's End Lighthouses

The Longships Lighthouse was the first of many built around this treacherous coast where for centuries many Cornishmen had lived by plundering wrecks. The original Longships was built in 1791 by men issued with special medals to protect them from press gangs. It was manned by four men each paid £30.00 a year to work in pairs, for a month at a stretch, living in primitive conditions. But the sea here was everything John Ruskin later said it to be – 'a dizzy whirl of rushing, writhing, tortured, undirected rage' – and in 1975 the original structure was replaced by the existing version as towering waves were found to engulf the lantern and obscure the light. Few neighbouring lighthouses made a cosier berth; Wolf Rock Lighthouse took its name from the fierce howling of the wind, and in one particularly powerful storm, waves racing up the side of the Bishop Stone Lighthouse tore a 550-lb fog bell from its fastenings at the top.

The Pendeen Lighthouse, established in 1900 and modernised in 1920, offers visitors the chance to learn something of life in a lighthouse at first hand. Reached by car from the village of St Just, it is generally open to the public any afternoon except Sundays, although it is advisable to telephone first to avoid disappointment. [T] Penzance (0736) 788418.

The Minack Theatre

Porthcurno, Penzance

No theatre could wish for a more dramatic site. Perched on Cornwall's granite cliffs, with the sea as a moving backdrop to the stage, Minack's heady, open-air setting and classical design make it unique in the British Isles. Though the style came from the ancient Greeks, Minack found its inspiration at home. In 1928 amateur thespians put on *A Midsummer Night's Dream* in a valley nearby, with local resident Rowena Cade making the fairies' wings. In 1932, when the company asked to produce *The Tempest* on her land, she devised a make-shift stage.

For the next fifty years, working with never more than three helpers, Rowena Cade improved on what she had begun, gradually turning a gorse-filled gully into a well-equipped theatre capable of seating 800 people.

Today the Minack Theatre Season runs from the end of May to mid-September, staging productions of drama and music by visiting companies and defying the elements by cancelling – on average – only three performances a year. Visitors may trace Minack's remarkable story in the new Rowena Cade Centre, and visit the theatre itself, providing no performance is in progress.

Guide to opening: April–October; [T] St Buryan (0736) 810471 for full details. Programme information is obtainable from the above address.

Mousehole

With stone houses set around a small, semi-circular harbour, Mousehole retains the air of a quaint fishing village. Its oldest building is the fifteenth-century Keigwin Arms, the only survivor of a vicious raid in 1597 when 200 Spaniards landed from four galleys, burning buildings and raping women. Despite such set-backs, deep-seated traditions clung on here; Polly Pentreath, buried here in 1777, was thought to be the last native speaker of the ancient Cornish tongue.

The Longships Lighthouse.

The Minack Theatre – Anneka joins a production of 'Amadeus'.

29

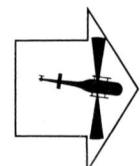

St Michael's Mount

Marazion, near Penzance

In the twelfth century, the Abbot of Normandy's Mont St Michel built a Benedictine priory here on this tiny granite island, which rises like a romantic vision from the bay. At first the site was not blessed with good luck: in 1275 the church collapsed in an earthquake, and 70 years later all but three of the monks died in an outbreak of the Black Death. By the fourteenth century the church had been rebuilt largely as it is today, and services are still held here on Sundays at 11 a.m.

The castle crowning the Mount also dates from the fourteenth century and reflects various styles; of particular interest are the Chevy Chase Room – once the monk's refectory which now sports hunting scenes – and the eighteenth century Blue Drawing Rooms, with fine rococo plasterwork and Chippendale furniture. The castle numbers works by Gainsborough, Kneller and other famous artists among its treasures together with collections of maps, weapons, silver, eighteenth-century clothes and such delightfully diverse items as a cannon salvaged from a French frigate and a model of the Mount carved out of champagne corks by an artistic butler before the war. A tall story centres on the castle's outside wall; legend has it that the marauding giant Cormoran who built the Mount was lured to his death here by the wiles of a local lad, 'Jack the Giant Killer'.

The Mount is owned by the National Trust, and is accessible by causeway at low tide, and by ferry at high tide.

Guide to opening: November – March, guided tours, April – Oct, free flow. [T] Penzance (0736) 710507 for full details. NT

St Ives

Artists and tourists love this picturesque harbour town of narrow streets and attractive cottages. When the pilchard trade declined (75 million were said to have been caught in one day in 1864), painting took its place: James McNeil Whistler and Walter Sickert captured nineteenth-century St Ives on canvas; and painter Ben Nicholson (1894–1982, sculptress Dame Barbara Hepworth (1903–75) and the potter Bernard Leach (1887–1979) established the town as a leading centre of contemporary art. The Leach Pottery still thrives, Barbara Hepworth's home is now a museum and art gallery, and one of her works is in the parish church.

Legends and landmarks here cover intriguing things: the fishermen's chapel of St Nicholas supposedly marks the spot where St Ia landed in his coracle from Ireland in the sixth century. Street names like Teetotal and Salubrious Place reflect Wesley's influence on the town. A hill-top monument commemorates a reformed smuggler, by whose decree two widows and ten little girls dance round it to the music of a fiddle once every five years . . .

TOURIST INFORMATION

Tourist Information Centres: Station Road, **Penzance** [T] (0736) 62341/62207 and The Guildhall, **St Ives** [T] (0736) 797600.

- **Cornucopia & Merlin's Magic Land, Lelant.**
- **Land's End Experience, Sennen.**
- **Paradise Park, Hayle.**
- **Pendeen Crafts & Mining Exhibition.**
- **Penlee House & District Museum, Geevor Mine, Pendeen.**
- **Trengwainton Garden, nr Penzance.**
- **Wayside Folk Museum & Mill, Zennor..**

St Michael's Mount – aerial view.

Avon/Wiltshire

START POSITION LACOCK ABBEY

CLUE ONE Tunnel vision will show the vessel of Guinevere's king. Watch out for obstacles, and the postman's walk will lead to high ratings.

Leads to **HMS ROYAL ARTHUR, CORSHAM**   Near Box Tunnel, at Corsham, is HMS Royal Arthur (Guinevere's king). The clue is attached to the 'postman's walk' on the obstacle course.

CLUE TWO In a Yorkshire-sounding place where the clink's on a crossing, make for an old tax-collecting storehouse and pull for a point between the Barton cutwaters.

Leads to **BRADFORD-ON-AVON**   There is a prison on a bridge in this Yorkshire-sounding town. The tithe barn (tax-collecting storehouse) leads to Barton bridge where the clue is hidden between the cutwaters, the wedge-shaped pier ends.

CLUE THREE Down by degrees to the home of the brave and the product of a quilting bee – Mrs Waterbury's Album.

Leads to **AMERICAN MUSEUM, CLAVERTON**   One of the exhibits in this American ('home of the brave' from the 'Star Spangled Banner') Museum is a patchwork quilt known as Mrs Waterbury's Album.

CLUE FOUR Now for a dash
        Past a statue of Nash
        Down the steps where a spring
        makes a splash.

Leads to **GREAT BATH, BATH**   Having landed in front of the Royal Crescent, Anneka is given a dashing ride in a police car to the Pump Room, where there is a statue of Richard Beau Nash. Spring water enters the Great Bath over some steps, where the clue is hidden.

CLUE FIVE Sally forth to old Lilliput, where a peel will pull the prize from the faggots.

Leads to **SALLY LUNN'S HOUSE**   Sally Lunn's house is in the street that used to be known as Lilliput Alley. The treasure is a bun which has to be pulled from the faggot oven, in the kitchen museum, with a baker's shovel called a peel.

Lacock Abbey.

CLUE SIX While still on the run, consider this obscure clue in a negative manner, but once it's clicked, whose room will you try for some positive results?

CLUE SEVEN Some of it's officially secret, so if you use this ammunition to guide you to your destination, you'll be dumped in it! Where is it?

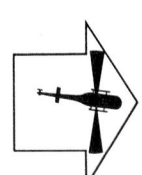

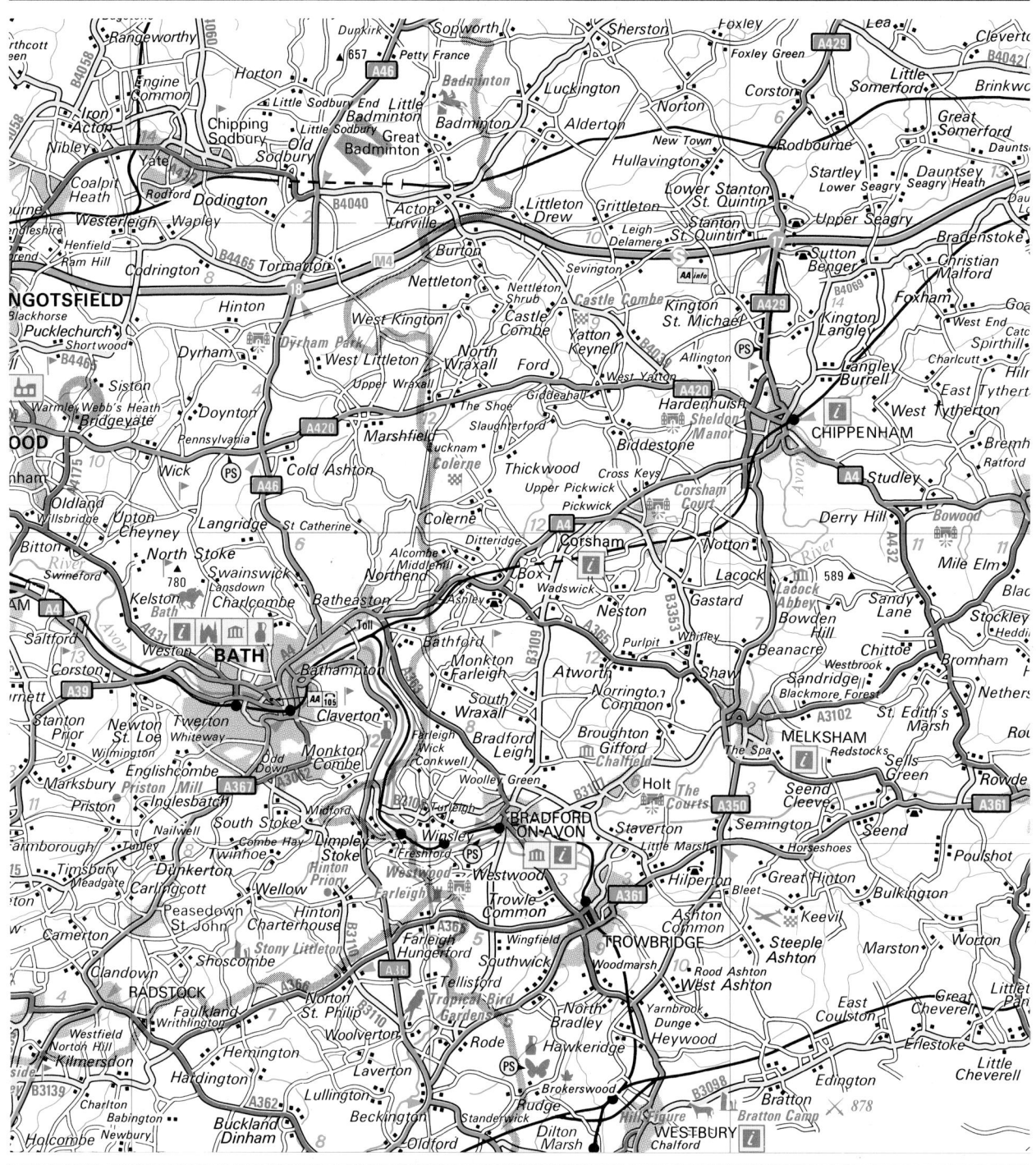

Lacock Abbey

Wiltshire

Lacock Abbey and its delightful village have grown up together over the past 700 years. The Abbey came first, founded in 1232 by Ela, Countess of Salisbury who was its abbess for 17 years. The last of all the religious houses in England to be suppressed, the abbey finally closed in 1539 whereupon the nuns were pronounced 'of virtuous living' and given pensions, and the abbey itself was sold as a private home.

Although the new owner destroyed the church, much of the original building remained, and in the seventeenth century it passed by marriage to the Talbots. In 1754 John Ivory Talbot added the Great Hall in Gothic style, and the house stayed in the family until 1944. Now much of the old house is open to the public, and an old barn has been converted to house a fascinating museum devoted to Henry Fox Talbot, the famous pioneering photographer who made the world's first photographic negative in 1835.

Like the Abbey, much of Lacock itself is owned by the National Trust. Twisting streets, gabled roofs and timber buildings make it one of the prettiest villages in England, with many houses dating from medieval times and none later than about 1800.

Guide to opening: Lacock Abbey, April to October. [T] Lacock (024 973) 227; Fox Talbot Museum, March to October. [T]·Lacock 459 for details. NT

Bradford-on-Avon

Wiltshire

This is a small market town, built of attractive local stone, with streets rising steeply from the banks of the River Avon. The town was a prosperous centre of the woollen cloth industry, which left behind a rich legacy in terraces of weavers' cottages, grander Georgian mansions of rich clothiers and mills built during the Industrial Revolution. It's most photographed feature is the Town Bridge with the tiny lock-up (formerly a chapel) mentioned in Clue 2.

Other interesting buildings here include one of the most complete of all Saxon churches in England (restored in the 1870s having been used as a charnel house, school and cottages) and a magnificent tithe barn, also mentioned in Clue 2. Built in the fourteenth century as a granary for Shaftesbury Abbey, and still retaining many of its original timbers, the barn measures an impressive 55 yards by 10 yards, divided into 14 bays with 4 projecting gabled porches.

Adjacent to the barn is 36-acre Barton Farm Country Park, complete with jogging track and trim trail. Both the River Avon and the Kennet & Avon Canal run through the park and provide a pleasant 1½-mile walk from the barn to Avoncliffe, where a classical Georgian aqueduct carries the canal over the river.

The American Museum

Claverton Manor, near Bath, Avon

Winston Churchill delivered his first political speech here at Claverton Manor in 1897, and the early-nineteenth-century house now provides an attractive home for the first comprehensive 'Museum of Americans' in Europe. Founded by Americans Dallas Pratt and John Judkyn to increase Anglo-American understanding, the museum illustrates the background to American life between the seventeenth and nineteenth centuries through a series of rooms each furnished in varying period styles. They include a borning room (used for childbirth), a Massachusetts tavern, a Mexican living room, a New Orleans bedroom and a Shakers' room which holds furniture made by the craftsmen of this nineteenth-century religious sect.

Rooms are devoted to special displays telling different stories of which Exploration and Colonisation, followed by American Indians and the Opening of the West are but two. Further parlours and bedrooms are furnished to illustrate specific themes such as craftsmanship in furniture, silver, pewter, and textiles. The textile room displays quilts featured on *Treasure Hunt*.

Even the grounds at Claverton Manor are in keeping with the theme; visitors will come across a tepee, a prairie wagon and the observation platform

The Town Bridge, Bradford-on-Avon.

of an American train. The park and formal gardens boast an American Arboretum, a Colonial Herb Garden and a replica of George Washington's rose and flower garden at Mount Vernon, Virginia. There is also a milliner's shop with a colourful collection of bandboxes, and the stable block has been converted to house a gallery of Folk Art. A tea-room selling American cookies rounds off any visit in perfect style.

Guide to opening: April to October. [T] Bath (0225) 60503 for details.

The Roman Baths & Museum

Bath, Avon

Here at the famous King's Bath spring, water heated to a constant temperature of 46.5°F bubbles out of the ground at a rate of 250,000 million gallons a day. At this Sacred Spring, the Celts worshipped the goddess Sulis and, when the Romans took over the site, they included her in the worship of their own goddess Minerva.

The 60s and 70s AD saw the start of a great religious complex here, centring on the temple of Sulis Minerva from which Roman Aquae Sulis took its name. People flocked here to ask help of the goddess. In addition to the coins which were offered for favours received, excavation of the spring has also yielded thin sheets of etched pewter on which citizens outlined an offence committed against them, and provided a list of suspects to enable the goddess to identify and punish the guilty party. These 'curses' throw an intriguing light on the social squabbles of the day!

Near the spring was the temple of Sulis Minerva which housed the statue of the deity. Religious ceremonies took place here – on the steps or in the precinct. Excavations show the partly-reconstructed altar which bears an inscription relating to the augur. It was the augur who sacrificed animals on the altar, often using their livers to fortell the future. Finds from the temple precinct now on display include marvellous sculpture such as the gorgon's head pediment and the famous gilt-bronze head of Minerva, which probably came from statue within the temple itself.

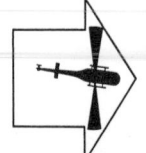

Linked to the temple was the great bathing complex which was one of the wonders of Roman Britain. This was the centre of social life, devoted to the complicated rituals of bathing, to gossip, gambling and entertainments of every kind. The centrepiece is still the original lead-lined Great Bath, and it was here, where the water flows in from the Sacred Spring, that Anneka found the *Treasure Hunt* clue. After the Emperor Hadrian banned mixed bathing in the second century AD other baths were added, finally creating a complex arrangement of swimming baths, cold plunges, saunas and Turkish baths serviced by the sophisticated systems of plumbing and underfloor heating which are visible today.

Guide to opening: all year, daily. [T] Bath (0225) 61111 for details.

The Pump Room

Bath, Avon

Written above the door of the Pump Room is a Greek motto meaning 'Water is best'. According to Sam Weller in the *Pickwick Papers* the curative water dispensed here tasted like 'warm flat-irons', yet visitors still sip it along with tea and Bath buns, to the accompaniment of live music from the Pump Room Trio. As shown on *Treasure Hunt*, a statue of Beau Nash now presides over the site where the great man himself once reigned supreme. As Master of Ceremonies, the Beau banished Bath's reputation at a haunt for pickpockets and gamblers, and imposed instead of elegance and order echoed in the new buildings of the town. Like Aquae Sulis, Georgian Bath was built from local stone which the genius of Yorkshireman John Wood used to stunning effect. In 1729 he designed Queen Square in the Palladian style and started on the Circus just before he died in 1754. John Wood the Younger carried on the good work, most notably in the Assembly Rooms and the majestic sweep of the famous Royal Crescent. No. 1 Royal Crescent (open to the public) has now been restored and refurnished in its original style.

Other historic buildings in Bath include the abbey (restored 1495–1503), Pulteney Bridge (designed by Robert Adam in the style of the Pontevecchio in Florence) and Sally Lunn's House, built in 1482 and now the oldest house in the city. Sally Lunn moved here in 1680 and gave her name to a type of bun which she made in the Kitchen Bakery – hiding place of the fifth *Treasure Hunt* clue. The kitchen is now open to the public together with excavations showing evidence of earlier Roman and medieval buildings which stood on the site.

The Great Bath.

TOURIST INFORMATION

Tourist Information Centres: Abbey Church Yard, **Bath** [T] (0225) 462831. 34 Solver Street, **Bradford-on-Avon** [T] (02216) 5797. The Neeld Hall, High Street, **Chippenham** [T] (0249) 65773. 25 Church Street, **Melksham** [T] (0225) 707424. St Stephen's Place, **Trowbridge** [T] (0225) 777054. The Library Car Park, **Westbury** [T] (0373) 827158.

- **Bath Postal Museum.**
- **Bowood House, Calne.**
- **Burrows Toy Museum, Bath.**
- **Chalcot House, Westbury.**
- **Claverton Pumping Station, nr Bath.**
- **Corsham Court.**
- **The Courts, Holt.**
- **Dyrham Park, Dyrham.**
- **Elms Cross Vineyard, Bradford-on-Avon.**
- **Farleigh Castle.**
- **Great Chalfield Manor.**
- **Iford Manor Gardens, nr Bradford-on-Avon.**
- **Monkton Farleigh Mine.**
- **Museum of Costume, Bath.**
- **National Centre of Photography, Bath.**
- **Tropical Bird Garden, Rhode.**
- **Victoria Art Gallery, Bath.**
- **Westbury/Bratton White Horse.**
- **Westwood Manor.**

TREASURE HUNT 8

Isle of Wight

START POSITION COWES

CLUE ONE To a majestic home with a Kipling connection where the game's afoot, what once was straining in the slips now stands stonily among the statues.

Leads to **OSBORNE HOUSE** The House was built for Queen Victoria, who later added the Durbar Room. John Kipling may have been consulted on its design. The reference to Shakespeare's *King Henry V* is on the subject of greyhounds, and the clue is hidden on a statue of a greyhound in front of the house.

CLUE TWO Churchill's 'intriguing parcel' was royally sealed here, and some donkey work ensures the next delivery.

Leads to **CARISBROOKE CASTLE** Charles I sought safety here; he was described by Churchill, in one of his letters, as an intriguing parcel. The water wheel of the castle's well is worked by donkeys, which go about their job and bring up the next clue.

CLUE THREE Cross an Arab-sounding watercourse to a hooded height where the Commando network leads Annie up the pole.

Leads to **ROBIN HILL ADVENTURE PARK** Across the River Medina is Robin (Hood) Hill (Height) Adventure Park. The clue is hidden on the climbing course; Annie has to climb over a rope bridge to reach a pole to which the clue is attached.

CLUE FOUR Past the Hiawatha man's fountain and a crustaceous pub to a seaside tradition in mint condition.

Leads to **OLD SHANKLIN ROCK SHOP** A fountain outside The Crab pub has a Longfellow (Hiawatha man) inscription. In the Rock Shop, a new batch of rock (in mint condition) is being made. The clue is on a stick of rock on the counter.

CLUE FIVE It's beside the point, but a smugglers' glen leads to an amazing finish with a little man from Zurich.

Leads to **BLACKGANG CHINE** West of St Catherine's Point is this ravine, a former haunt of smuggling gangs. Now an amusement park, one of its attractions is a maze. In the middle is a tree up which the treasure, a gnome (little man from Zurich) is climbing!

Sailing at Cowes.

CLUE SIX Move the decimal point one place to the left and you'll get the scale of the setting. When you arrive, you'll think you're seeing double, or even treble! To which lofty village have you come?

CLUE SEVEN Seafarers – you can try turning these familiar, lonely sails to the wind, but look out! Perched on top of a circle, that's the only way they'll go! Where are they?

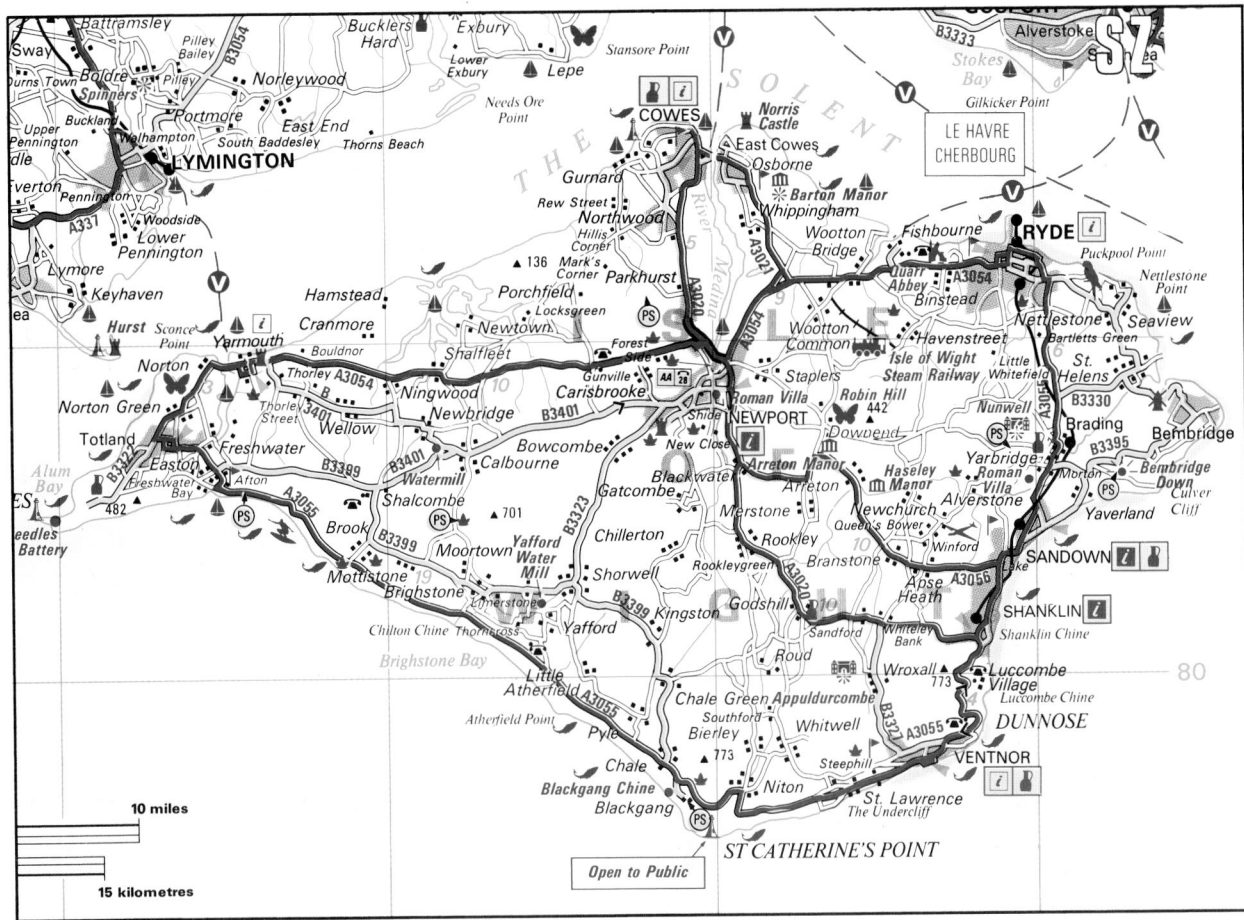

Osborne House

East Cowes

Designed by Prince Albert himself, 'Her Majesty's Marine Residence at Osborne' was the home where Queen Victoria and her family could be free from the ceremony of state. The Prince Consort lavished his taste and attention on the house, planning its gardens and dictating the decoration of its rooms even to the extent of designing the elaborate motifs on the billiards table. In 1861, the widowed Queen took refuge at Osborne determined to keep both house and contents just as he would have known them, and after her own death things remained unchanged. As a result, original pictures, furniture and bric-a-brac now form a perfect period piece of Victorian taste.

Osborne's second royal home is half a mile east of the main house. In the Swiss Cottage – brought in sections from Switzerland – the princes learnt carpentry and gardening, and the girls practised cookery and keeping house; it, too, is fully furnished with all its original items.

Guide to opening: April to October. [T] Cowes (0983) 200022 for details. EH.

Carisbrooke Castle

Near Newport

Carisbrooke offers the chance to explore impressive earthworks, substantial castle ruins, well-preserved domestic buildings and an interesting museum all in one 7-acre site. Seventy-one steps lead up the side of a Norman motte surmounted by a twelfth-century stone keep, and from the base of the motte twelfth-century curtain walls encircle the castle and provide wonderful views from the 'wall walk'. Within the courtyard are the domestic buildings: the Great Hall, the Chapel of St Peter, the Great Chamber and the Upper Gallery, the ruins of the Elizabethan officers' quarters and kitchens, and a sixteenth-century well-house where the wheel is still worked by donkeys.

As befits a castle, Carisbrooke was always 'in the wars' but its greatest fame comes from its association with Charles I of whom it has many reminders. In 1647, the King fled to Carisbrooke expecting to find support but was instead taken prisoner here. After two escape attempts he eventually left the castle in 1649 on a journey which was to end at the block in Whitehall. St Nicholas' Chapel was built as a memorial to him, and at the Carisbrooke Castle Museum various personal items are on display including the lace nightcap he wore the night before his execution and a piece of the cravat he wore on the day. Also on show is a lock of hair which belonged to his 14-year-old daughter, Elizabeth, who died at Carisbrooke in 1650 having caught a chill whilst playing on the bowling green.

Guide to opening: all the year. [T] Newport (0983) 522107 for details. EH.

Robin Hill Adventure Park

Arreton, near Newport

The island's largest tourist attraction offers a happy blend of wildlife and holiday adventure in 80 acres of magnificent woods and downlands. Fallow deer, marmots, wallabies, peacocks and wildfowl roam freely in walk-through enclosures, with llamas, ostriches, miniature horses and many tame animals.

Bennet's Rock, known as the Stone of Light, not only affords splendid views over the island but also enables visitors to take stock of the rest of Robin Hill, which includes water gardens, a lake stocked with Giant Carp, a woodland walk with a Nature Trail quiz sheet, a Commando-style Assault Course (where Annie found the clue), a Continental Trim Course, and an Activity Area, which includes BMX, archery, boating and an 80-foot slide.

Guide to opening: early March to late October. [T] Newport (0983) 527352 for details.

Shanklin Old Village

Adding an old-world touch to one of the island's most popular resorts, Shanklin Old Village is a picturesque cluster of well-kept thatched cottages dating from Tudor times. The Rock Shop featured in the *Treasure Hunt* stands just across the road from The Crab, an attractive old inn once a favourite haunt of smugglers. From here, steep paths wind down through the green ferns and lush vegetation of Shanklin Chine, past an interesting new Heritage Centre and onto the beach – and more pubs – below.

Osborne House – the dining room.

Blackgang Chine Fantasy Theme Park

Blackgang

The name Blackgang probably relates to smugglers and wreckers once active on this shore. A 'chine' is a gorge formed by the action of the weather, and this one at Blackgang provides panoramic views and a steep but spectacular setting for a variety of fantasy worlds.

The Dinosaur Park boasts life-size models of prehistoric giants such as *Stegosaurus* or *Tyrannosaurus Rex*. In Jungleland, Zulu warriors rub shoulders with lions, rhinos and other wild beasts. Frontierland recreates the Wild West of Buffalo Creek in faithful detail from the bank to Boot Hill. Like the tanks and rockets in the Adventure Park, everything is for climbing on, and the smallest visitors find something just their size in the Fairy Castle, Nursery Land or in the model village which features most of the famous buildings on the island.

Guide to opening: all the year; floodlit evenings June to September. [T] Niton (0983) 730330 for details.

TOURIST INFORMATION

Tourist Information Centres: **Cowes** [T] (0983) 291914. Town Lane Car Park, **Newport** [T] (0983) 525450. Western Esplanade, **Ryde** [T] (0983) 62905. The Esplanade, **Sandown** [T] (0983) 403886. 67 High Street, **Shanklin** [T] (0983) 862942. 34 High Street, **Ventnor** [T] (0983) 853625. The Quay, **Yarmouth** [T] (0983) 760015.

- **Arreton Manor.**
- **Barton Manor Vineyard & Garden.**
- **Bembridge Maritime Museum.**
- **Bembridge Windmill.**
- **Brading Roman Villa.**
- **Brickfields Horsecountry & Isle of Wight Shire Horse Centre, nr Ryde.**
- **Butterfly World, Wootton.**
- **Calbourne Water Mill & Museum of Country Life.**
- **Flamingo Park Waterfowl & Water Gardens, Seaview.**
- **Godshill Model Village.**
- **Golden Hill Fort, Freshwater.**
- **Isle of Wight Steam Railway, Ryde.**
- **Haseley Manor & Pottery, Arreton.**
- **Isle of Wight Zoo, nr Sandown.**
- **Lilliput Museum of Antique Dolls & Toys, Brading.**
- **The Needles Pleasure Park, Alum Bay.**
- **Nunwell House & Gardens, nr Brading.**
- **Osborn-Smiths Wax Museum, Brading.**
- **Tropical Bird Park, St Lawrence.**
- **Ventnor Botanic Garden.**

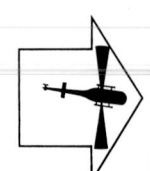

TREASURE HUNT 9

Dorset

START POSITION OLD HARRY ROCKS

CLUE ONE Where the defender of Mafeking pitched camp, his successors have blazed a trail. So be prepared!

Leads to **BROWNSEA ISLAND** Lord Baden-Powell, the Defender of Mafeking, was founder of the Boy Scouts (motto: be prepared). At a Scout and Guide camp on the island, the clue is at the end of the Scouts' trail.

CLUE TWO At the scene of the deed that made an unready boy king, take a square look at a martyr's memorial.

Leads to **CORFE CASTLE** Edward was murdered here and Aethelred, the Unready, became King. In the village square is a memorial to Edward the Martyr.

CLUE THREE Rule Britannia! Pass over the composer for a fly past the powerful one that's on top of the waves.

Leads to **WAREHAM CHANNEL** Fly over Arne (the composer of Rule Britannia) to Wareham Channel. On top of a speedboat dashing up the Channel is written the next clue.

CLUE FOUR Caterpillar country near A.C. Shaw's home. Your alien Panther is flanked by Tigers.

Leads to **BOVINGTON TANK MUSEUM** A.C. Shaw (Lawrence of Arabia) lived at Cloud's Hill, which is en route to the Tank Museum. Between two Tiger tanks is a German Panther tank on which the clue is hidden.

CLUE FIVE Between the Puddles and the Piddle
lived the Martyns, man and boy.
Amid the leaves yew'll solve this riddle,
Close by the House of Joy.

Leads to **ATHELHAMPTON** Situated near the River Piddle, between Puddletown and Tolpuddle, this former home of the Martyn family has a summer House of Joy. The treasure is hidden in a nearby yew tree.

CLUE SIX Well, head to a place with a beautiful bridge and seek out the setting for Hardy's wedding-night confession.

CLUE SEVEN Take to the air now, and let the skipper lead you to a limestone location where two bays are separated by an arch. What is its name?

Old Harry Rocks – from the helicopter.

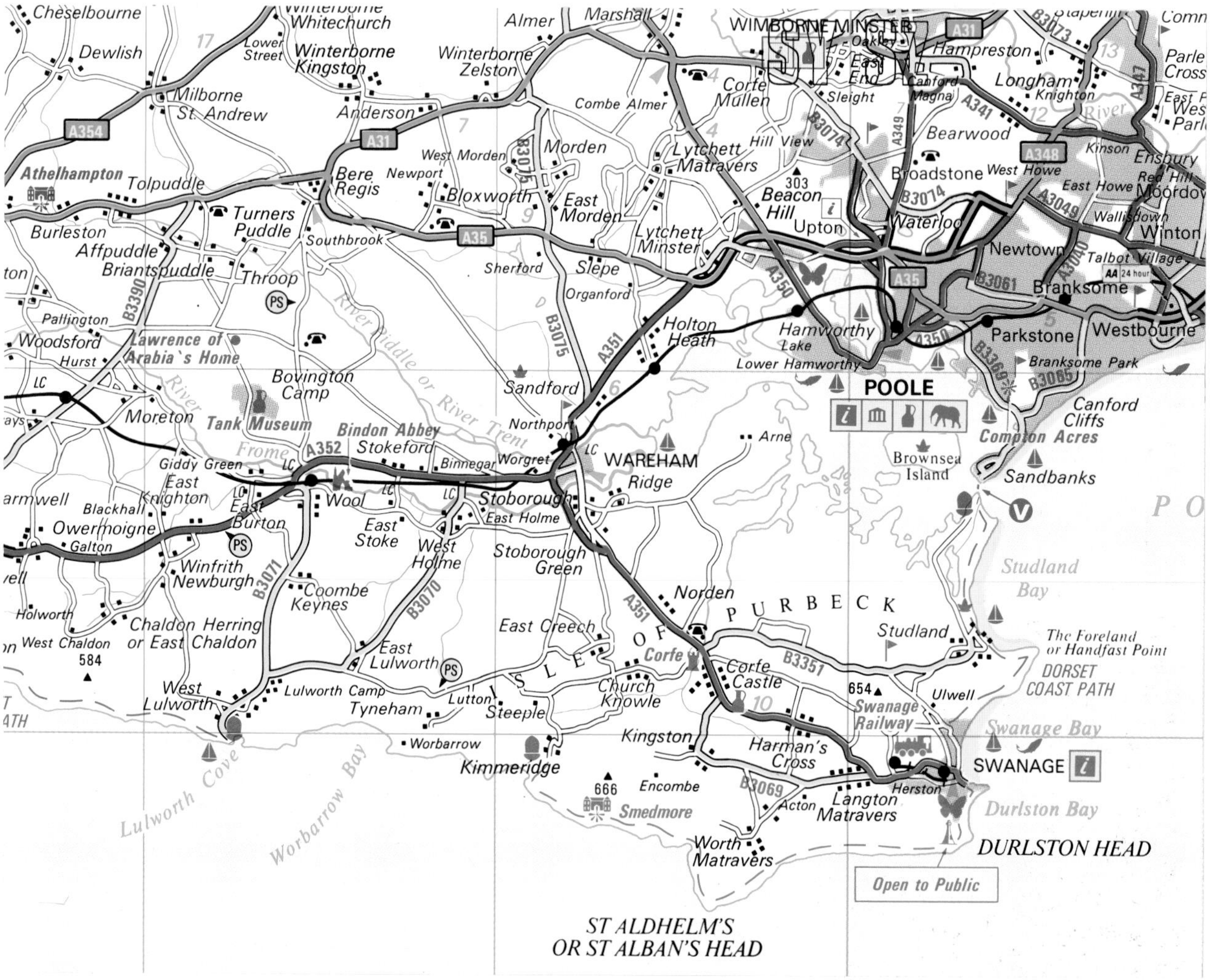

Brownsea Island

Poole Harbour

Brownsea, which is 1½ miles long and ¾ mile wide, dominates the entrance to the land-locked harbour of Poole, the largest natural harbour in the world. Visitors come here to enjoy its quiet beaches and the peace and beauty of 500 acres of heath and woodlands with their shady glades, nature trails and superb views of the Dorset coast. Brownsea is owned by the National Trust, and part of it is leased to The Dorset Trust for Nature Conservation as a Nature Reserve providing sanctuary for ducks, geese, waders, herons and gulls on marshes, lakes and a salt-water lagoon. The rest of the island is also a haven for naturalists; red squirrels and peafowl still breed here, and an earlier venture into bulb growing on the island now results in marvellous displays of daffodils in the spring. Facilities on the island include a cafeteria and two small shops, and services are held at the church here every Sunday in summer; the castle is not open to the public.

Visitors may land their own boats at Pottery Pier at the western end of the island (accessible in all tides) and the Tourist Information Centre at Poole (0202 673322) can provide details of regular boat services from Poole Quay and Sandbanks.

Guide to opening: tours of the Nature Reserve are available from April to September; please ring Canford Cliffs (0202) 709445. NT

Corfe Castle

Near Wareham

High on a dramatic hilltop site, the romantic ruins of Corfe Castle stand guard over an attractive village of mellowed stone cottages grouped below. This fine strategic site was fortified many centuries ago, and excavations have revealed the Saxon building where, according to legend, the Saxon king Edward was murdered in AD 978 at the command of his step-mother who sought to advance her own son Ethelred the Unraed, or 'ill-advised'. Domesday Book records a castle here built by William the Conqueror, and the present tower-keep dates from Norman times. From then on defences were improved by the addition of outer walls, mural towers and a deep ditch dug by local miners and quarrymen in 1214 until, by the end of that century, the castle was considered able to withstand any attack. It met its severest test in the Civil War when it became the last Royalist stronghold between London and Exeter – it

Corfe Castle.

withstood several sieges until treachery forced its final surrender in 1646.

The village of Corfe Castle itself offers a museum of village relics, and a Model Village with a scale replica of the castle as it stood in 1645. The village also bears the distinction of being the centre of the oldest trade union in the world: the Company of Marblers and Stone-Cutters of the Isle of Purbeck.

Guide to opening: all year. [T] Corfe Castle (0929) for details. NT.

The Tank Museum

Bovington Camp, Wareham

Over 200 examples of tanks, armoured cars, scout cars and half tracks make up Bovington's awesome collection of armoured fighting vehicles – the largest in the world. Exhibits from many countries illustrate the story of the tank from the turn of the century to the present day, with separate halls devoted to different periods of development. All the famous makes of tanks are represented here such as the Mark 1 Male Tank (the first tank used in action), and the renowned Matilda, considered virtually invulnerable in the early years of the Second World War.

The museum encourages everyone to make the most of what they see; visitors are allowed to climb in some of the tanks, to walk through a Centurian which has been sliced in half, and to feel the thrill of driving a tank from the safety of special simulators, while audio visual displays and contemporary photographs help put the whole experience into context. A variety of special events are also staged here each year, giving enthusiasts the chance to watch some of these veterans in action once more.

Guide to opening: all the year. [T] Bindon Abbey (0929) 462721 for details.

Athelhampton

Puddletown

The 'most picturesque house in the country' has been a family home for the last five centuries. A serene and beautiful building of well-weathered stone, Athelhampton stands on the legendary site of the palace of the Dark Age king Athelstan, described by contemporaries as 'the very celebrated king who ruled all England, which prior to him many kings shared between them.' It was also the model for Thomas Hardy's Athelhall in *The Waiting Supper*, yet its very real charm has little to do with links such as these. The house was built in 1485 by Sir William Martin, Lord Mayor of London, with a 'new wing' added in the reign of Henry VIII and has remained largely unchanged since then. The fifteenth-century Great Hall, with its hammerbeam roof, oriel window, heraldic glass and linenfold panelling is one of the finest in the country, and the Great Chamber, all panelling and carved stone, boasts a magnificent four-poster bed and other splendid pieces. The public may also visit the eighteenth-century Dining Room, the Tudor Bedroom, Wine Cellar and exhibition room, together with two secret rooms and hidden stairs set into the thickness of the walls.

Encircled by the River Piddle, Athelhampton's 12 acres of gardens are also a delight. There are 8 architectural and water gardens offering fountain-pools, waterfalls, pavilions and terraces, a circular dovecote and rare plants and trees. One of the most striking features here is a series of yew pyramids, each 30 feet high.

Guide to opening: Easter to mid-October. [T] Puddletown (0305 84) 363 for details.

TOURIST INFORMATION

Tourist Information Centres: Enefco House, Poole Quay, **Poole** [T] (0202) 673322. Shore Road, **Swanage** [T] (0929) 422885. Town Hall, East Street, **Wareham** [T] (09295) 2740.

- **Clouds Hill, Bere Regis.**
- **Compton Acres, Poole.**
- **Cranborne Manor Gardens, nr Wimborne.**
- **Deans Court, Wimborne Minster.**
- **Kingston Lacey, Wimborne Minster.**
- **Lulworth Castle.**
- **Merley Bird Garden.**
- **Merley House & Model Museum.**
- **Poole Aquarium.**
- **Poole Lifeboat Museum.**
- **Poole Maritime Museum.**
- **Poole Park Zoo.**
- **Smedmore House, Kimmeridge.**
- **Tolpuddle Martyrs Museum, Tolpuddle.**
- **Wareham (Teddy Bears) Exhibition**.

Anneka aboard a tank, Bovington, Camp Wareham.

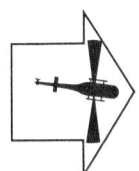

West Sussex

START POSITION EAST HEAD, WEST WITTERING

CLUE ONE Where Canute got his feet wet, it's All Hands – 216 to be precise – on deck.

Leads to **BOSHAM QUAY**　It is here that Canute is said to have commanded the tide to turn back. In the harbour is the yacht 'All Hands' (number 216) with Michael Bentine aboard; he has the clue.

CLUE TWO Find a nominal association with a round-the-world lepidoptera, and make for a central octagon and all that jazz. Search for a sousaphonic note.

Leads to **CHICHESTER**　Sir Francis Chichester sailed round the world in Gypsy Moth IV. A strolling jazz band is playing by the octagonal Market Cross. The clue is in the sousaphone.

CLUE THREE Trundle over a gloriously racy spot to a rural recreation, where Titchfield has a lot at stake.

Leads to **WEALD & DOWNLAND MUSEUM** Beyond 'Glorious Goodwood' racecourse

and Trundle Hill is this open air museum. Sheep are being auctioned by 'Titchfield', and the auctioneer has the clue.

Reposition **LITTLEHAMPTON BEACH**

CLUE FOUR Where an East Anglian duchess met Imran last April, there's a catch in the 86 county captain. Go on, Annie, be silly!

Leads to **ARUNDEL CASTLE CRICKET CLUB**　The castle is the home of the Duchess of Norfolk. Early in the cricket season, the Duchess's XI play host to the touring test team – in this instance Pakistan, captained by Imran Khan. When Annie reaches the ground a match is in progress. She stands at SILLY mid ON to catch the ball and receives the clue from the Sussex captain.

CLUE FIVE Over the northern scarp, the name of a fairy-tale illustrator points to a theatrically decorated gallery, with a horsey memento of the last Stuart king.

Leads to **PARHAM HOUSE**　Across the northern scarp of the South Downs near (Arthur) Rackham, is Parham House. The treasure, a riding crop, is placed on James II's saddle in the Long Gallery.

CLUE SIX Unwinding robing will reveal the home of the Tuppers' tesserae. Over a winged panel, her head in a cloud, a complementary lady looks down. Who is she?

CLUE SEVEN South and East will guide you up to 'Bladesover', the home of a little Queen Anne residence. To which large residence have you been guided?

Skyrunner with crew in hot pursuit, Parham House

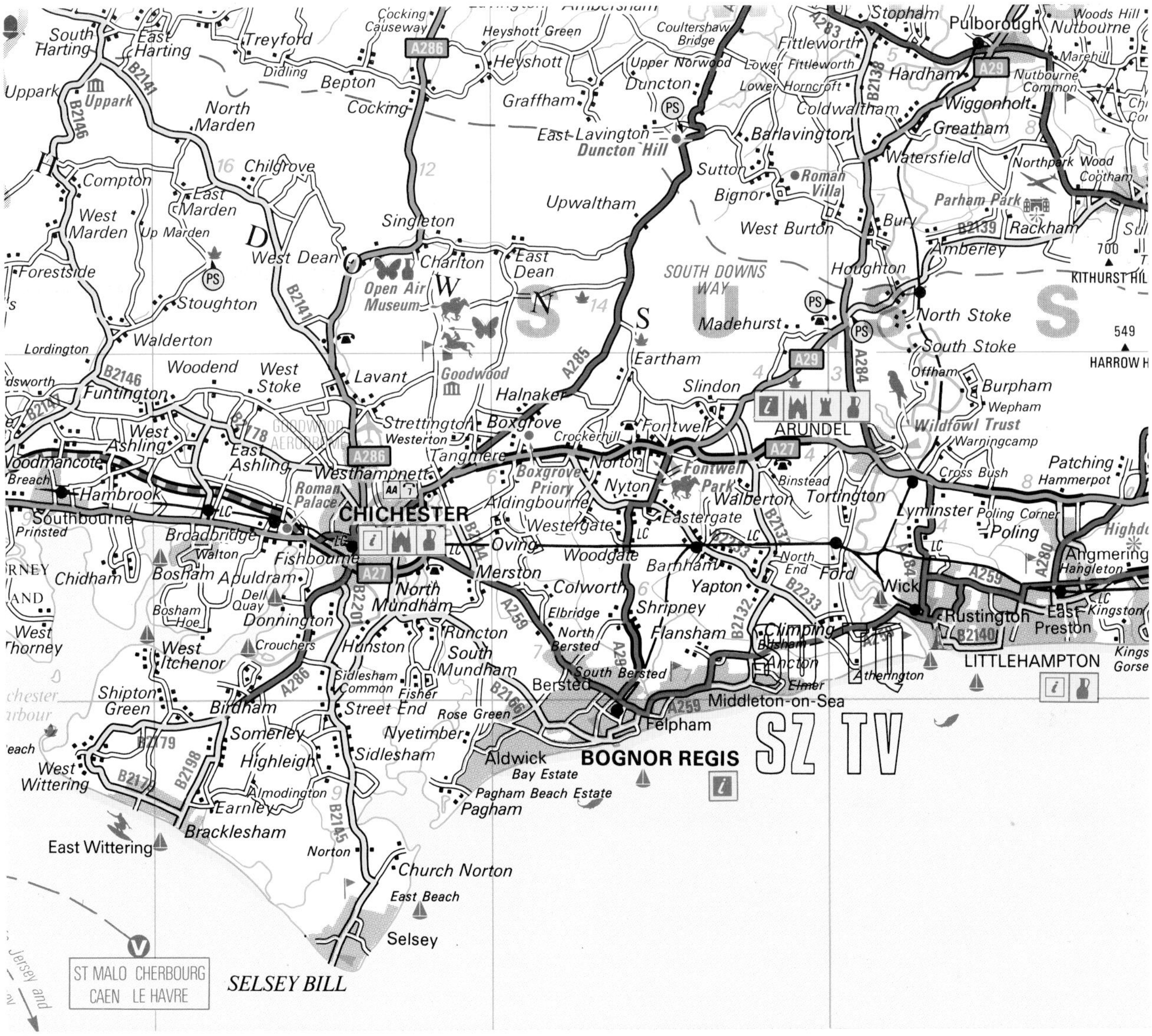

Bosham

An attractive village where pretty cottages reach down to the water's edge, Bosham lies in a sheltered channel off Chichester Harbour, regarded as one of the finest sailing areas in the country. It was here at Bosham that Canute (c.994–1035) the Danish King of England bade the waves recede in order to show flatterers the limits of his power and one of his daughters is buried here. The church itself bears traces of pre-Norman work, and the Bayeux Tapestry shows further proof of a Saxon church on the site.

Chichester

The Romans built their town of Noviomagus here together with the superb palace at nearby Fishbourne, which has some of the finest mosaics in the country. The Saxon leader Cissa took over the Roman 'ceaster' thus giving the city its present name, and the Normans left their magnificent mark in the cathedral built between 1091 and 1123 of stone brought from the Isle of Wight.

Alterations followed a major fire in the twelfth century and a spire was added in the thirteenth/fourteenth centuries, but this collapsed in 1861 after a violent storm and was replaced in 1866. The bell tower dates from the fourteenth/fifteenth centuries, and is unique in being the only one in the country to be detached from the main cathedral building. The twentieth century has made some additions of its own: the John Piper tapestry behind the altar and Graham Sutherland's painting 'Noli me tangere' in the Chapel of St Mary Magdalen. The pennant flown by Sir Francis Chichester on his round-the-world voyage in Gipsy Moth IV is on view in the Sailors' Chapel.

The Market Cross stands at the heart of the city at what was the crossroads of North, South, East and West streets. The gift of Edward Story, Bishop of Chichester from 1478–1503, it was built of Caen stone with eight octagonal arches grouped around a central pillar and topped by a stone cupola supported at the base with elegant flying buttresses. Though restored, it largely retains its original shape and

43

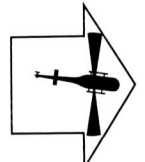

character and is considered to be one of the finest structures of its kind in the country. It makes a convenient starting point from which to explore Chichester's many fine Georgian buildings. Most notable of these are the beautiful merchant's houses in West Street and the Pallants; Pallant House itself, a Queen Anne residence built in 1712, is now a gallery housing a first-class collection of paintings and sculptures.

Chichester Festival Theatre, opened in 1962, now enjoys an international reputation. The Festival Season (April/May to the end of September) features four of the Company's own productions. Casts include world-famous actors, and several successful plays have had their world premier here. At other times of the year the spotlight is on ballet and music as the theatre plays host to top-class touring companies and visiting artists. In October and November 'Jazz International' presents the very biggest names in the world of jazz.

[T] Chichester (0243) 781312 for programme details.

Joining the band at the Chichester Festival.

Weald and Downland Open Air Museum

Singleton, near Chichester

Forty acres of wooded weald and open downland provide a marvellous open-air setting for a wide variety of vernacular buildings from the South of England. Since 1967 the museum has been rescuing traditional local buildings and re-erecting them here to form one of the most fascinating collections of historic buildings in the country. Houses, barns, rural craft workshops and agricultural buildings are among over 30 major exhibits. A medieval timber-framed farmhouse from Chiddingstone with open hall and upper chamber, Titchfield's sixteenth-century market hall with its open arcade for stalls and council chamber above, and West Wittering's elementary school (in use up to 1851) number but a few. There are workshops of blacksmiths, plumbers and carpenters, a working watermill for grinding corn, an animal pound and a windpump, in fact something of

everything from a charcoal burner's camp to a seventeenth-century treadwheel. The museum also has extensive collections of artefacts representing country crafts and industries, building trades and agriculture, many of which are on show in relevant buildings. Some feature in annual events such as the steam threshing and ploughing with heavy horses and vintage tractors which takes place in October; other events include Novice Sheep Dog Trials in May, Heavy Horses at Work in June and a Rare Breeds Show in July.

Guide to opening: all the year; [T] Singleton (0243 63) 348 for details of opening, regular demonstrations and special events.

Arundel Castle

Arundel

This great castle is set in superb grounds overlooking the River Arun. It was built in the late eleventh-century for the Earl of Arun, and has been the seat of the Dukes of Norfolk (England's Premier Duke) and their ancestors for over 700 years. Badly damaged during the Civil War in 1643, the castle was largely restored and rebuilt in the eighteenth and nineteenth centuries on magnificent lines. It was then that it gained the breathtaking Barons' Hall, a vast 133-foot long and 50-foot high, together with the Private Chapel considered to be the finest Victorian room in the castle and one of the most perfect monuments of the nineteenth century Catholic revival in England. From the extravagant gilt bed made for Queen Victoria, to a case of stuffed owls of an extinct breed which once flourished in the Keep, the castle is a treasure house of fascinating and fine things. A number of special family treasures are also on show; these include the prayer book, gold rosary and cross which Mary Queen of Scots carried at her execution, and the fourth Duke of Norfolk's death warrant signed by Elizabeth I – the outcome of his part in the Ridolfi Plot which aimed to set Mary Queen of Scots on the throne.

The wall walk around the castle gives excellent views along the river, towards the coast and over the Cathedral and town, including the Cricket Club featured on *Treasure Hunt*.

Guide to opening: April to late October. [T] Arundel (0903) 883136 for details.

Parham House and Gardens

Parham, near Pulborough

This grey-stone house was built largely in Elizabethan times by the Palmer family, who had bought the Parham estate and other properties from Henry VIII for £1,225. 6s. 5d. Queen Elizabeth is thought to have dined here in 1593, and certainly no visitor to Parham can doubt the Tudor origins of most of the house. On view is the Great Hall where the house-

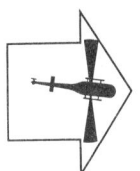

Arundel Castle.

hold ate their meals; the Great Parlour, once the family's private sitting room; the Great Chamber used as a reception room and dining room and the 160-foot Long Gallery, with its wonderful views over the deer park to the South Downs. In Tudor times the gallery was used for walking, recreation and games (during the Napoleonic scares, the Parham Troop of Yeomanry was also drilled here on rainy days).

These rooms provide an impressive setting for collections of Elizabethan, Stuart and Georgian portraits, furniture and china and rare needlework. Among the riches many single items stand out, ranging from needlework attributed to Mary Queen of Scots to a narwhal tusk, thought by Elizabethans to be the horn of a unicorn. The Long Gallery brings together a Roman cistern, a Jacobean font and Charles I's saddle cloth, while the Green Room offers a painting of a kangaroo by George Stubbs who is said to achieved the likeness by inflating a kangaroo skin to serve as a model.

Guide to opening: April to October. [T] Storrington (09066) 2021 for details.

TOURIST INFORMATION

61 High Street, **Arundel** [T] (0903) 882268. Belmont Street, **Bognor Regis** [T] (0243) 823140. St Peter's Market, West Street, **Chichester** [T] (0243) 775888. Windmill Complex, Seafront, **Littlehampton** [T] (0903) 713480.

- **Arundel Cathedral.**
- **Arundel Museum & Heritage Centre.**
- **Arundel Toy & Military Museum.**
- **Bignor Roman Villa.**
- **Chalk Pits Museum, Amberley.**
- **Chichester Cathedral.**
- **Corps of Royal Military Police Museum, nr Chichester.**
- **Denmans, Fontwell.**
- **Fishbourne Roman Palace & Museum.**
- **Goodwood House.**
- **Mechanical Music & Doll Collection, Chichester.**
- **Smarts Amusement Park, Littlehampton.**
- **Tangmere Military Aviation Museum, Chichester.**
- **Uppark, South Harting.**
- **West Dean Gardens, nr Chichester.**
- **Wildfowl Trust, Arundel.**

TREASURE HUNT 11 & 12

Kent

HUNT 11

START POSITION **LULLINGSTONE CASTLE**

CLUE ONE **Fly-drive to the pits, and between 4 and 6, stop Tim, 22, clutching Lola, 30, and let's hope they've got the message.**

Leads to **BRANDS HATCH**   Having been dropped at the gates by helicopter, Annie drives to pit number 5 and asks the pit marshall to call in Lola racing car, number 30, driven by Tim Jones, aged 22. The clue is in the passenger space.

CLUE TWO **Between a Sole and a Thong look for another sign of leather, where Mr Pickwick took refreshment, and the clue is in the bag.**

Leads to **THE LEATHER BOTTLE INN, COBHAM** Made famous by the *Pickwick Papers* this pub (with its sign of leather) now has a Pickwick Restaurant. On the wall, holding the clue, hangs Dickens' leather bag. The village is situated between Thong and Sole Street.

CLUE THREE **In Edwin Drood's Cloisterham there's a message in a piece of Switzerland near Uncle Pumblechook's shop.**

Leads to **CHARLES DICKENS' SWISS CHALET.** Rochester becomes Cloisterham in Dickens' *The Mystery of Edwin Drood*. Not far from the High Street premises of 'Uncle Pumblechook' is Eastgate House with the Swiss chalet in its garden. The clue is hidden in a letter rack inside.

CLUE FOUR **South to the riparian ford of a band of brothers, then follow the scent to the rosaceae where the lady is over the moon.**

Leads to **THE FRIARY, AYLESFORD**   South of Rochester, on the River Medway, the village of AylesFORD provides the setting for this abbey. At the Shrine of the Assumption of the Glorious Virgin, a statue depicts Our Lady as the woman with the moon at her feet. Annie sniffs out a vase of roses standing nearby and finds the clue.

CLUE FIVE **Len will lead to a Northern-sounding castle. Potted near Anne Boleyn's chamber,**

something worn by Mr Pratt's best friend encloses the treasure.

Leads to **LEEDS CASTLE**   Head towards LENham for this 'Yorkshire' castle. The Queen's Room is near Fountain Court, where the treasure, a dog, is in a flower pot. It is encircled by a dog collar which bears the inscription 'I belong to Mr Pratt'.

Anneka with a hop-picker at the Whitbread Hop farm.

CLUE SIX Past caring? Then proceed at a stately pace to a palace complex where you will be transported by the delightful collection of a former Mayor whose name it bears. What is the name?

CLUE SEVEN Now go full tilt at this final clue; Try not to fall off, though, whatever you do! It's not to the north or to the south.; Where is this unique target that knights would joust?

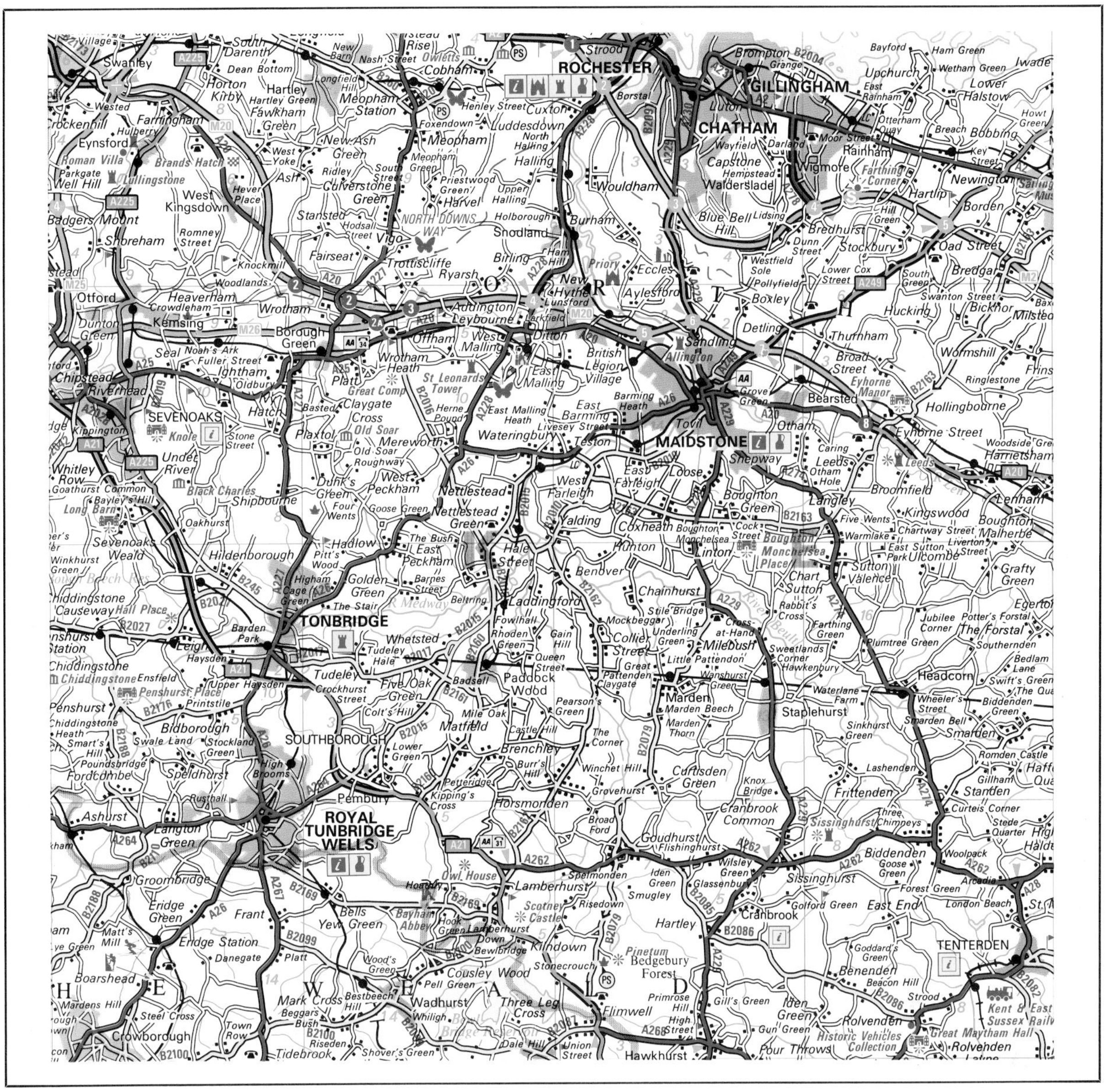

[Map of Kent region]

Lullingstone Castle

Eynsford

This historic family mansion is still lived in by descendants of the original owners who built it 500 years ago. It was begun in the reign of Henry VII by courtier Sir John Peche, later a favourite and constant companion of Henry VIII who often visited the new house here. Sir John was noted for his prowess in the lists; his jousting helmet is still on display in the Dining Room, and the site of his personal jousting ground is clearly visible near the Gate House. Constructed on massive lines in 1497, the Gate House itself is thought to be one of the first of its kind to be built in brick. In the eighteenth century Queen Anne was a regular visitor to Lullingstone, and many impressive alterations and additions made to the house were for her benefit.

According to tradition it was here at Lullingstone Castle that the rules of lawn tennis were drawn up by Sir William Hart-Dyke, grandfather of the present owner, and until recently Lullingstone was also known as the home of the famous silk farm which had supplied the silk for many royal occasions since the time of Queen Mary.

Guide to opening: April to the end of October. [T] Farningham (0322) 862114 for details.

Brands Hatch International Racing Circuit

Swanley

Well known for the race meetings held here on most weekends, this famous circuit is kept very busy in between. A variety of specialist schools offer tuition to individuals in the follow subjects: clay pigeon shooting and parascending; racing saloons and single seaters; racing 400cc bikes; racing 250cc carts; skid-control (taught in a skid pan or computerized car) and racing round Le Mans, courtesy of simula-

47

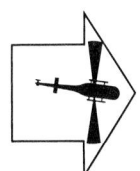

tors. There is also a popular School of Defensive Driving, teaching chauffeurs and security guards how to avoid kidnap situations and other pitfalls of the profession.

Guide to opening: [T] Gravesend (0474) 872367 for details concerning cars, bikes and carts and (0474) 337600 for other courses.

The Dickens Centre

High Street, Rochester

Here in sixteenth-century Eastgate House, imaginative displays using light and sound recreate Charles Dickens' world. Visitors to this award-winning centre come face to face with life-size models of famous characters such as Mr Pickwick and Miss Haversham, all placed in convincing settings which range from a Victorian slum tenement to the opium den featured in *Edwin Drood*. Impressive 'Talking Tableaux' introduce speaking likenesses of Lady Deadlock, Scrooge and other well-known characters. In the grounds of the Centre is the Swiss Chalet Dickens used as a study when he lived at nearby Gad's Hill; the chalet was the hiding place for the third *Treasure Hunt* clue.

Guide to opening: all the year. [T] Medway (0634) 44176 for details.

Aylesford Friary

Aylesford

A Carmelite Friary stood here beside the River Medway from 1242 until its dissolution in 1538. The next 400 years saw the Friary buildings in private hands, until in 1949 the same Carmelite Order bought them back. Now the Friary is a place of pilgrimage to the Shrine of Our Lady and St Simon Stock, a local man from the Kentish community. The Shrine Chapels were built between 1960 and 1965, and are richly decorated with ceramic works on religious themes by the artist Adam Kossoski who died in 1987.

Guide to opening: all the year. [T] Maidstone (0622) 77272.

Fagin ponders life in the Dickens Centre.

Leeds Castle.

Leeds Castle

Near Maidstone, Kent

Leeds Castle boasts a fairy-tale setting on two small islands in a glassy lake. The first stone castle was built here in 1130, and this was later expanded and surrounded by an enormous moat. Eleanor of Castile, wife of Edward I, bought the castle in 1278, and thus began Leeds' long association with England's queens. In 1321 Isabella, 'she-wolf of France' and wife of Edward II, sought a lodging here and, when she was turned away by castellan Thomas Colepeper, the king's forces beseiged the castle and hanged the hapless Colepeper from the Gate Tower. In 1403

Henry IV and his wife Joan of Navarre came to Leeds escaping the plague and, as the accounts show, Joan lived on here in high style spending some £13 a week. Under Henry VIII the castle was extended and improved, the additions including a tower to house the royal maids-of-honour one of whom was Anne Boleyn. In 1632 the castle passed back to the descendants of the ill-fated Colepeper, and in the 1660s it was used to house captured French and Dutch sailors. In 1926, the castle's last private owner Olive, Lady Baillie, began restoration.

Guide to opening: all the year. [T] Maidstone (0622) 65400 for details.

TOURIST INFORMATION

Tourist Information Centres: The Gatehouse, Old Palace Gardens, **Maidstone** [T] (0622) 602169/ 673581. Eastgate Cottage, High Street, **Rochester** [T] (0634) 43666. Buckhurst Lane, **Sevenoaks** [T] (0732) 450305.

- Allington Castle, nr Maidstone.
- Boughton Monchelsea Place, nr Maidstone.
- Chatham Historic Dockyard.
- Emmetts, nr Sevenoaks.
- Eynsford Castle, nr Farningham.
- Fort Amherst, Chatham.

- Great Comp Gardens, Borough Green.
- Igtham Mote, nr Sevenoaks.
- Knole, nr Sevenoaks.
- Leeds Castle, nr Maidstone.
- Meopham Windmill, nr Cobham.
- Museum of Kent Rural Life, Maidstone.
- Owletts House, Cobham.
- Riverhill, nr Sevenoaks.
- Rochester Castle.
- Rochester Cathedral.
- Royal Engineers Museum, Chatham.
- Upnor Castle, nr Rochester.

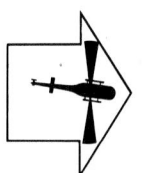

HUNT 12

START POSITION PENSHURST PLACE

CLUE ONE Off the rails to the south, a Beatle takes on the stones. If you know the ropes you'll beat Flotsam and Jetsam.

Leads to **HARRISON'S ROCKS**   Near the railway line at Groombridge, south of the start point, Penshurst Place, are Harrison's (one of the Beatles) Rocks. One of the climbs is known as Flotsam & Jetsam: the clue is at the top.

CLUE TWO Near Queen Henrietta's campsite, take to the Tuscan columns for the chalybeate source and duck down by the dipper.

Leads to **ROYAL TUNBRIDGE WELLS**   Queen Henrietta Maria camped here when taking the spa (chalybeate spring) waters. In the Pantiles, an Italianate colonnade, is the Dipper's Well, where the clue is hidden under a duckboard.

CLUE THREE Hop over a line at an olde worlde Toad Wood to 25 cowls. Head for the poles, and when you're one over the eight try walking a straight line.

Leads to **WHITBREAD HOP FARM**   The hop farm, with 25 oast houses, is beyond the railway line near Paddock (toad) Wood. In the hop field, tied up high on the ninth row of poles, is the clue, which is retrieved by a stilt-walker tending the crop.

CLUE FOUR Here's a Teiser: St Paul's railings should help you forge ahead to a claustral cluster where the clue is rooted beyond the sedilia.

Leads to **BAYHAM ABBEY**   The abbey (claustral cluster) is on the River Teise, near an old forge. Beyond the sedilia (block of stone seats) and the altar, the roots of a tree have grown into the abbey wall – the clue is hidden here.

CLUE FIVE Listen for the sound the poet heard on Innisfree and fall for the fellow who's got a rosy half-century under way.

Leads to **BEWL WATER**   Yeats heard lake water lapping, so the hunt is on for water. A pink-sailed wind-surfer (No. 50) is skimming along with the treasure, a scarf. The draught from the helicopter brings down the surfer and Anneka jumps into the lake to rescue the treasure.

CLUE SIX Although it's no longer how Roger de Ashburnham imagined it, Gilpin's adjustments have transformed this garden into a fairy-tale setting. Which garden is it?

CLUE SEVEN Them that asks no questions isn't told a lie. Watching the wall, though, won't help you get to the bottom of this poser. If they were alive today, these gentlemen, who once put the locals on edge, would be rather on edge themselves! Who were they?

A dash through Royal Tunbridge Wells.

Penshurst Place

Near Tonbridge

The story of Penshurst begins in 1340 with the building of a manor which now stands at the centre of the house. Visits to Penshurst start here, in the magnificent hall which has remained unaltered since that date. With its central hearth, great Gothic windows, gallery and a roof so high that hawks would roost there, it is thought to be the finest domestic hall in Britain. Over the centuries the rest of the house with its splendid state rooms and Long Gallery has spread out around it, never more than one room deep, and by the mid-sixteenth century the house had gained its final form. Later changes were made, but these too followed the Gothic style in which the house was begun.

It has been said of Penshurst that a list of its owners reads like the *dramatis personae* of all of Shakespeare's historical plays, but the name of Sir Philip Sydney (1554–86) stands out amongst them all. A poet and courtier, man of letters and man of action, he typified the Renaissance ideal of the complete gentleman.

The grounds at Penshurst include Tudor gardens, recently restored, a Venture Playground, nature trail, Farm Museum and Toy Museum.

Guide to opening: April to October. [T] Penshurst (0892) 870307 for details.

Harrison's Rocks

Near Groombridge

Harrison's Rocks are part of a series of sandstone outcrops which are a feature of the Tunbridge Wells area. Together with Bowles Rocks, High Rocks and Bulls Hollow they provide a mecca for climbers, providing testing routes of every grade. For non-climbers, the finest of all the outcrops is High Rocks, 2 miles south-west of Tunbridge Wells. Here, pathways wind round 40-foot cliffs with rustic bridges spanning chasms at the top.

Royal Tunbridge Wells

Prior to the early seventeenth century there was nothing at Tunbridge Wells but trees. Then, in 1606, the water from the local spring was discovered to contain iron and other minerals and word of its medicinal properties soon reached the court. In 1630 Henrietta Maria came here just after the birth of the future Charles II and found herself camping in a field, but following the royal visit building soon got underway. Ironically the first of its churches, built in 1679, is that of St Charles the Martyr, dedicated to Henrietta Maria's husband Charles I. The church stands close to the famous Pantiles, a broad, tree-lined walk flanked with elegant shops set back under colonnades. As the second *Treasure Hunt* showed, visitors to the Pantiles can still sample water dispensed by 'the dipper' in the building called The Chalybeate Spring.

By the time the famous Pantiles had been laid Tunbridge Wells was already a flourishing spa, and after Beau Nash arrived here from Bath in 1735 and took on the role of Master of Ceremonies, the town enjoyed many years as a fashionable centre with buildings to match. Many of the substantial Georgian and Victorian houses remain, and together with several beautiful parks and a 250-acre common (where the *Treasure Hunt* helicopter landed) they still give the town an elegant air. A perfect adventure playground for children, the Wellington Rocks on the common are the small relations of Harrison's Rocks featured in Clue 1.

Whitbread Hop Farm

Beltring, Paddock Wood

Whitbread's working hop farm grows more than a quarter of the hops needed to satisfy the brewery's thirsty customers. The centrepiece of the farm is a wonderful complex of white-coned Victorian Oasts, the largest group of its kind in the world. No longer used for drying hops, the Oasts and galleried barns now house displays of carts, harness and agricultural machinery, and a museum of 'hopping' and rural crafts. The farm also provides a country retreat for some of Whitbread's famous Shire Horses, still used for deliveries in the City of London and to pull the coaches of the Lord Mayor and the Speaker of the House of Commons on ceremonial occasions.

Guide to opening: April to October. [T] East Peckham (0622) 872068 for details.

Bayham Abbey

Lamberhurst

Set in the wooded valley of the River Teise, the picturesque remains of St Mary's Abbey and claustral buildings make what Pevsner describes as 'the most impressive monastic ruin of Sussex'. The abbey was built in the thirteenth century by Premonstratensian canons, using a smaller but similar plan to that favoured by the Cistercians. Elizabeth I sold the abbey to two brothers, one 'a gentleman', the other 'a grocer', and from then on Bayham stayed in private hands. In the late eighteenth century the ruins were seen to have Romantic appeal: a Gothic villa was built nearby and the ruins landscaped to enhance its view. At the same time the stream was dammed, and the gatehouse became a summerhouse by the new lake. In 1870 a mansion was built on the slope opposite the villa which in turn became incorporated into the present Dower House.

The abbey ruins include walls of the church and gatehouse rising to a fairly substantial height, and remains of the dormitory range, refectory and other buildings in the cloisters.

Guide to opening: April to September. [T] Lamberhurst (0892) 890381 for details. EH.

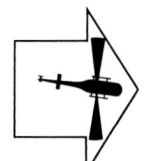

Bayham Abbey.

Bewl Water

Lamberhurst, Tunbridge Wells

Constructed in the 1970s, this 770-acre reservoir is now the scene of numerous leisure activities both on and off the water. From April to October the reservoir is generously stocked with brown and rainbow trout, making this the premier trout fishery in southern England. Permits for flyfishing, and boat hire, are available at the Fishing Lodge, and a series of one-day courses are held during the season for more experienced anglers. Sailing and canoeing are limited to members of organised groups and clubs, but individual board sailors are welcome providing they obtain a permit from the Recreation Office and can

also show a certificate of competence. The S.S. Frances Mary provides regular 45-minute cruises from April to October; a network of footpaths and riding tracks surrounding the reservoir provide ample scope for walking and riding; 127 acres have been set aside as a nature reserve accessible to people conducting scientific investigations; and there is also a special hide for ornithologists. An adventure playground is adjacent to the car parks and picnic areas. In the midst of them is the Visitor Centre, which can provide full information on all the facilities available here.

Guide to opening: all year. [T] Tunbridge Wells (0892) 890661 for details.

TOURIST INFORMATION

Tourist Information Centres: Vestry Hall, Stone Street, **Cranbrook** [T] (0580) 712538. Town Hall, High Street, **Tenterden** [T] (05806) 3572. Town Hall, High Street, **Tunbridge Wells** [T] (0892) 26121.

- **Benenden Walled Garden, nr Cranbrook.**
- **Biddenden Vineyards.**
- **Chiddingston Castle, nr Tonbridge.**
- **Finchcocks, Goudhurst.**
- **Lamberhurst Vineyard.**
- **Great Maytham Hall, Rolvenden.**

- **Kent & East Sussex Railway.**
- **Owl House Gardens, nr Tunbridge Wells.**
- **Penshurst Vineyards.**
- **Rare Farm Animals of Hollanden, Hildenborough.**
- **Scotney Castle Gardens, Lamberhurst.**
- **Sissinghurst Castle Garden.**
- **Smallhythe Place, nr Tenterden.**
- **Sprivers, Lamberhurst.**
- **Stocks Mill, nr Tenterden.**
- **Tenterden Vineyards.**
- **Union Mill, Cranbrook.**

TREASURE HUNT 13

East Anglia

START POSITION KENTWELL HALL, LONG MELFORD

CLUE ONE He lived and worked in Bath, painted many portraits; but where he was born you will see a painting of a church and get a clue under a horse.

Leads to **GAINSBOROUGH'S HOUSE, SUDBURY** Thomas Gainsborough was born in this house which now displays many of his works, including a painting of Hadleigh Church and Deanery and a sculpture of a horse. The clue is under the horse.

CLUE TWO Behind a table tomb in the churchyard by the Deanery is something Gainsborough would have like to paint.

Leads to **HADLEIGH CHURCH** Reference has been made already to this church and the deanery. Behind a table tomb in the churchyard is a blue ribbon.

CLUE THREE Two were millers' boys, two painted portraits and all painted horses. The clue is pinned to something pink, which is really red, where one of them worked.

Leads to **SIR ALFRED MUNNINGS ART MUSEUM, DEDHAM** Munnings and Constable were the millers' boys and Gainsborough and Munnings the portraitists. Munnings worked at Castle House, now the museum, where the clue is pinned to a red (hunting pink) riding jacket.

Constable's inspiration – Flatford Mill.

CLUE FOUR Stand where the other miller's boy stood to paint The Haywain and his neighbour's house and your treasure is a mahlstick concealed on your left, by a gate.

Leads to **FLATFORD MILL** Standing where Constable stood to paint 'The Haywain' and Willy Lott's Cottage, Anneka sees a gate to her left, as forecast. On the gate is a mahlstick, which is used to support the hand in painting.

CLUE FIVE Where the neighour is buried, the bells are in a cage; touching the tenor (very gently) gets the prize.

Leads to **EAST BERGHOLT CHURCH** Willy Lot is buried here. Money ran out before the bell tower had been completed, so the church bells have hung, since the fifteenth century, in a wooden cage in the churchyard. The bell ringers are waiting, and when Annie arrives they start ringing, so the prize is not as gentle as expected!

CLUE SIX Black cherries and a black deed both brought fame to a quiet village where, unlike poor Maria's cottage, the scene of the crime no longer stands. Where in the village was the crime committed?

CLUE SEVEN While ladies stepped out in Woolsey, their men sported a more hard-wearing cloth from a neighbouring village. Still evident today is the great prosperity that its popularity brought to the village. Where is it?

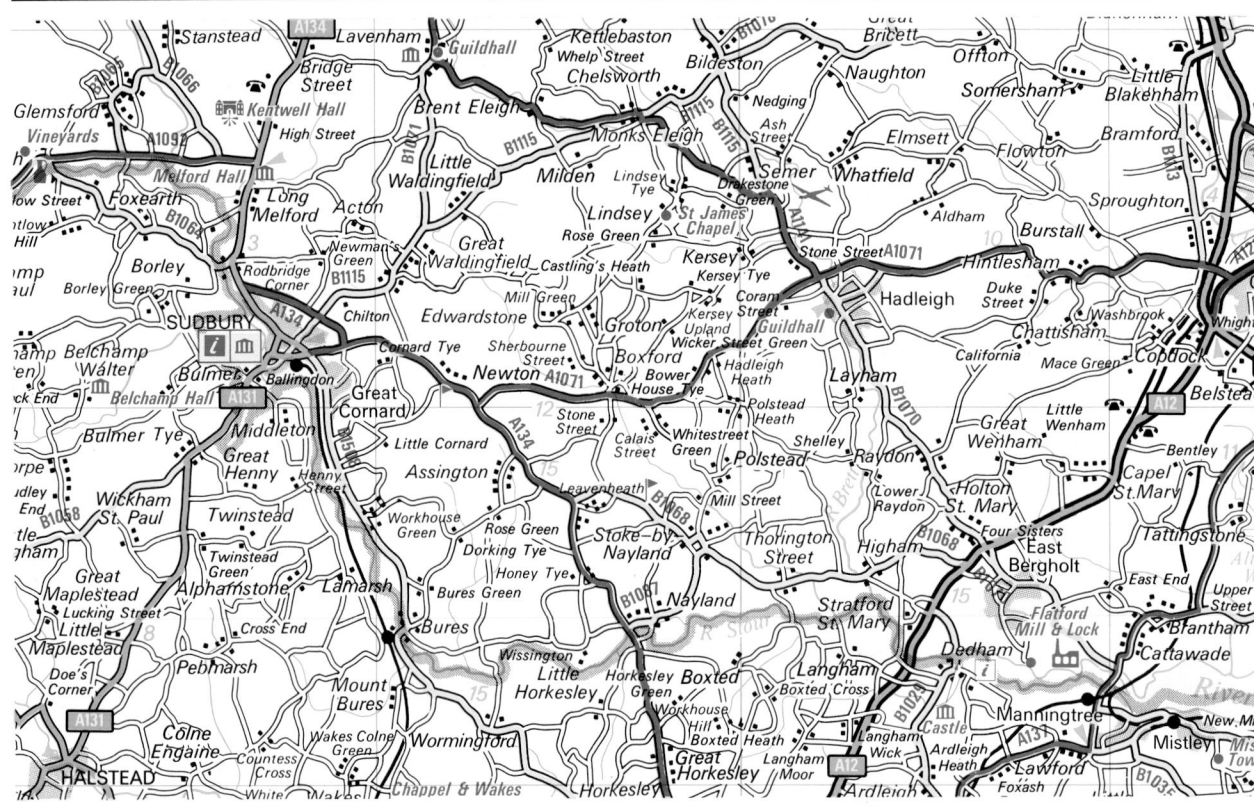

Gainsborough's House

Sudbury, Suffolk

Thomas Gainsborough once remarked that both he and 'old, pimply nosed Rembrandt' had been born in a mill, and his birthplace here in Sudbury did in fact serve as a workshop for his father who was a weaver of woollen shrouds. The famous artist was born here in 1727, and Sudbury was his home until he went to London to study at the age of 13. After his marriage in 1746 he returned and stayed for nearly four years before moving on to Ipswich, Bath and London. Although his portraits brought him fame and fortune, Gainsborough was happiest when painting land- scapes and, while these were not accepted as 'art' during his lifetime, by 1789 (the year after his death) they were selling for up to £500 each.

Today the house where Gainsborough was born contains more of his works than any other gallery, and includes a particularly fine collection of portraits of the local landed gentry painted during his Suffolk period. Additional displays here include modern sculpture, a Print Workshop and various temporary exhibitions.

Guide to opening: all the year. [T] Sudbury (0787) 72958 for details.

Hadleigh

Suffolk

A picturesque market town, Hadleigh displays a wealth of medieval buildings reflecting the prosperity brought by the wool and cloth trades. Many cluster round the Church of St Mary, which itself dates from the fourteenth/fifteenth centuries. The clock bell outside the tower is thought to be the oldest in the country, and a tomb in the south aisle is the legendary burial place of the Saxon king Guthrum, who died in AD 889. Beside the church is the Deanery Tower, a survival of an archbishop's palace built in 1495, and nearby is the fifteenth-century Guildhall, a superb half-timbered building with two overhanging storeys. The former town hall in the Market Place dates from 1851, and the High Street offers a further exceptional variety of fine buildings of brick, timber and plasterwork.

The Sir Alfred Munnings Art Museum

Castle House, Dedham, Essex

Born in 1878, Alfred Munnings was the son of a Suffolk miller. At 14½ he was apprenticed to a firm of lithographers in Norwich working as a poster artist promoting Caley's Chocolates and while still an apprentice he had the first of many pictures hung by the Royal Academy, of which he was later to become the president. Despite losing the sight of his right eye at the age of 20, Munnings developed his artistic career rapidly, first painting 'horses, village charac- ters, hunting themes and landscapes' and then serving as an official war artist with the Canadian Cavalry Brigade in France. In 1919 he bought the 'house of his dreams' here in Dedham and soon found world-wide fame painting racehorses.

A spacious Tudor and Georgian house set in

pleasant grounds, Castle House is still furnished as it was when Munnings lived here. Two galleries have been added to the house and here, as well as in the rooms where he lived and worked, some of his finest pictures are on display.

Guide to opening: May to October. [T] Colchester (0206) 322127 for details.

Flatford Mill

East Bergholt, Suffolk

The inspiration for many of Constable's paintings, Flatford Mill and Willy Lott's Cottage still look very much as they do on his canvas. Built in 1733, the mill passed to Constable's father in 1765, and after leaving school in Dedham the budding artist worked here in an attempt to learn the miller's trade before giving up to study at the Royal Academy schools in London. In 1802 he returned to East Bergholt as a professional painter, and after moving to a cottage in Hampstead in 1819 he returned regularly to the Stour Valley, sketching and seeking inspiration from nature, 'the source from whence all originally must spring'.

Facing Flatford Mill is Willy Lott's Cottage, which served as Constable's viewpoint when painting the famous Haywain. It was written of the cottage in 1843 that 'Willy Lott, its possessor, was born in it; and it is said, has passed more than 80 years without having spent four whole days away from it.' The 'Cottage' is in fact a fairly substantial house owned by the National Trust together with the Mill and the Mill House. The buildings are used by the Field Studies Council to accommodate residential courses promoting understanding and appreciation of 'Constable Country'. At nearby Bridge Cottage (a replacement of the one he loved to paint) there is a National Trust shop and tea garden open to the public, together with displays devoted to the artist's work.

Guide to opening: Bridge Cottage, open April to October [T] (0206) 298260 for details. NT. Courses at Flatford Mill Field Centre [T] Colchester (0206) 298283.

Gainsborough's House, Sudbury.

Hadleigh Parish Church.

East Bergholt. In 1774 Constable's father moved from Flatford Mill to the village, and a plaque now marks the site of the house where the artist was born in 1776. The church at East Bergholt is of particular note. Willy Lott is buried in the churchyard here.

TOURIST INFORMATION

Tourist Information Centres: Toppesfield Hall, **Hadleigh** [T] (0473) 822922. The Guildhall, **Lavenham** [T] (0787) 248207. County Library, Market Hall, **Sudbury** [T] (0787) 72092.

- **Belchamp Hall, nr Sudbury.**
- **Cavendish Manor Vineyards, nr Sudbury.**
- **East Bergholt Lodge.**
- **Kentwell Hall, Long Melford.**
- **Lavenham Guildhall.**
- **Lavenham Priory.**
- **Little Hall, Lavenham.**
- **Melford Hall, nr Sudbury.**

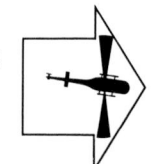

TREASURE HUNT 14

Norfolk

START POSITION WINDMILL HOUSE, HORNING

CLUE ONE At a capital place, broadly speaking, make a crafty move to St Ambrose's emblem, and pick up a bank note.

Leads to **BEEHIVE, WROXHAM**   Wroxham is 'Head of the Broads'. Having arrived here by helicopter, Annie has to take a boat to reach the Beehive, a half-timbered, thatched house; it has a distinctive weather vane which incorporates a beehive, a flower and a bee (St Ambrose's emblem). The clue (bank note) is hidden in some flowers near the river bank.

CLUE TWO Where Crome set up a school, fruitful market research into C63 and the Old Man of Hoy will lead to Annie's cue.

Leads to **NORWICH MARKET**   John Crome was the founder of the Norwich School of Painting. In the Market Square, an examination of stall C63, run by Dot and Geoff Hoy, reveals a cucumber bearing Annie's name and the clue.

CLUE THREE Hotfoot to an alley with a prison connection, shop for something that made Bottom's eyes water.

Leads to **MUSTARD SHOP, NORWICH**   The helicopter is not needed to reach Bridewell (house of correction) Alley and the Mustard Shop. Annie shops here for a jar of the spice that made Bottom's eyes water, and on it finds the clue.

CLUE FOUR North, and east of a Belgian battlefield, a navigational limit has signs of dawn and a heron by a staithe.

Leads to **COLTISHALL**   North of Norwich, and east of Waterloo, is Coltishall, the navigational limit of the River Bure. Near to the Rising Sun (sign of dawn) pub, the clue is attached to another sign which depicts a heron.

CLUE FIVE The Boleyn family were to the manor born; and an equestrian Romanov will spur you on to victory.

Leads to **BLICKLING HALL**   At one time this estate was owned by the Boleyn family. A later owner named a room after Peter the Great, the equestrian, one of the Romanov dynasty. The treasure is in Peter the Great's room, near a large tapestry, a gift from Catherine the Great.

CLUE SIX A weaver, a Saint, a ploughman, a manor and a duel commemorate a coronation. When you have found the connection between Harry's subjects, put down the sign!

CLUE SEVEN Preston and Richmond may be rather distant, but they both made an impression on this one-time home of an Englishman with Russian associations. Which home is it?

A taste of Norwich – the Mustard Shop.

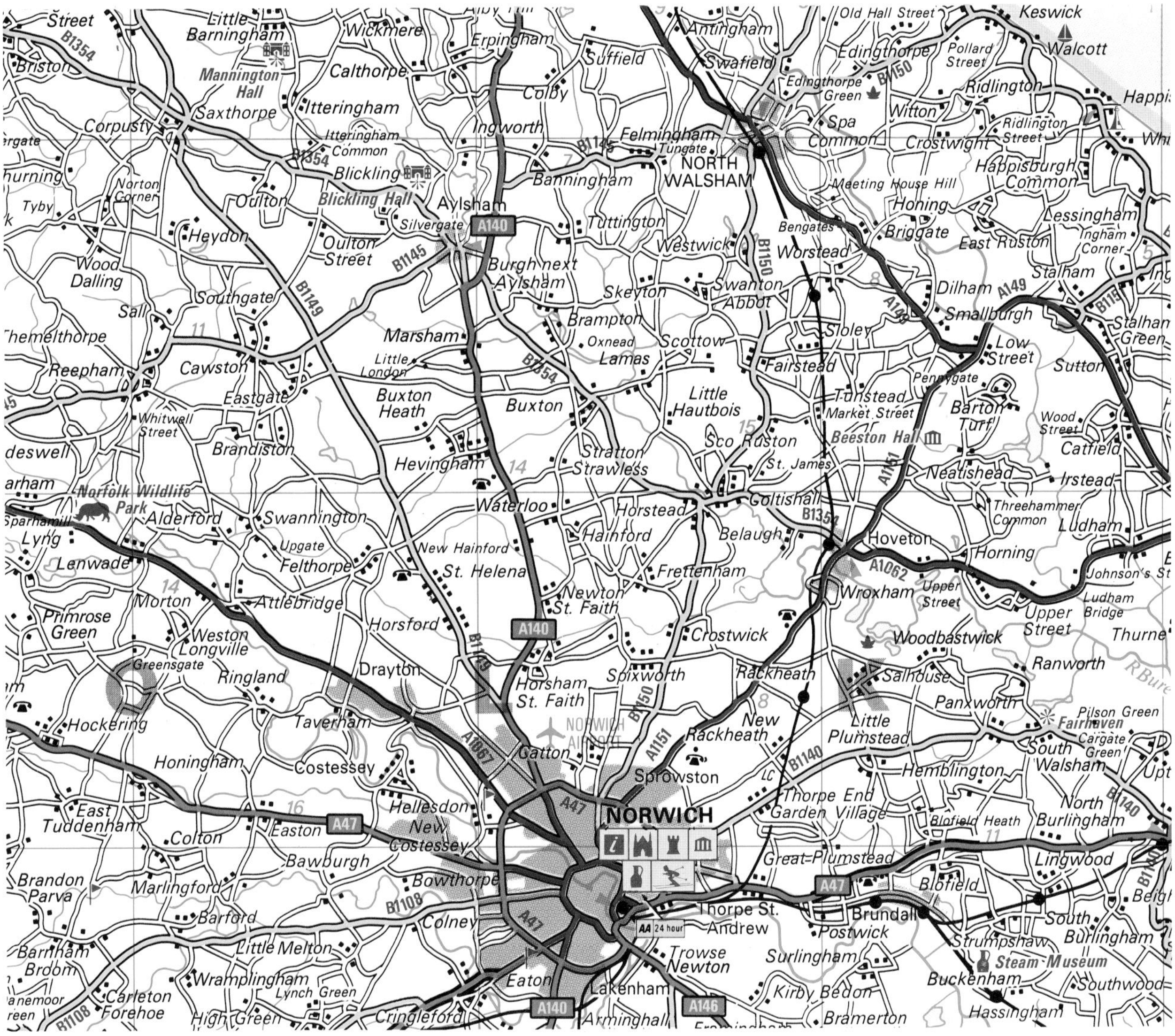

[Map of Norfolk showing Norwich and surrounding area including the Norfolk Broads, with towns such as North Walsham, Aylsham, Wroxham, Horning, Hoveton, and road networks A140, A149, A47, A146, etc.]

The Norfolk Broads

The Norfolk Broads are made up of 108 square miles of fens, woodlands and marshlands between Norwich and the coast, with inland lakes and rivers which find an outlet to the sea at Great Yarmouth and Lowestoft. The Boards are, in fact, flooded peat pits dug by early inhabitants, and together with connecting rivers these reedy channels now form 124 miles of navigable waterways entirely free of locks. The busy boating centre of Wroxham, 'Head of the Broads', and riverside Horning, are typical of the waterside communities which grew up here. Originally Broadland had few roads, and shallow barges known as Norfolk wherries provided the main link between towns and villages, but in the 1920s working wherries began to be adapted as pleasure craft, and the great Broads boating industry was born. Now the waterways are alive with yachts, launches and motor cruisers available for hire by the hour, day or week from many riverside boatyards. Details of these may best be obtained from the East Anglia Tourist Board (see page 7).

Broadland retains many delightful, traditional features. The area boasts some very fine churches (often with the distinctive Norfolk round tower) and many local buildings are thatched with Norfolk reeds, which are still cut for commercial use. Windpumps once used to drain the marshes are another hallmark of the landscape. Although, to a large extent, superceded by electric and diesel pumps, many still stand and some have been restored and opened to the public. Busy as they are, the Broads also remain a notable area for wildlife; they provide the last refuge for the Swallowtail Butterfly and the Southern Marsh Orchid and one of the few remaining nesting ground for the 'booming' bittern. Another rarity found here is the Norfolk Hawker dragonfly, the chosen symbol of the Broads Authority.

Norwich

Set snugly in a loop of the River Wensum, the buildings of this ancient city reflect nearly 900 years of history. Founded by the Normans in 1096, Norwich's graceful cathedral was one of the first arrivals on the scene. It represents a harmonious blend of Romanesque and late Gothic styles, with a

57

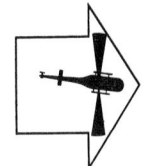

soaring fifteenth-century spire, elegant Perpendicular vaulting, and a wealth of wonderful detail. One of its greatest glories is the roof of the nave, decorated with intricate painted bosses carved between 1465 and 1510, each depicting a biblical scene to illustrate the story of mankind from Creation to the Day of Judgement. Similar bosses in the cloisters (also carved by workmen slung in hammocks) depict subjects ranging from devils to saints with amazing vigour and imagination.

The Normans also built the castle here (now a museum) and the fourteenth century saw the addition of the flint walls which then encircled the city. The oldest part of Norwich lies within the limits of these ancient walls – medieval cobbled streets like Elm Hill and Tombland, and a wealth of interesting individual buildings. Norwich also boasts a remarkable number of old churches; they include St Andrews and Blackfriars Halls, once part of monasteries, the non-conformist Old Meeting House of 1693, the Octagon Chapel of 1756 and the Roman Catholic Cathedral, built in 1884.

Leaflets available at the Tourist Information Centre outline a variety of tours and trails introducing different aspects of the city. One of these is the aptly named Macabre Trail. This takes in Tombland, the burial ground for victims of the Great Plague which killed over half the population here, Bishopgate where prisoners doomed to be burned alive carried faggots to the stake, and some 20 other sites. The Castle Museum exhibits the death masks of prisoners executed here, and outside the south door of the cathedral is the grave of Red Cross Nurse, Edith Cavell, tragically executed in the First World War for helping allied soldiers to escape from Belgium.

The Mustard Shop

Bridewell Avenue, Norwich

Large department stores and numerous antique shops make Norwich a first-class shopping centre. In particular, visitors love to explore 'character' shops tucked away in narrow medieval streets, and Bridewell Alley and The Mustard Shop come high on the list.

Jeremiah Colman started milling mustard in 1814 at Stoke Holy Cross, 4 miles south of Norwich, and bright yellow mustard fields supplying Colman's soon became a feature of the East Anglian landscape. In 1854 the firm moved to Carrow on the outskirts of the city, where they have been producing mustard ever since. In 1973 Colmans opened the Mustard Shop in Bridewell Alley, one of the oldest parts of Norwich. A faithful replica of Victorian trade premises, the shop stocks an extensive range of mustards (including some made especially for the shop) together with a wide selection of mustard pots and spoons, original posters and other related items. A small Mustard Museum explains the history of mustard, and the Colman family's involvement in it. The Mustard Shop also runs a thriving mail order service.

Guide to opening: [T] Norwich (0603) 627889 for details.

Norwich Cathedral, viewed from the Close.

Norwich Market

Market Place, Norwich

The centre of a rich agricultural area, Norwich has always been an important market town. The Saxons held their market in Tombland, but by the fourteenth century it had become established in the present Market Place. Earliest accounts of trading here tell not only of stalls selling meat, fish and vegetables, but also 'cloth, hats, shoes, stockings . . . rope, soap, books and ballads.' Entertainment was provided by organ grinders, dancing bears, Punch and Judy shows and even a 45-year old rattle snake, forming a light-hearted contrast to activities of the dentist who also operated here. Today the market is still one of the largest in the country; protected from the elements by bright canvas awnings, it operates all the year round, every day except Sunday.

The Norwich Museums: The Castle Museum displays archaeology, art, ceramics and glass, natural history and social history plus a lively programme of temporary exhibitions. Exhibits include the world's finest collection of Lowestoft porcelain, and paintings by John Sell Cotman and other well-known artists of the Norwich School. Strangers' Hall Museum, Charing Cross evokes the homes of prosperous citizens from the Middle Ages onwards. The Bridewell Museum, St Andrews Plain holds displays illustrating the trades and industries of Norwich during the past 200 years. St Peter Hungate, Elm Hill is a church museum and brass rubbing centre in a notable fifteenth-century church.

Blickling Hall

Blickling

With its warm brickwork, imposing leaded windows, extravagant gables and turrets with gilded vanes, Blickling Hall presents a perfect example of the Jacobean style, yet its history begins long before the present house was built. The original manor belonged to Harold Godwinson, last of the Saxon kings, and successive houses were built on the site. In 1616 the existing building was incorporated into a new home designed by Robert Lyminge who 12 years earlier had designed Hatfield House. Although other houses of the period were showing signs of the new Palladian style, Blickling Hall was wholly Jacobean.

Much of the interior, however, was remodelled in the 18th century by the second Earl of Buckinghamshire. Two of the most important rooms created at this time are the Peter the Great Room and its adjoining State Bedroom. The finest survival from Jacobean times is the Long Gallery.

Blickling's gardens are equally noteworthy, showing evidence of the changing styles of centuries.

Guide to opening: April to October. [T] (0263) 733084 for details. NT.

TOURIST INFORMATION

Tourist Information Centres: The Guildhall, Gaol Hill, **Norwich** [T] (0603) 666071.

- **Barton House Narrow Gauge Railway, Wroxham.**
- **Beeston Hall, nr Wroxham.**
- **Bridewell Museum of Trades and Industries, Norwich.**
- **Broads Conservation Centre, Ranworth**
- **Fairhaven Garden Trust Woodland and Water Garden, South Walsham.**
- **Mannington Hall & Gardens, nr Blickling.**
- **Norfolk Wildlife Park & Play Centre, Great Witchingham.**
- **Redwings Horse Sanctuary, Frettenham, nr Norwich.**
- **Royal Norfolk Regiment Museum, Norwich.**
- **Sainsbury Centre for Visual Arts, Norwich.**
- **St Peter Hungate Church, Norwich.**
- **Strumpshaw Hall Steam Museum, Strumpshaw.**
- **Sutton Windmill & Broads Museum.**
- **Swannington Manor Gardens, nr Norwich.**
- **Wolterton Hall Gardens, nr Erpingham.**

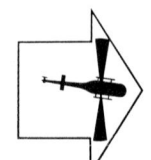

Blickling Hall – home to Shakespeare's Falstaff.

TREASURE HUNT 15

Hertfordshire

START POSITION **Brocket Hall**

CLUE ONE **Connect Harare and England's tallest spire with an Elizabethan childhood, and take your cue from an anteprandial royal entrance.**

Leads to **OLD PALACE, HATFIELD**   Salisbury (the former name of Harare and England's tallest cathedral spire) leads to Hatfield House, which was built by the first Earl of Salisbury. An Elizabethan banquet is about to start, and the Queen enters carrying the clue.

CLUE TWO **Near the first British martyr's shrine, a gateway gives access to academic heights. Where there's still life, there's hope!**

Leads to **ST ALBAN'S SCHOOL**   Near to St Alban's Abbey, the school is situated in the gatehouse. On the first floor, an art class is working on a still life. The clue is well hidden under one of the paintings.

CLUE THREE **A green place for green fingers and what Browning's patriot found all the way. Aim for gold following a French May.**

Leads to **GARDENS OF THE ROSE**   Chiswell GREEN is the home of this gardener's (green fingers) delight, and it is roses all the way! The clue is hidden in a climbing Maigold rose.

CLUE FOUR **Between two home grounds – Adrian IV's and Elton's – a jetsetter will play host to a circus bird, so watch out.**

Leads to **LEAVESDEN AERODROME**   Leavesden is situated between Bedmond (Adrian IV's) and Watford (Elton John's football club). Having made a dramatic appearance alongside the helicopter, a Harrier jump jet (the circus bird) lands at the aerodrome (owned by Rolls Royce – makers of jet engines) and its pilot hands over the clue.

CLUE FIVE **It sounds like another circus, by Parsley's place! Be a sport, try Falstaff's tipple – and you're up for the cup.**

Leads to **CHIPPERFIELD COMMON**   The manor house here was once owned by John Parsley. Anneka joins in a children's sack (Falstaff's tipple) race, which is taking place on the common. The treasure is the prize – a silver cup.

CLUE SIX Its owners have included Thomas a Becket, the Black Prince and now the Duchy of Cornwall. Which is this property at which Geoffrey Chaucer was once Clerk of Works?

CLUE SEVEN To the east, by the ruins of an essayist's house, has risen the seat of the Grimston family. What is it called?

Eureka! A triumphant Skyrunner at the Old Palace, Hatfield.

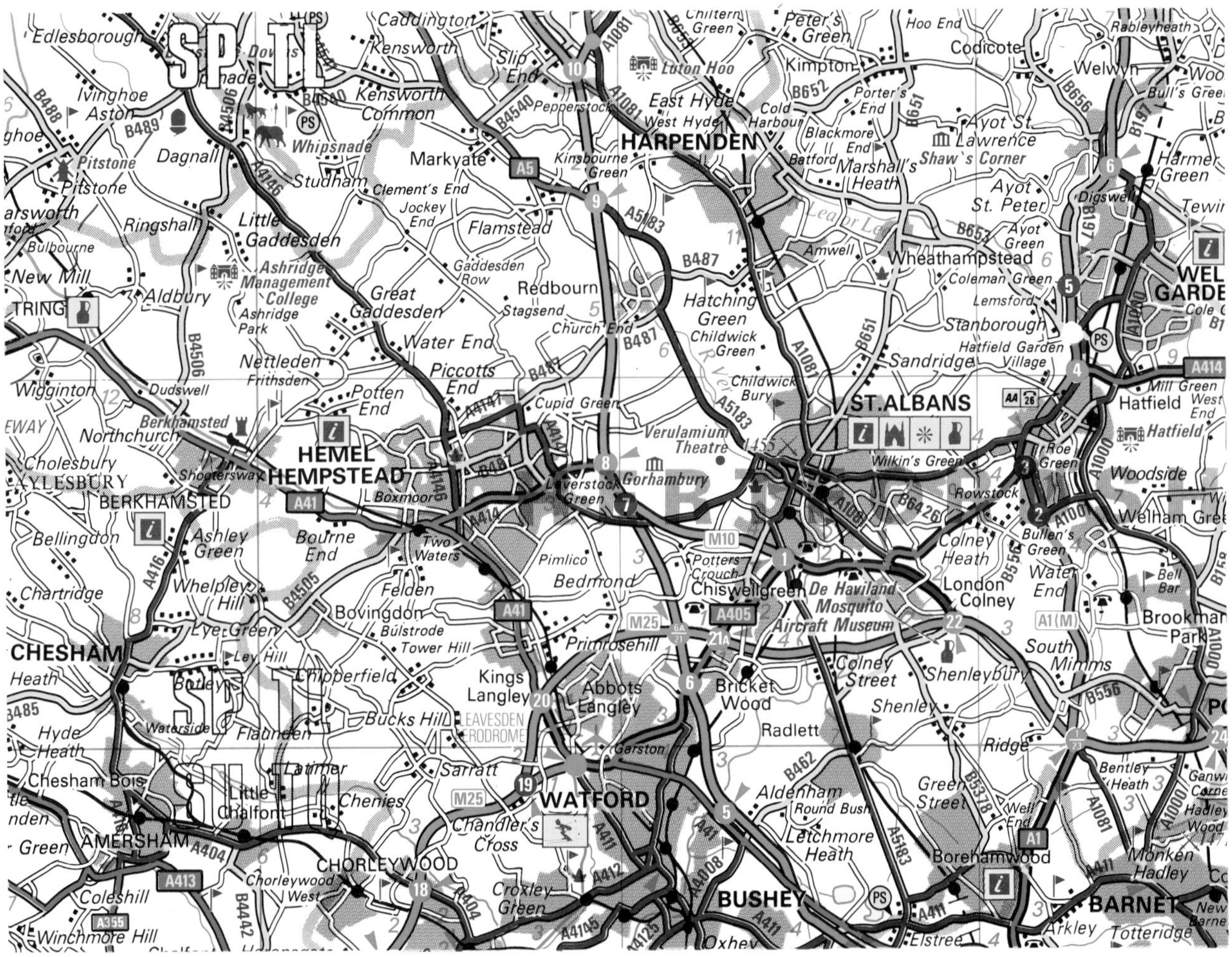

[Map of Hertfordshire area showing towns including Tring, Hemel Hempstead, Berkhamsted, Chesham, Amersham, Watford, Bushey, St Albans, Harpenden, Welwyn Garden City, Barnet, and surrounding villages with road networks]

Hatfield House, Old Palace and Gardens

Hatfield

History, house and contents combine to make Hatfield a fascinating place. The original Old Palace was built in 1497 by Cardinal Morton, Bishop of Ely, and the side which contained the Banqueting Hall still stands today. When Henry VIII claimed church properties the Palace became home to his children, and there are poignant stories of their lives here. In Mary's reign Elizabeth became a virtual prisoner at Hatfield, and she was sitting in the park here when news arrived of her accession. 'It is the Lord's doing,' she said, 'and it is marvellous in our eyes.' Her successor, James I, gave the house to the Cecil family, and it was Robert Cecil, first Earl of Salisbury, who pulled down most of the Old Palace and built the present Jacobean house in the 'E' shape popular in Elizabethan times.

The Cecils established Hatfield as a social and political centre; Charles I came as a prisoner *en route* to London, and James II (then Duke of York) came here fleeing anti-Catholic agitation, only to find the Protestant third Lord Salisbury had purposely deserted the house and left the royal party without so much as a candle. The sixth Earl (1713–1780) gained

a different kind of notoriety acting as a public coachman on the run from London to Hatfield, but the wife of the first Marquess (1748–1823) carried eccentricity still further by tossing gold coins to the poor from a velvet bag, and presiding over gambling parties which left the floor of the Long Gallery ankle-deep in cards. She died in a fire which destroyed the interior of the west wing, but her portrait by Reynolds still hangs in the King James' Drawing Room. Her son made good the damage, and Hatfield continued its distinguished role, entertaining Victoria and Albert, Edward VII and leading political figures of the day.

Tours of Hatfield today take in the superb Marble Hall and Minstrels' Gallery, the elaborately carved Grand Staircase, the 180-foot Long Gallery, the Library with its 10,000 books, the Chapel, Armoury and much else besides.

Guide to opening: late March to early October. [T] Hatfield (07072) 62823/65159 for details.

St Albans

In AD 209, a citizen of Verulamium named Alban sheltered a priest fleeing from persecution, and was converted by him to Christianity. Refusing to deny his new faith, Alban himself was put to death on a hill

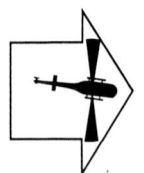

61

overlooking the town, and was later canonised as Britain's first Christian martyr. By the time the Romans left Britain a shrine had been set up to mark the place of his execution, and in 793 this was chosen for the site of a Benedictine abbey. The abbey church was dedicated to St Alban and, in due course, the town which grew up there also took his name. Thus history links the abbey and the Roman town which are now side by side on the 'tourist trail'.

Verulamium covers some 200 acres beside the River Ver and was the third largest town in Roman Britain. It is estimated that at its peak the population reached about 25,000, and as a 'municipium' its inhabitants enjoyed the same rights as the citizens of Rome. The original town was destroyed in AD 60 by Boudica and was rebuilt on a grander scale, but suffered again from a large fire in AD 155. Fifth-century Verulamium provided a last glimpse of civilised Roman society in Britain.

Visible remains of the town (now a part of Verulamium Park) include the foundations of the London Gate, the remains of the City Wall and a hypocaust which provided the heating system for a private suite of baths. Set slightly apart are the remains of a large Roman theatre, town house and shops; built in AD 140–180, the theatre had a stage rather than an amphitheatre, and was therefore unique in Britain.

Verulamium Museum in St Michael Street features interpretive displays of the Roman town together with a wide variety of finds from the site. These include jewellry and coins, some very fine wall plasters and mosaics and two fourth-century skeletons.

Guide to opening: all year, daily. [T] St Albans (0727) 54659.

Cathedral and Abbey Church of St Alban. In 1077 the Normans demolished the Saxon abbey and started building one of their own, often (as seen in the tower) using red tile-like bricks salvaged from the Roman town. Because of the fame of the shrine of St Alban the abbey grew rich, flourishing as a centre of art and culture until in 1539 the Dissolution of the Monasteries meant most of its treasures were broken or removed, and the monastery buildings destroyed. The local people bought the abbey church for £400 to use as their parish church, and in the mid-nineteenth century it was restored, becoming a cathedral in 1877.

At 275½ feet, the cathedral's nave is the longest in England while its arches and pillars reflect three clearly different styles – Norman, Early English and Decorated. Beyond the Presbytery, which has the oldest wooden ceiling vault in England, an elaborate stone reredos separates the altar from the Shrine of St Alban. The gem-encrusted shrine was destroyed during the Reformation, and only the broken pedestal of Purbeck marble remains where once pilgrims came, and miraculous cures were reported. Overlooking it is a wooden Watching Chamber from which monks safeguarded the treasures of the shrine.

The Garden of the Rose, Chiswell Green.

The Gardens of the Rose

Chiswell Green, St Albans

At the showground of the Royal National Rose Society, 12 acres of mature gardens stocked with over 30,000 roses provide a marvellous spectacle for the casual visitor, and endless fascination for the real rose enthusiast. The gardens contain one of the most important single collections of roses in the world, a living 'catalogue' of plants which aims to include representatives of all roses past and present. Alongside this, the search goes on to find the flowers of the future; the Society made its first award to a new rose in 1883, and since then it has established its own trial grounds where worldwide varieties undergo a three-year scrutiny to assess their value as garden plants.

Guide to opening: mid June to late October; British Rose Festival, early July. [T] St Albans (0727) 50461 for details.

TOURIST INFORMATION

Tourist Information Centres: County Library, Kings Road, **Berkhamsted** [T] (04427) 4545. The Pavilion, Marlowes, **Hemel Hempstead** [T] (0442) 64451. 37 Chequer Street, **St Albans** [T] (0727) 64511. Campus West, The Campus, **Welwyn Garden City** [T] (0707) 332880.

- **Ashbridge House Gardens, nr Hemel Hempstead.**
- **Berkhamsted Castle.**
- **Chenies Manor, nr Amersham.**
- **Gorhambury House, St Albans.**
- **Kingsbury Water Mill, nr St Albans.**
- **Knebworth House, nr Welwyn.**
- **Luton Hoo, nr Luton.**
- **Organ Museum, St Albans.**
- **Piccotts End Medieval Wall Paintings, nr Hemel Hempstead.**
- **Pitstone Tower Mill, nr Tring.**
- **St Albans City Museum.**
- **Shaw's Corner, Ayot St Lawrence.**
- **Tring Zoological Museum.**
- **Whipsnade Zoological Park.**

TREASURE HUNT 16

Cambridge

START POSITION WIMPOLE HALL, LIBRARY

CLUE ONE Not a Barrett home, but Elsie's, whose bedtime stories were just so, there's a *déjà vu* feeling under the lantern, where a torchère has a message.

Leads to **WIMPOLE HALL, YELLOW DRAWING ROOM** Elsie, daughter of Rudyard Kipling (*Just So Stories*) once lived here. Anneka has to retrace her steps through the hall (hence the *déjà vu* feeling) to the Drawing Room where the clue is hidden on a torchère.

CLUE TWO Get a telescopic sight, then join the Army, but Annie forget your gun. The enemy are all clued up.

Leads to **BARTON ROAD RIFLE RANGE** The telescopic sight is the real hint to this destination, where the Army is practising. Annie has to borrow a pair of binoculars to read the clue, which is on the helmet of one of the targets.

CLUE THREE Among the regal groves of Academe, an exact science describes a fluvial arc. To figure it out, Annie must float off the fellows' backs.

Leads to **MATHEMATICAL BRIDGE, CAMBRIDGE** If you can't put two and two together, you'll never figure out this one! Annie does, though. Then she has to punt off from The Backs to reach the clue, which is suspended from the Queens' College end of the bridge.

CLUE FOUR Stands the church clock at ten to three?
Cherries and honey hold the key.

Leads to **GRANTCHESTER CHURCHYARD** Words from Rupert Brooke's 'The Old Vicarage, Grantchester' point to this churchyard where the clue is in a pot of honey, hanging from a cherry tree.

CLUE FIVE At the house of Hobson's choice, 9,000 have met their Waterloo. The treasure lies below a Constable connection.

Leads to **ANGLESEY ABBEY** The Abbey, once owned by Thomas Hobson, the carter, has a library of 9,000 books. In the library hangs Constable's painting 'The Opening of Waterloo Bridge', and the clue is hidden beneath it.

CLUE SIX A classic strip in a thoroughbred town takes its name from a royal aficionado. What is it called?

CLUE SEVEN A long haul, in formation maybe, to the west of south, could take you on a trip down memory lane. Your precise target on this sortie, though, is something civil of the modern day. E – what an agreeable way to end! What is your target?

Wimpole Hall.

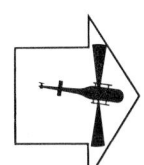

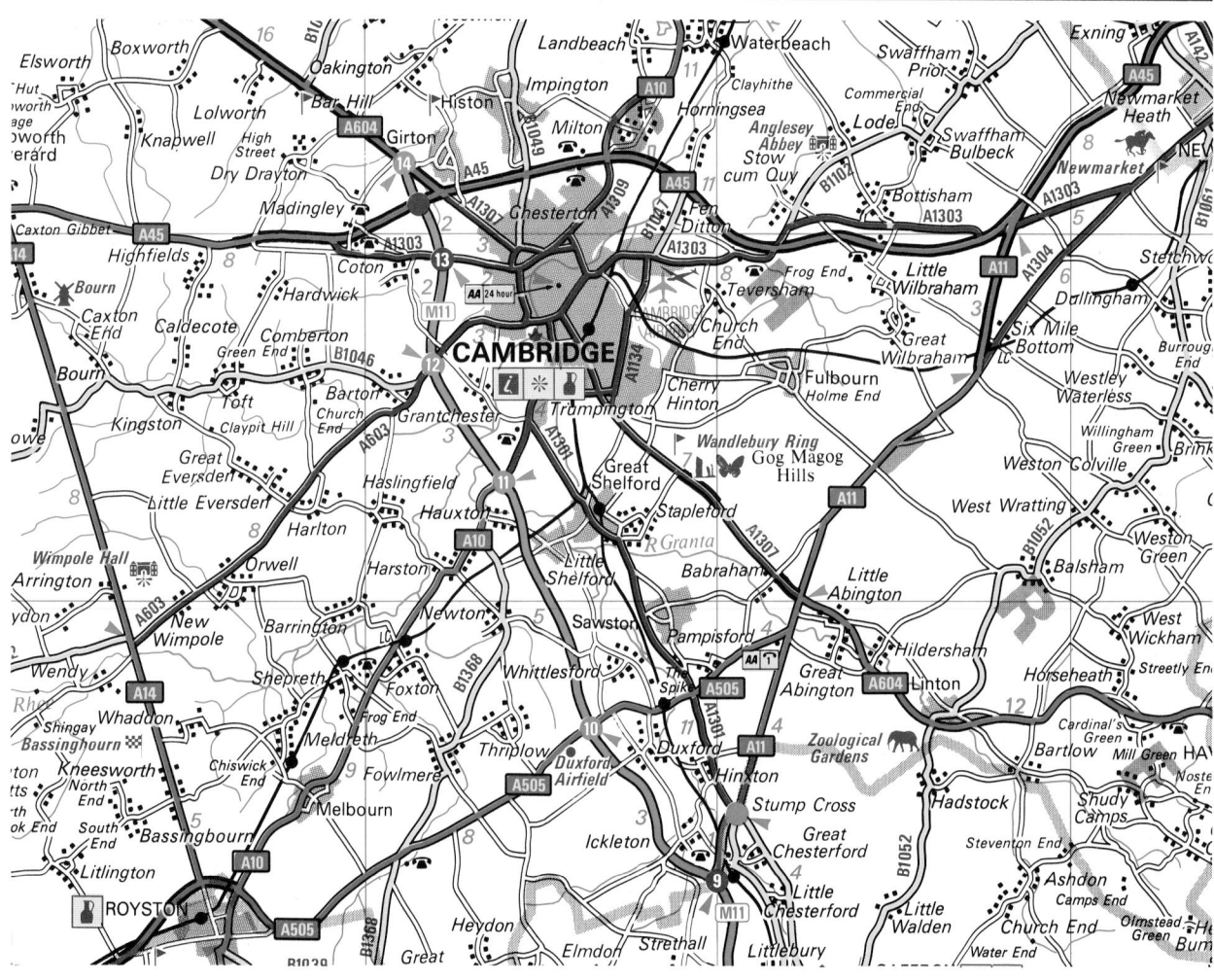

Wimpole Hall

Arrington, Cambridgeshire

The largest house in Cambridgeshire, Wimpole is also the most important if only for the number of famous architects and landscape gardeners who worked here. The first house was built between 1640 and 1670, and altered between 1713 and 1721 under the guidance of architect James Gibbs; the additions which he made include the magnificent 50-foot library, almost a double cube, and the chapel with its great Baroque interior, decorated by Sir James Thornhill for a fee of £1,350.00. The 1740s saw the house altered again, this time by Henry Flitcroft; his greatest contribution was the Gallery, a noble 62 feet long. On several occasions the cost of lavish plans resulted in Wimpole Hall's having to be sold, and by 1938 the house was unlived-in and almost empty. In this sorry condition it was bought by Captain George Bambridge and his wife, the daughter of Rudyard Kipling; it was she who restored and furnished the Hall, leaving it to the National Trust at her death.

The garden and park at Wimpole reflect the changing fashions of English gardens from 1690 to 1830. In the 1720s Charles Bridgeman extended the existing gardens with avenues, ha-has and ponds; in 1767 Capability Brown extended the park, built the Gothic Tower and made a chain of lakes between it and the house, and Humphry Repton altered the park yet again between 1801 and 1809. More recently the National Trust has restored the eighteenth-century Home Farm to house rare breeds, old farm equipment, a museum and film loft, and now both house and grounds are used regularly to stage a variety of indoor and outdoor events.

Guide to opening: April to October. [T] Cambridge (0223) 207257. NT

Cambridge

Cambridgeshire

Cambridge grew up around a fording place on the River Cam, where fens and forests once met. Romans and Saxons built on the site and the Normans raised a castle here from which to tackle the Saxon rebel Hereward the Wake who had his lair in the Isle of Ely. Students began to gather in Cambridge as early as 1209, and in 1284 the Bishop of Ely founded Peterhouse, the first of the university colleges; five more followed in the 14th century, ten in the fifteenth-sixteenth centuries and so on steadily until the opening of Robinson College in 1977 brought the final number to thirty-two. Although each of the colleges has something splendid to offer, King's College Chapel is the gem of them all. Built between

St John's College, Cambridge.

College. Brooke joined the navy in 1914 and died of blood poisoning on board a hospital ship without having seen action, but the idealist patriotism of his wartime poetry had already made him a national figure. 'The Old Vicarage, Grantchester', written in Berlin in 1912, creates a romantic and aching nostalgia for the rural charms of his favourite village.

Anglesey Abbey

Near Lode, Cambridgeshire

Dating from around 1600, the house is built on the site of an Augustinian priory which had fallen into ruin following the Dissolution in 1535. In the early seventeenth century it was owned by Thomas Hobson, whose practice of hiring out horses without allowing clients to select their own animal gave rise to the saying 'Hobson's Choice', but after that the history of the house remained undistinguished until this century. In 1926 Anglesey Abbey was bought by Huttleston Broughton, later the First Lord Fairhaven. An immensely wealthy man and notable patron of the arts, he restored the Abbey and made it a fitting home for the priceless Fairhaven Collection of paintings, tapestries, books, mosaics, bronzes and furniture. Besides many English pieces the collection includes *objets d'art* from ancient Egypt, the Ming dynasty and Renaissance Europe which together form the most wide-ranging display to be found at any country house.

Lord Fairhaven also created gardens to match the splendours of the house, transforming 100 acres of rather flat fenland into a masterly blend of formal and free landscaping incorporating walks and avenues, an arboretum, a magnificent herbaceous garden, a large collection of statuary and a working water mill, demonstrated on the first Sunday in each month. The Visitor Centre houses a graphic display which shows how the gardens were developed.

Guide to opening: April to October. [T] Cambridge (0223) 811200 for details. NT

1446 and 1515, its delicate fan vaulting, glorious stained glass windows and richly carved screen and choir stalls make it a supreme achievement of Gothic architecture. Behind the altar, Rubens' 'Adoration of the Magi' provides the crowning touch.

Most colleges are open to visitors except during the examination period (early May to mid June) and individuals may also join guided tours which leave the Tourist Information Centre at set times.

The 'Backs', a pleasant stretch of riverside lawns and gardens behind the colleges, also reward visitors with excellent views of many of the university buildings. From Easter to October rowing boats, punts and canoes may be hired from Quayside (beside Magdalene Bridge).

Grantchester

Near Cambridge, Cambridgeshire

A popular village with thatched and timbered cottages set around the River Granta (the Roman name for the Cam), Grantchester has long been a part of Cambridge university life. Chaucer, Spenser, Milton, Dryden and Byron all came to write at the spot now known as Byron's Pool, and Rupert Brooke lived and wrote here at the Old Vicarage after leaving King's

---

TOURIST INFORMATION

Tourist Information Centre: Wheeler Street, **Cambridge** [T] (0223) 322640.

- **Bourne Windmill.**
- **Chilford Hundred Vineyard, nr Linton.**
- **Denny Abbey, Waterbeach.**
- **Docwra's Manor Gardens, Shepreth.**
- **Imperial War Museum, Duxford.**
- **Linton Zoo.**
- **Lode Water Mill.**
- **National Horseracing Museum, Newmarket.**
- **Unwins Seeds Trial Grounds, Histon.**
- **Wandlebury Rings Iron Age Fort.**
- **Willers Mill Wild Animal Sanctuary & Fish Farm, Shepreth.**

TREASURE HUNT 17 & 18

Warwickshire / Cotswolds

HUNT 17 (WARWICKSHIRE)
START POSITION HENLEY-IN-ARDEN

CLUE ONE **Twenty-one locks secure a capital diamond centre, but a bouyant hero of Khartoum has the key.**

Leads to **HATTON LOCKS**   Hatton Garden, London's diamond centre, leads to these locks where 'General Gordon' (hero of Khartoum), a boat, has the clue.

CLUE TWO **Gatecrash a Kingmaker's family house party, head for the sound of music, then inspect the still life.**

Leads to **WARWICK CASTLE**   Richard Neville, Earl of Warwick, was the Kingmaker. In the music room of his castle, a waiter, looking like one of the waxworks, has the clue on a salver. Anneka has the shock of her life when he moves!

CLUE THREE **In Shallow ground where young Will poached**
Are the crested seats on which Lucy was coached.

Leads to **CHARLECOTE PARK**   Having been caught stealing deer in the park, young Will (Shakespeare) was brought to account before the owner, Sir Thomas Lucy. Justice Swallow is Shakespeare's caricature of Sir Thomas. The clue is in the Lucy coach.

CLUE FOUR **'The play's the thing Wherein I'll catch the Blessed role of king.'**

Leads to **ROYAL SHAKESPEARE THEATRE**   This hint of Hamlet could mean only one place – the Royal Shakespeare Theatre. Actor Brian Blessed, in kingly role, has the clue.

CLUE FIVE **Bedtime for the future bride of Aston Cantlow, and all's well that ends well.**

Leads to **MARY ARDEN'S HOUSE**   Mary Arden was married at Aston Cantlow. In the bedroom is the treasure, a miniature edition of *All's Well That Ends Well*.

CLUE SIX A ladder turns, but not on a table, in this peaceful home, where a postman may utter an impressed 'coo' on seeing the accommodation. What is it called?

CLUE SEVEN An arrow will help you find the Seymours and your well-plastered destination, but once there, all you have to look for is water! To whose design is this envious expanse laid out?

Warwick Castle.

66

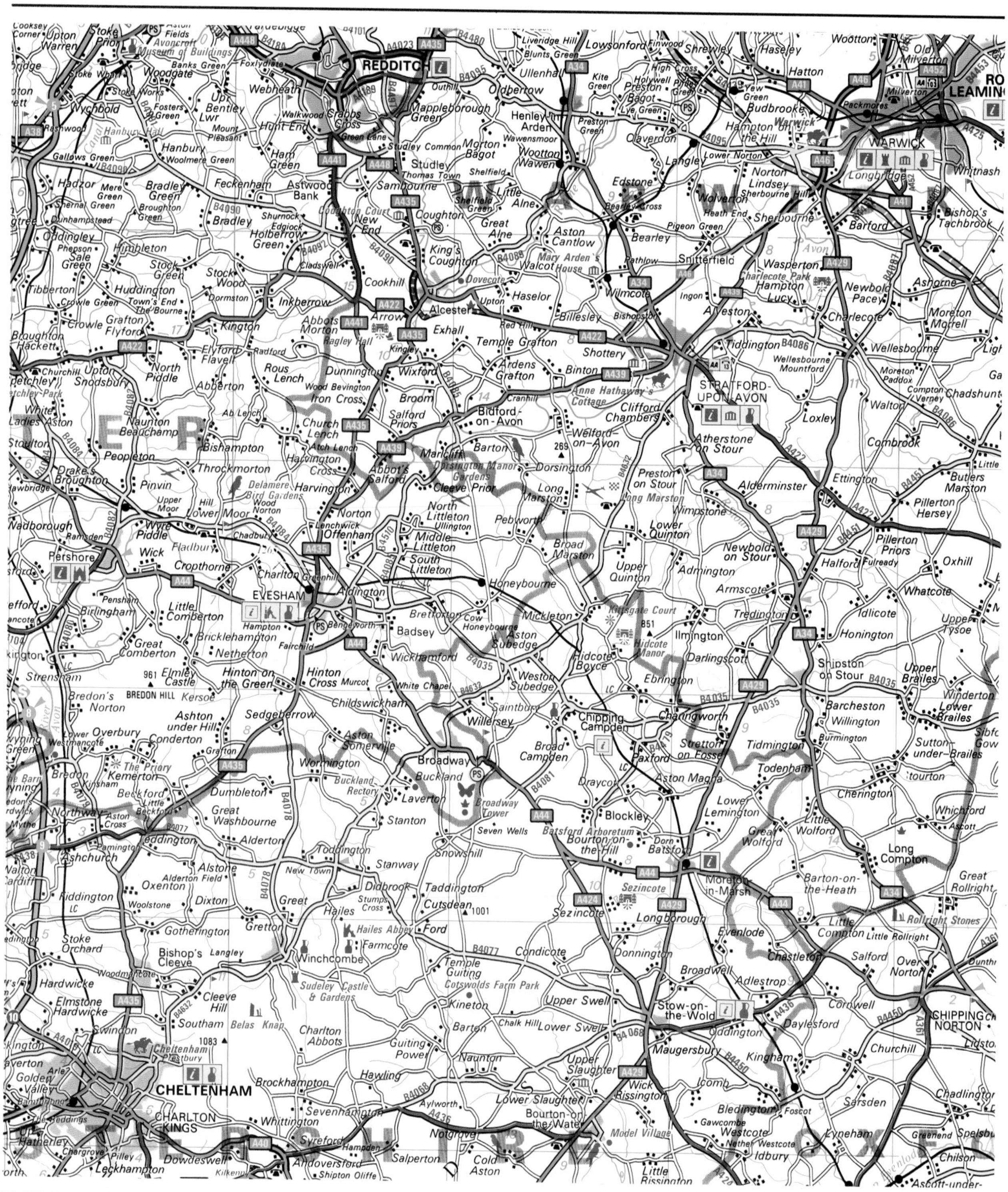

[Map of Warwickshire and surrounding area showing towns including Redditch, Warwick, Stratford-upon-Avon, Evesham, Cheltenham, Chipping Norton, and the surrounding villages and road network.]

Hatton Locks

Hatton

Known as 'The Stairway to Heaven', Hatton's dramatic flight of 21 locks poses a tough challenge to boatmen tackling this stretch of the Grand Union Canal. Navigating the formidable flight takes a good 2½ hours, and most boats like to wait for company. In the 1930s all locks between Napton and Knowle were widened in an attempt to speed up traffic but faced with competition from other forms of transport tonnage figures soon declined.

Warwick Castle

Warwick

Set on a sandstone cliff overlooking the Avon, 'the finest medieval castle in England' is a sturdy sight. The entrance is through a massive Gatehouse and Barbican flanked by two fourteenth-century corner towers – Guy's Tower, now a favourite viewpoint, and Caesar's Tower which houses the well-used dungeons, torture chamber and sinister *oubliette*. The Clarence Tower and Bear Tower (where bears for baiting were kept) watch over the north wall, and the

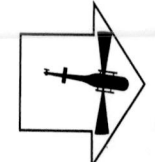

67

Watergate Tower, or Ghost Tower, guards the gateway to the river (the ghost is that of the hapless Sir Faulke Greville, murdered by his manservant in a particularly unpleasant way).

Within this mighty, military shell are the castle's awesome armoury and the state rooms. Largest of them all is the Great Hall, built in the 14th century and remodelled in the 1830s. The Library, Music Room, Card Room, Boudoir and various bedrooms now hold 'A Royal Weekend Party, 1898' as recreated by Madame Tussaud's. A series of 17th-century staterooms are also on view.

Guide to opening: all the year. [T] Warwick (0926) 495421 for details.

Charlecote Park

Warwick

Charlecote Park was the home of the Lucy family from the twelfth century until the house was given to the National Trust in 1945. The most famous of its owners was Sir Thomas Lucy, the local magistrate thought to have fined young William Shakespeare for poaching deer from the park.

The present Charlecote Park dates from 1558, when it was built on the site of Sir Thomas' house of which only the gatehouse and a two-storey Renaissance porch survive. Between the 1820s and 1860s, both the interior and exterior of the house were largely rebuilt and improved in what is acknowledged to be one of the finest examples of the Elizabethan Revival style. The parklands surrounding the house were 'improved' by Capability Brown in 1760s, and still support the famous 'Shakespeare' deer and Jacob sheep.

Guide to opening: April to October. [T] Stratford-upon-Avon (0789) 840277. NT

Stratford-upon-Avon

William Shakespeare was born in Stratford-upon-Avon in 1564, went to school at the Grammar School which still remains, retired here to New Place, died here in 1616 and was buried in Holy Trinity Church. It is therefore not surprising that Stratford-on-Avon is very much his town.

The **Royal Shakespeare Company**, one of the best known and largest theatre companies in the world, stages a varied repertorie at its three riverside theatres in Stratford, and in London's Barbican Centre. The Stratford Season runs from late March/early April to January, during which time the Royal Shakespeare Theatre (which seats 1,500 people) presents the works of the Bard himself, the Swan Theatre (an Elizabethan-style playhouse seating 430) stages plays by his contemporaries, and The Other Place (seating 150) features new plays.

Guide to opening: [T] Stratford-upon-Avon (0789) 295623 for details.

Shakespeare's Birthplace in Henley Street is a half-timbered Elizabethan building where Shakespeare was born and spent his early years. His mother was the daughter of a prosperous local farmer and his father was a glover and wool dealer who became Bailiff, or Mayor, of Stratford, and part of the house was used in connection with his trade. Today the living room, kitchen and bedrooms have period furniture appropriate to a middle-class home, and the other half of the house contains an exhibition on Shakespeare's life and work and on the history of the house itself.

Charlecote Park – east front.

Mary Arden's House, Wilmcote.

New Place/Nash's House (Chapel Street/Chapel Lane). Although Shakespeare spent his professional life in London, he bought New Place in 1597 and later retired here. The site and foundations of the house are preserved in an Elizabethan garden setting, entered via the adjoining Nash's House which belonged to the first husband of Shakespeare's grand-daughter, Elizabeth Hall. Furnished in period style, the house also has a museum of local history.

Hall's Croft, located in Old Town, is set in a beautiful walled garden. This house belonged to medical man Dr John Hall, the husband of Shakespeare's daughter, Susanna. The period furniture includes some particularly fine Elizabethan and Jacobean pieces, and special displays illustrate Dr Hall's career and the medical background of the time. Prize exhibit is a dispensary complete with apothecaries' jars, herbs and surgical instruments.

Mary Arden's House and Shakespeare Country Museum (Wilmcote, 3 miles from Stratford). The hiding place of the fifth *Treasure Hunt* clue is a Tudor farmstead with stone dovecote and half-timbered farm buildings. The house boasts some rare pieces of country furniture and farming utensils, and various outbuildings join with the neighbouring Glebe Farm complex in accommodating a unique museum of old farming implements and other bygones associated with the local countryside. Further attractions include a working smithy and displays of country crafts.

Anne Hathaway's Cottage (Shottery, 1 mile from Stratford). This picturesque thatched cottage belonged to Shakespeare's wife before her marriage. The family came from farily well-to-do yeoman stock, and the 'cottage' was, in fact, a 12-roomed farmhouse. The buttery, the kitchen with its open fire and bake-over, and the old-fashioned garden and orchard provide some of Old England's most photogenic subjects.

Guide to opening; all five properties listed above are open all the year round, and may be visited individually or on one joint ticket. [T] Stratford-upon-Avon (70789) 204016 for details.

TOURIST INFORMATION

Tourist Information Centres: Civic Square, Alcester Street, **Reddich** [T] (0527) 60806. Judith Shakespeare's House, 1 High Street, **Stratford-upon-Avon** [T] [0789) 293127. The Court House, Jury Street, **Warwick** [T] (0926) 492212.

- **Arms & Armour Museum, Stratford.**
- **Coughton Court, nr Alcester.**
- **County Museum, Warwick.**
- **Kinwarton Dovecot, Alcester.**

- **Lord Leycester Hospital, Warwick.**
- **Movie Memorabilia, Warwick.**
- **Oken House Doll Museum, Warwick.**
- **Ragley Hall, nr Alcester.**
- **Stratford Butterfly Farm & Jungle Safari.**
- **Stratford Brass Rubbing Centre.**
- **Stratford Motor Museum.**
- **Warwickshire Museum of Rural Life, Moreton Morrell.**
- **Warwickshire Yeomanry Museum, Warwick.**

HUNT 18 (COTSWOLDS)

START POSITION STANWAY

CLUE ONE **Head south west towards a musical link with the Planets, and above the Cloud watch this space – for Longfellow's strange device, perhaps!**

Leads to **CLEEVE HILL** Gustav Holst, composer of the Planets Suite, was born at Cheltenham, which is south west of the start point at Stanway. *En route* to Cheltenham is Cleeve Hill. At Cleeve Cloud, on the Hill, a light aircraft trails a banner (Longfellow's strange device) giving the first words of the next clue.

CLUE TWO **ON A PARR WITH BLANDINGS: look for a field or, two bends gules.**

Leads to **SUDELEY CASTLE** Katherine Parr is buried at Sudeley Castle, setting of P.G. Wodehouse's *Blandings Castle*. A medieval fair is taking place, and the clue is hidden on the gold (or) shield with two diagonal red stripes (bends gules) carried by one of the knights.

CLUE THREE **At a Power-point for Jacobs and Old Spots, Billboy will put Annie on the horns of a dilemma.**

Leads to **COTSWOLDS FARM PARK** Situated near the village of Guiting Power, the farm is the home of Jacob sheep, Old Spot Pigs and other rare breeds, including an Old Gloucester bull, Billboy. The clue is on one of his horns.

CLUE FOUR **An aquatic rookery in Little Venice, and royalty on the rocks? Sounds fishy.**

Leads to **BIRDLAND** Bourton-on-the-Water is known as the Little Venice of the Cotswolds. The clue is on a tray of fish which is to be fed to the colony (or rookery) of King penguins.

CLUE FIVE **After a swell flight, an academic has a head start in a race for a yard in a tun.**

Leads to **DONNINGTON BREWERY** A flight over Lower and Upper Swell leads to DONnington Brewery where the treasure, a yard of ale, is hidden in a large cask or tun.

CLUE SIX So – you know your onions and you want to crow about it! Something that inspired the Prince Regent could be just the place for you to do it! Where is it?

CLUE SEVEN A man of the willow, hitting boundaries, indicates the scene of a border incident, but hush – don't shout about it! Locate a lone detachment from the army, and note it down.

Tackling a yard of ale at the Donnington Brewery.

Sudeley Castle

Winchcombe, Gloucestershire

The inspiration behind fiction's famous *Blandings Castle*, is now as picturesque and peaceful as P.G. Wodehouse showed it to be. Though tucked away in the heart of the Cotswolds, the castle has played its part in a thousand years of history.

Sudeley's first royal owner was Ethelred (the 'Unready') who prized the estate for its oak trees and its deer, but it was the Tudors who really put Sudeley on the map. Following his marriage to Jane Seymour, Henry VIII made her brother Thomas Lord Seymour of Sudeley, and on Henry's death in 1547 it was he who married the royal widow Katherine Parr. But Seymour was soon making advances to the Princess Elizabeth, then only 15, and Katherine retired to Sudeley together with her ladies-in-waiting, one of whom was Seymour's neice, Lady Jane Grey. Katherine Parr died at Sudeley in 1548 after giving birth to a daughter, and was buried here in St Mary's Church; Seymour's rash ambitions soon ended with his execution in the Tower of London, and in 1554 Lady Jane Grey – the 'Queen for Nine Days' – followed him to the block. The castle's royal connections did not end there; Elizabeth I, who had known Sudeley as a child, returned three times as queen, and Charles I made a base here in the Civil War. As a result the castle was 'slighted' by the Parliamentarians in 1643, and left to decay.

In 1837 rebuilding began and now the castle boasts works by Turner, Constable, Rubens and Van Dyke, together with a wealth of antique furniture, artefacts, arms and armour and an interesting variety of things relating to Katherine Parr. Still Sudeley continues to add to its attractions, with an adventure playground for children, regular falconry displays, and a permanent exhibition of designer craftsmen at work. The castle also stages special events throughout the season including music and drama and various forms of 'period' entertainment.

Guide to opening: April to October. [T] Cheltenham (0242) 602308/604103 for details.

Cotswolds Farm Park

Guiting Power, Gloucestershire

This 25-acre farm has the most comprehensive collection of Rare Breeds of British farm animals in the country. The animals on show are selected from larger flocks and herds reared on the surrounding Bemborough Farm to form a 'living exhibition' of rare breeds, and a shop window for the vital work of conservation. Compared with the 'specialist' hybrids which farming demands today, most of the animals here have a decidedly distinctive look, and background information on the breeds is full of fascinating details too.

There are Iron Age pigs, Exmoor ponies (still just like their ancestors who came to Britain with the Celts) and rare Golden Guernsey goats (whose survival was due solely to a woman who protected them during the German occupation of the island),

while characters amongst the cattle include White Parks, once sacrificed by the Druids, diminutive Dexters, specially bred for small farms, and Gloucesters such as Billboy, guardian of the *Treasure Hunt* clue. Visitors may also enjoy the adventure playground, picnic sites, cafe and gift shop.

Guide to opening: April to September. [T] Guiting Power (04515) 307 for details.

Birdland

Bourton-on-the-Water, Gloucestershire

Home to many colourful characters, Birdland lends an exotic touch to one of the Cotswolds' most picturesque villages. Since *Treasure Hunt* was filmed here Birdland has found a new riverside site in the centre of the village just behind the car park. Numerous aviaries have bene completed, and more are on their way, but in the meantime most of the old favourites are still on show. The flamingoes have exchanged their lawn enclose for an idyllic stretch of the River Windrush, which they share with a large variety of wildfowl. Popular free-flying birds include the brilliant Macaws and Cockatoos.

Birdland's penguins, who held the key to the *Treasure Hunt* clue, are now rehoused in another rocky setting, this time with a low wall where the public can reach in and stroke their glossy backs.

Guide to opening: all the year. [T] (0451) 20689 for details.

TOURIST INFORMATION

Tourist Information Centres: Public Library, **Alfreton** [T] (0773) 833199. Old Market Hall, Bridge Street, **Bakewell** [T] (062 981) 3227. The Library, Church Street, **Bolsover** [T] (0246) 823179. Peacock Information Centre, Low Pavement, **Chesterfield** [T] (0246) 207777. The Pavilion, **Matlock Bath** [T] (0629) 55082.

- **Arkwright's Cromford Mill.**
- **Bakewell Old House Museum.**
- **Bolsover Castle, nr Chesterfield.**
- **Gulliver's Kingdom Family Theme Park, Matlock Bath.**
- **Hardwick Hall, nr Chesterfield.**
- **High Tor Grounds, Matlock.**
- **Lea Gardens, nr Matlock.**
- **Matlock Bath Aquarium.**
- **Middleton Top Engine House, Middleton-by-Wirksworth.**
- **Midland Railway Centre, Butterley Station, Ripley.**
- **The Museum Townscape & Stephenson's Railway, Crich.**
- **Peacock Heritage Centre, Chesterfield.**
- **Peak District Mining Museum & Temple Mine, Matlock Bath.**
- **Riber Castle Wildlife Park, nr Matlock.**

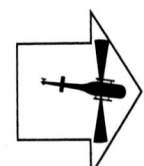

TREASURE HUNT 19

Derbyshire

START POSITION Alport Height

Clue One Where Stephenson made tracks, your quarry – via a moving reminder of old Paisley – is waiting in suspense at the bridge.

Leads to **National Tramway Museum, Crich** George Stephenson originally developed this site as a railway link between the local limestone quarry and the main line railway. As the Paisley District Tramways' open-top car passes under a bridge, the clue, hanging beneath, is caught from the top deck.

Clue Two Ascend Alpine-style to the scene of Wolfe's victory, then seek shade on the terrace.

Leads to **Heights Of Abraham** General Wolfe launched an attack from the plains of Abraham. After taking a cable car to the top of the Heights, the clue is to be found under an umbrella in the visitors' centre.

Clue Three Manners are important here, so when you find the man who was Whistler's Long Gallery boy, Annie say your grace.

Leads to **Haddon Hall** Manners is the family name of the Duke of Rutland, whose home this is. Hanging in the Long Gallery is a landscape by Rex Whistler, which portrays the ninth Duke and his son, the present Duke. Beside the painting stands the tenth Duke, from whom Annie receives the clue after introducing herself.

Clue Four In a town of good cooks, shop around for the proof of the pudding.

Leads to **Bakewell** Good cooks bake well – especially in the Old Original Pudding Shop! The clue is well-hidden in a pudding that has 'Annie' written on its top.

Clue Five Where Devonshire meets Derbyshire, look for a violin that's a bit of a fiddle.

Leads to **Chatsworth** In the State Music Room of this home of the Duke and Duchess of Devonshire is a *trompe l'oeil* of a violin. The treasure, a real violin, is placed nearby.

Cable car, Heights of Abraham.

Clue Six In a village to the west of the twisted spire is another ecclesiastical eye-catcher. No matter how late you arrive at this probable birth-place of a founding physician, you'll always have minutes to spare! Where are you?

Clue Seven Now look for a hall more glass than wall. Beneath its famous silhouettes, however, there is wall-space enough in the Blue Room to display a woven set. What is the set called?

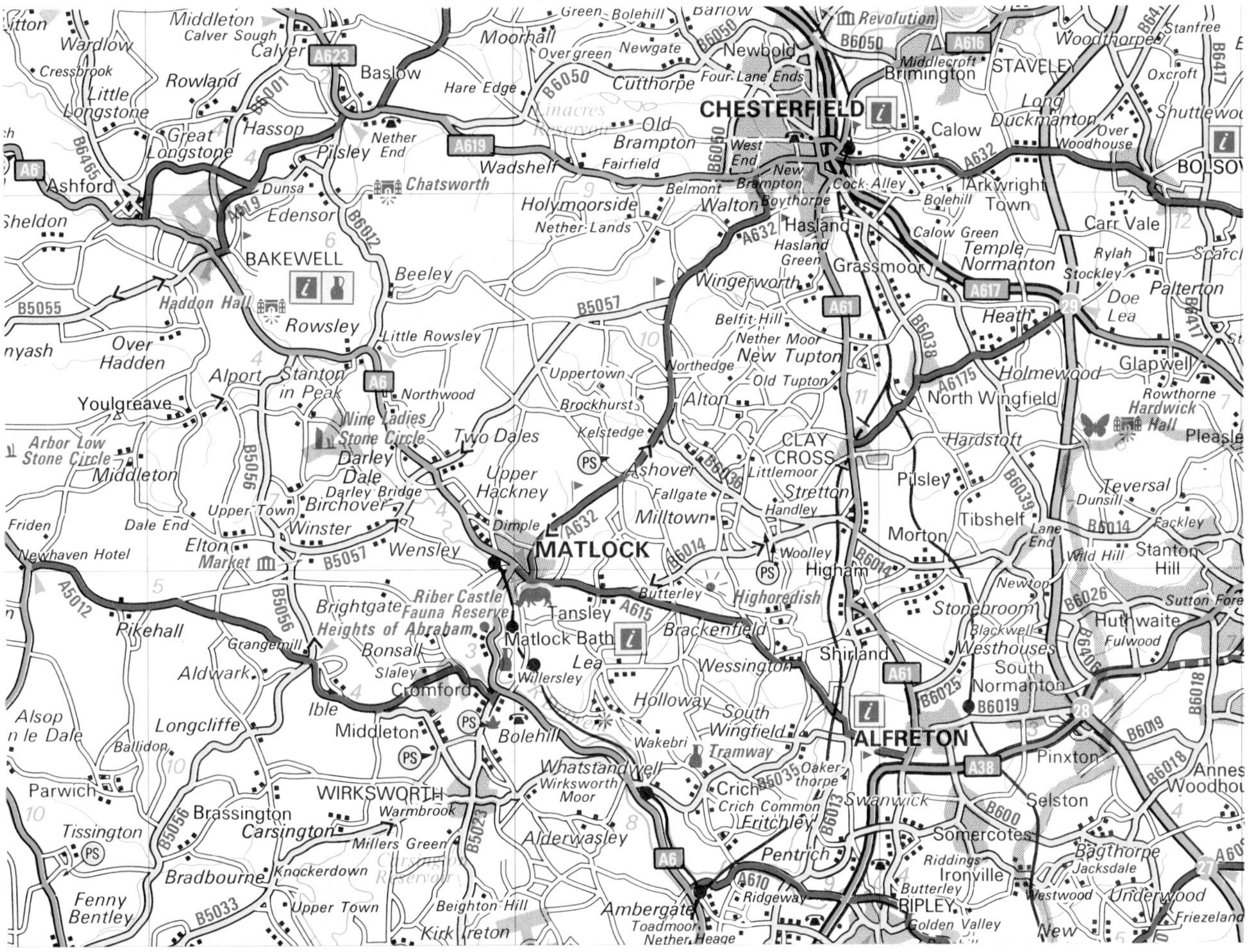

[Map of Derbyshire showing Chesterfield, Bakewell, Matlock, Alfreton and surrounding areas]

The National Tramway Museum
Crich

This unique museum was set up to preserve a form of transport which reigned supreme in many of our cities from the 1890s to just after the Second World War. In 1959 the Tramway Museum Society acquired the site of a former mineral railway, built by the great George Stephenson, and set about adapting it as a home and showground for their historic tramcars, together with their attendant depots and workshops. Now the collection at Crich comprises over 50 horse, steam and electric tramcars built between 1873 and 1953; a third of them are in full working order, and normally two or three are in operation each day, offering scenic rides with lovely views across the Derwent valley. The centrepiece of the Museum is a 'period' townscape in keeping with the heyday of trains and skilfully assembled with paving stones, granite setts, working gas lamps, cast-iron tram shelters and other authentic items. In addition to its collection of tramcars, the Museum also features various special exhibitions and displays, and a variety of events are staged here at weekends.

Guide to opening: April to October. [T] Ambergate (077 385) 2565.

Heights of Abraham
Matlock Bath

The cable car from Matlock Bath offers a spectacular way of scaling these heady Heights, and a range of attractions greet visitors at the top. Chief amongst them are the Great Masson Cavern and the Great Rutland Cavern-Nestus Mine, both excavated by lead miners in the seventeenth century. There's plenty to see above ground too; the Woodland Trail which links the caverns winds on down the steep face of the hill; Prospect Tower, a Victorian folly, gives panoramic views over five counties, and the Tree Tops Centre provides a gift shop and refreshments in a chalet setting perfectly appropriate to an area nicknamed 'Little Switzerland'.

Guide to opening: February to December. [T] Matlock (0629) 2365 for details.

Haddon Hall
Bakewell

The Derbyshire seat of the Dukes of Rutland, this enchanting medieval manor house is a romantic vision of grey-stone walls, towers and turrets of which none is less than 400 years old. A combination of grandeur and simplicity, it is sturdily built of local

73

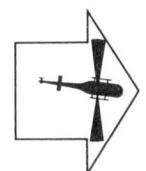

stone and home-grown oak with not a trace of brick, marble or any other 'foreign' material to be found. Such stout construction has served it well, and beyond the deep stone threshold of the main gateway, well-worn with hundreds of years of use, much of the house has survived just as it was. Visitors are allowed to roam through much of the house: into the dining room with its original carved panelling, up the stairs, past the priceless tapestries probably made for Charles I, and into the Long Gallery, built above existing walls in 1611. 110 feet long and panelled entirely in oak decorated with carved walnut, it is one of the loveliest rooms of its kind in the country. From here visitors find themselves out in the grounds; set between a wooded hillside and the fast-flowing River Wye, Haddon's beautiful terraced gardens are stocked with an abundance of roses and other old-fashioned flowers and herbs.

Guide to opening: April to September. [T] Bakewell (062 981) 2855.

Bakewell

A small riverside town built of soft, brownish stone, Bakewell lies in a sheltered wooded valley in the heart of some wonderful walking country. It has been a market town since 1313, and the traditional Monday market still attracts local residents and tourists alike. Jane Austen was a visitor here and it is thought that she stayed at the Rutland Arms whilst working on *Pride and Prejudice*; if the Bakewell was indeed 'Lambton' then some of the scenes of the novel must have been set in this hotel.

Though Bakewell's name has nothing to do with its puddings, its fame undoubtedly has. The true Bakewell Pudding is sold at The Original Bakewell Pudding Shop in The Square, and bears no relation to the mass-produced pies which borrowed its name. A light and deliciously eggy affair, the genuine article is made from a secret recipe devised by accident 120 years ago. Whilst making a jam tart, the cook at the White Horse Inn mistakenly put the egg mixture on the jam instead of in the pastry; impressed with the results, a friend adopted the recipe and opened the shop which exists today. Since then its fame has spread, and Bakewell's puddings are now sent to individual customers all around the world.

Guide to opening: [T] Bakewell (062 981) 2193 for details.

Chatsworth House

Bakewell

It is easy to see why the 'Palace of the Peak' has always drawn the crowds. The first house at Chatsworth was begun in 1552 by Bess of Hardwick and served as a prison for Mary Queen of Scots on several occasions between 1569 and 1584. In 1686 the first Duke began to tinker with the house and found the work so delightful that despite a general shortage of funds (and the threat of a huge fine incurred for tweaking a political opponent's nose) he went on

The Chatsworth Violin – trompe l'œil at Chatsworth House.

building until by 1707 a new Chatsworth had emerged. Succeeding Dukes added and altered in turn, and today only the Chapel and State Dining Room (1690s) and the Great Dining Room and Sculpture Gallery (1830s) are just as they were built. Many rooms are open to the public, and magnificence is the hallmark of them all.

The gardens at Chatsworth are as splendid as the house. Capability Brown worked on the park in 1761, but the present gardens are mainly the creation of architect Sir Jeffry Wyatville and Joseph Paxton, who later designed the Crystal Palace. Paxton's Emperor Fountain sends a jet of water 290 feet into the air, and water still flows down the impressive 'staircase' of the Cascade, just as it has done since 1696.

Guide to opening: April to October. [T] Baslow (024 688) 2204 for details.

TOURIST INFORMATION

Tourist Information Centres: 1 Cotswold Court, **Broadway** [T] (0386) 852937. Municipal Offices, Promenade, **Cheltenham** [T] (0242) 522878. Woolstaplers' Hall Museum, **Chipping Campden** [T] (0386) 840289. The Almonry Museum, **Evesham** [T] (0386) 6944. 37 High Street, **Pershore** [T] (0386) 554711. Talbot Court, **Stow-on-the-Wold** [T] (0451) 31082. Town Hall, **Winchcombe** [T] (0242) 602925.

- **Batsford Arboretum, Moreton-in-Marsh.**
- **Bourton-on-the-Water.**
- **Chastleton House, Moreton-in-Marsh.**
- **Cheltenham Museum & Art Gallery.**
- **Donnington Fish Farm, Stow-on-the-Wold.**
- **Hailes Abbey, nr Winchcombe.**
- **Holst Birthplace Museum, Cheltenham.**
- **Kiftsgate Court, nr Chipping Campden.**
- **Pitville Pump Room Museum, Cheltenham.**
- **Snowshill Manor, Broadway.**
- **Sezincote House, Moreton-in-Marsh.**
- **Spetchley Park, nr Pershore.**

TREASURE HUNT 20

Oxfordshire

START POSITION DAY'S LOCK AND WEIR

CLUE ONE Before you come to power, halt for a run on historic lines. A coach for the track event has chocolate and cream.

Leads to **DIDCOT RAILWAY CENTRE** It is not the steaming engine that holds the clue, but one of the dining cars. Travellers in period dress are being served by one waiter and some waitresses. It is the waiter who has the clue on his tray.

CLUE TWO To Peter Cook's *alma mater's* bank, where you'll need to shell out for the wet bobs' hero.

Leads to **RADLEY COLLEGE REGATTA** It is regatta time at Peter Cook's old college, in Radley, south of Oxford. On the river bank, Annie discovers that the only way to retrieve the clue from the umpire's boat ('Hero') is to take to the water herself (shell out) with a rowing four.

CLUE THREE Look in on the bibliopolist opposite the Encaenia location and ask for a note on Dodgson's Liddell account.

Leads to **BLACKWELL'S BOOKSHOP, OXFORD** The bookshop is opposite the Sheldonian Theatre where the annual commemoration of founders and benefactors is held. Hidden in an *Alice in Wonderland* display in the window is the clue. Dodgson (Lewis Carroll) wrote the book for Alice Liddel.

CLUE FOUR Fair Rosamund's tomb and a Schubert quintet bring you to a branch of *cuprous fagus*.

Leads to **THE TROUT, GODSTOW** The ruins of a nunnery, where Rosamund is said to have been poisoned, and Schubert's 'Trout Quintet' lead to this pub. The clue hangs from a branch of a large copper beech tree (*cuprous fagus*).

CLUE FIVE Connect Southey's old Kaspar and a proposal to Miss Hozier, then use a communications room to come face to face with Mrs Freeman's father-in-law.

Leads to **BLENHEIM PALACE** 'Old Kaspar' features in Southey's poem, 'The Battle of Blenheim'. Connect this to the location where Sir Winston Churchill proposed to Clementine Hozier, and Blenheim Palace it must be! In the Green Writing (communications) Room is a picture of the first Sir Winston Churchill, father-in-law of Mrs Freeman. The treasure, a little soldier, sits on top of the painting.

CLUE SIX Has Mallard been switched into the sidings? No – but its less powerful namesake might well have been in this border-line spot. In which village is it?

CLUE SEVEN An old Military College to the south west witnessed the initial success of a future benefactor's smartly rounded design. Which other College also bears witness to that success?

The roof-scape of Oxford, from St Mary's Church.

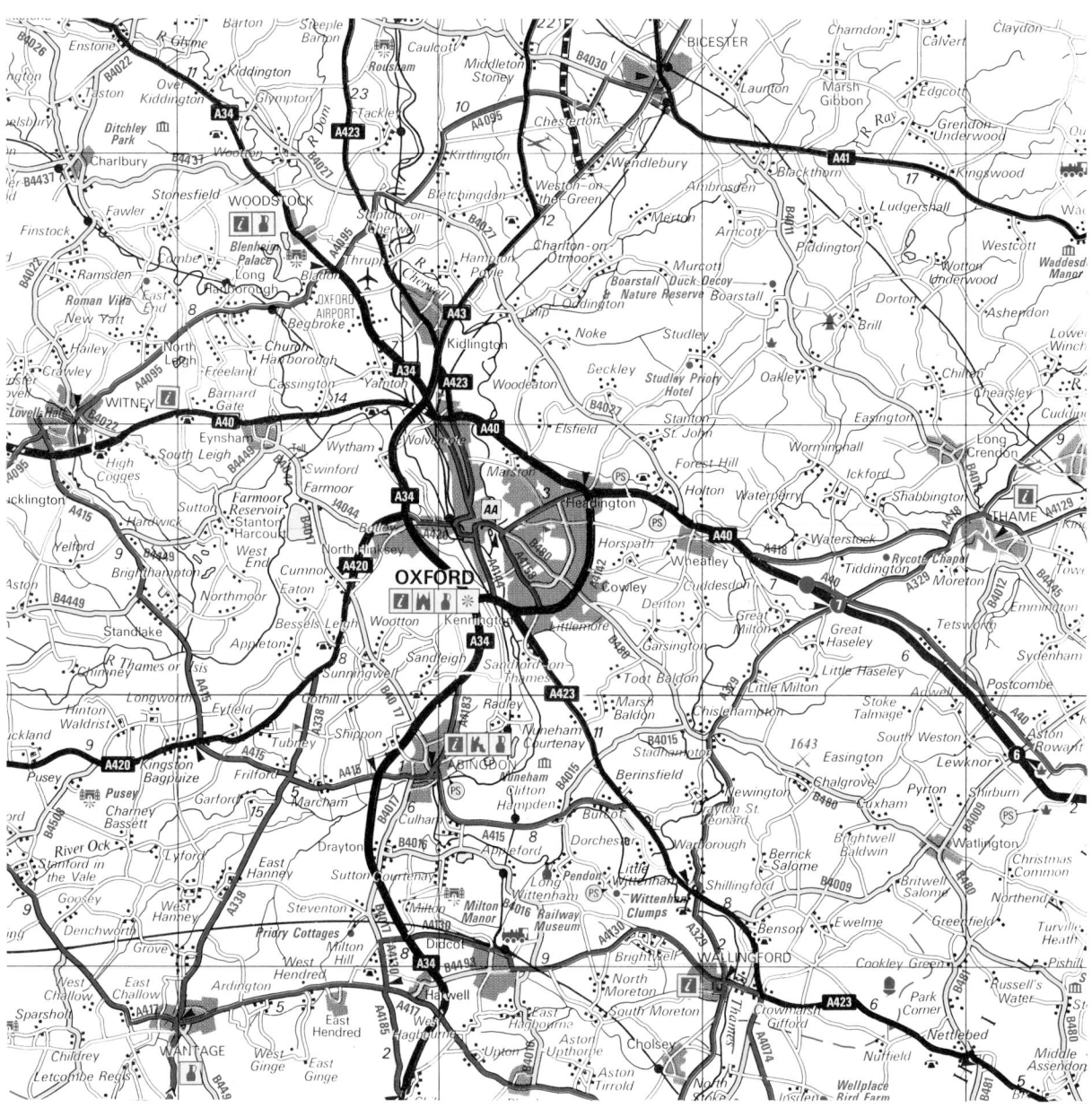

Didcot Railway Centre

Didcot

In 1835, Isambard Kingdom Brunel started designing and building a railway linking London and Bristol, giving it broad tracks, bridges, viaducts and stations on a grand scale. To many enthusiasts, this Great Western Railway was, as Brunel had promised, the 'finest railway in the world.' Now members of the Great Western Society are recreating its golden age here at Didcot alongside Brunel's original line. Visitors enter through the station and cross the shunting lines to find themselves in the nostalgic world of steam. Here are all the attendant buildings: coaling stage, engine shed, lifting shop, locomotive works, turntable, and carriage shed together with a typical branch line country station and signal box, and a recreation of Brunel's broad gauge track. There

is also a Small Relics Museum displaying uniforms, tickets, posters, nameplates and other diverse items. Last, but not least, are the locomotives and carriages themselves, lovingly restored. Locomotives include such imposing characters as 'Earl Bathurst' and 'Bonnie Prince Charlie', 'Hinterton Hall' or 'Burton Agnes Hall', while the pride of the coaches are the 'Prince Elizabeth' and 'Queen Mary' Super Saloons. Didcot Steamdays show them all at their best, offering rides on demonstration tracks and other activities such as coaling, watering and turning engines on the turntables. On special occasions lunch is served in the Super Saloons, and on selected Saturdays from April to September the public may also wine and dine here.

Guide to opening: March to December. [T] Didcot (0235) 817200 for details.

Oxford

Our oldest university began as an informal scattered community with masters and scholars hiring rooms around the town. By 1209 friction between the townspeople and students had already caused the university to close, but without it business was bad and in 1214 the academics were invited back. From the mid-thirteenth century, college buildings of golden stone began to shape the town, and today a wealth of styles are documented here with over 900 buildings of architectural or historic interest within one square mile of the city alone.

Cradled in the embrace of the Cherwell and the Isis (the Latin name given to this part of the Thames) are the 'dreaming spires' of the famous colleges. The grandest is probably Christ Church with its Wren tower housing Great Tom, its huge quadrangle and a magnificent chapel which is also Oxford's Cathedral. University College and Merton are among the oldest colleges; Merton's fourteenth-century Mob Quad is the oldest in the university, and its library may be the oldest in the country. Nearby Oriel is thought to have taken its name from an 'oriel' or upper-floor bay window in the original building, and Brasenose takes its odd name from the brazen nose of a bull on its original door knocker. Magdalen College boasts a river walk, deer park and series of glorious lawns of its own; these and other college gardens are said to give Oxford the best concentration of urban gardens outside Japan.

Besides the colleges, other university buildings of note include Wren's Sheldonian Theatre (used for matriculation and degree ceremonies and for concerts), the Divinity School (a fifteenth-century purpose-built lecture room now housing some of the Bodleian's treasures), the eighteenth-century Radcliffe Camera (a round reading room belonging to the Bodleian) and the Bodleian Library itself. With five million books this is one of the greatest libraries in the world, and one of only five entitled to a copy of every new book printed in the United Kingdom.

For the visitor, Oxford is an easy place to get to know; the 'Oxford experience' at the church of St Mary the Virgin provides a fascinating audio-visual introduction to the city, and the 'The Oxford Story' in Broad Street uses dramatic and imaginative presentations to bring the story of the university to life. There are also several ways of viewing Oxford's architectural treasures: the Sheldonian Theatre, the Carfax Tower and the church towers of St Mary the Virgin and St Michael give superb roof-top views; boat trips are available from Folly Bridge in the summer and punts may also be hired there and at Magdalen Bridge; while the Tourist Information Centre can supply details of a variety of bus tours and walking tours conducted around the city.

B.H. Blackwell's the Bookseller

Broad Street, Oxford

Blackwell's is outstanding in a city renowned for its bookshops. This family firm was first established here in 1879, and since then has earned an international reputation as one of the finest and largest bookshops in the world. It carries a stock of over 200,000 new titles in every academic and general subject, and the Norrington Room (built under the quadrangle of neighbouring Trinity College) boasts the largest display of books for sale in one room anywhere in the country. Blackwell's also organise an extensive programme of literary events throughout the year; these range from a visit by Winnie the Pooh to the children's bookshop, to signing sessions and readings, literary luncheons and dinners.

Guide to opening: Monday to Saturday, 9am – 6pm; [T] Blackwell Central Marketing, Oxford (0865) 792792 for details of events.

Blenheim Palace

Woodstock

Blenheim has been described as 'the most splendid relic of the age of Anne . . . which perfectly preserves its original atmosphere' but in one sense the original atmosphere was far from perfect. In 1704, following the Battle of Blenheim, Queen Anne gave the Manor of Woodstock to the Duke of Marlborough, indicating that she would build him a house there. Vanbrugh was chosen as architect, and he set out to create what he saw as 'a monument of the Queen's glory'. In 1705, when work began, Sarah Duchess of Marlborough was a close friend of the Queen, but by spring 1710 she had fallen from favour, and in 1712 work at Blenheim stopped, with bills of £45,000 still owing. From 1712–14 the Marlboroughs lived abroad in a 'sort of exile', returning the day after the queen died. Only then were Blenheim debts paid (in part) by the Crown, and the Duke continued building at his own expense. Soon Grinling Gibbons and other craftsmen had downed tools after being asked to lower their rates and in November 1716 Vanbrugh

Anneka adopts the local transport, Broad St, Oxford.

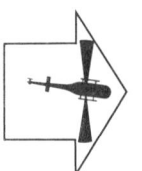

The Treasure Hunt team drop in on Blenheim Palace.

walked out, never to see the finished building.

In the end, it was a monument indeed: the imposing Great Hall is topped by Thornhill's ceiling, depicting the Duke's famous victories; the Green Drawing Room and two rooms beyond it have ceilings by Hawkesmoor, and the Saloon has murals and ceilings by Laguerre; three further State Rooms are hung with enormous tapestries illustrating the Marlborough campaigns, and the Long Library provides a loft setting for an impressive collection of books and personal manuscripts.

Sir Winston Churchill was born here and proposed here too; as he himself commented, 'at Blenheim I took two very important decisions: to be born and to be married; I am happily content with the decision I took on both these occasions.' Memorabilia of the great man is on display in a Churchill Exhibition near the birthroom, ranging from paintings and letters to the beribboned curls which he parted with at the age of five. The public may also visit his grave, at nearby Baldon Church.

Guide to opening: March to October. [T] Woodstock (0993) 811325.

TOURIST INFORMATION

Tourist Information Centres: 8 Market Place, **Abingdon** [T] (0235) 22711. St Aldates, **Oxford** [T] (0865) 726871. 9 St Martin's Street, **Wallingford** [T] (0491) 35351. Town Hall, Market Square, **Witney** [T] (0993) 4379. Hensington Road, **Woodstock** [T] (0993) 811038.

- **Ardington House.**
- **Ardington Pottery.**
- **Cogges Farm Museum, nr Witney.**
- **Dorchester Abbey.**
- **Milton Manor.**
- **Kingston House.**
- **Kingston Lisle Park.**
- **Minster Lovell Hall.**
- **Newington House.**
- **North Leigh Roman Villa.**
- **Nuneham Park.**
- **Pusey House Gardens.**
- **Rycote Chapel.**
- **Wallingford Castle.**
- **Waterperry Horticultural Centre, Wheatley.**

TREASURE HUNT 21

Shropshire/Worcestershire

START POSITION LUDLOW CASTLE

CLUE ONE Treasures 'teme' at a Cornwall family home. Our quest: a ruby from Gravetye, a cultivated traveller's joy.

Leads to **BURFORD HOUSE GARDENS**   Now the home of the Treasure family, this former home of the Cornwalls is on the River Teme. Traveller's Joy is the wild clematis. Here, a ruby red cultivar, Gravetye, conceals the clue.

CLUE TWO The end of the road for a Shropshire lad, a sign of the Prince of Wales, and finally the hustings.

Leads to **FEATHERS HOTEL, LUDLOW**   The ashes of poet A.E. Houseman, who wrote 'A Shropshire Lad', are in Ludlow churchyard. Hanging from the balcony (hustings) of the Feathers (sign of the Prince of Wales) is a hotel sign to which the clue is attached.

CLUE THREE Add fuel to the fire, say, as a fortification before the next station, and ask at the ticket office for a cross reference to a peephole.

Leads to **SOLAR AT STOKESAY CASTLE**   Just before the next stop on the railway line, is STOKEsay CASTLE. From the ticket office, Annie gets a postcard of the Solar on which is marked (cross reference) a peephole. The clue is hidden in it.

CLUE FOUR Across the valley of the apes to a scene of Scott-ish horsepower, where B.P.'s Robinsons will send you up the wall.

Leads to **ACTON SCOTT WORKING FARM MUSEUM**   Across Ape Dale is the Acton Scott Working Farm Museum where horses are busy in the yard. The clue is in the wall-hung trough in the pig (Beatrix Potter's Robinson) sty.

CLUE FIVE S.W. TOTS A WIN. **Plough that up and fill a jug of home brew.**

Leads to **THE PLOUGH, WISTANSTOW**   Unravel (plough up) this anagram and there is only one possible destination! The clue is under a pint of bitter.

CLUE SIX Cross back over your tracks to seek out something you would expect to find far to the west! Here it shows how the way of life has changed over the centuries. What is it?

CLUE SEVEN A long march to the south west will bring you to an Iron Age fort said, by some with local knolledge, to be the site where Caractarus made his last stand against the Romans. What is the name of the hill?

Ludlow Castle – Norman stronghold against the Welsh.

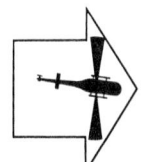

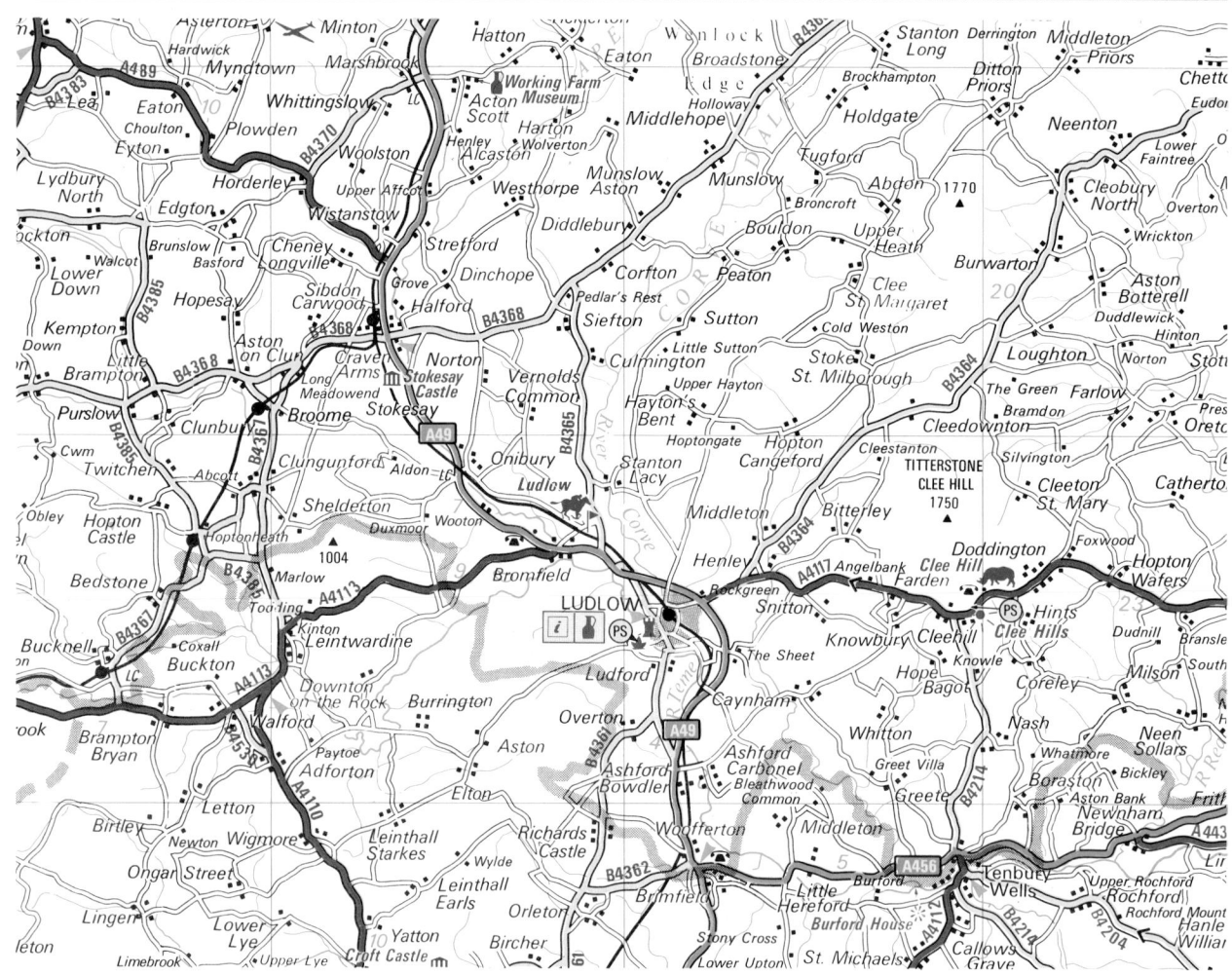

Ludlow Castle

Ludlow, Shropshire

Ludlow was one of the greatest of all the Norman castles built to hold the English frontier against the unconquered Welsh, and its substantial ruins are still a noble sight today. The oldest part of the castle is the inner bailey, built from 1086–94, together with the Great Tower dating from 1130; the larger outer bailey was built mainly in the late twelfth century, and the domestic buildings were added in the late thirteenth – early fourteenth centuries.

In 1306 the castle passed by marriage to the ambitious nobleman Roger Mortimer, who entertained Queen Isabella (wife of Edward II) here, with 'great expense in feasts, tilting and other recreations.' In the Wars of the Roses this was the main stronghold of Richard, Duke of York, which resulted in Ludlow being captured by the Lancastrians in 1459 when looting soldiers 'went footshode in wine', destroying much of the town in the process. In 1473 the castle was home to Edward, Prince of Wales, and thus was chosen as the seat of the powerful Council of the Marches of Wales. The Tudor Prince Arthur died here, and his heart was buried in Ludlow church.

Guide to opening: February to November. [T] Ludlow (0584) 3947 for details.

Burford House Gardens

Tenbury Wells, Worcestershire

The gardens of Georgian Burford House enjoy a beautiful setting beside the River Teme. The house itself was bought by the Treasure family in 1954, and immediately John Treasure started to redesign the 4-acre grounds, laying out lawns and pools, paved pathways and quiet corners of shady trees. He began to amass a vast collection of plants, many of them rare and usual, and in 1960 the adjoining nursery was formed to meet the growing demand for the wonderful range of plants and trees established in the gardens. Since the 1970s, Gold Medal winning exhibits at the Chelsea Flower Show have brought the 'Treasures of Tenbury' a larger following still, prompting yet a further increase in the number and variety of plants grown. Now, the well-known Tenbury Clematis and other plants are on sale in the nursery.

Though Burford House itself is not open to the public, meals and refreshments are served in the tea-room here, and visitors may trace the history and development of the gardens in a small Gardening Museum housed in the stable block.

Guide to opening: Gardens, March to October; Nursery, all the year. [T] Tenbury Wells (0584) 810777 for details.

The Feathers Hotel

Ludlow, Shropshire

In the thirteenth century the town which had grown up around the castle found prosperity as a centre for the wool and cloth industry, and the wealth from this financed the parish church, one of the largest and finest in the country. In 1459 the Lancastrians destroyed many of its contemporary companions, but the political importance of the Council of the Marches soon saw the building of other fine properties here. Woodcarvers and joiners flourished, and today Ludlow's superb display of black and white timbered houses is a tribute to their art. Chief among them is the Feathers Hotel; the building was refronted in 1619, and its balcony was added in the nineteenth century for electioneering purposes. By that time Ludlow had 46 licensed premises, 1 for every 60 adults; this was quite in its old tradition, for in 1632 the town was noted as being 'full of temptations, and much given to tippling and excess.'

Stokesay Castle

Craven Arms, Shropshire

A fortified manor house rather than a castle, Stokesay is a unique and delightful survival from the thirteenth century. Sturdy and sound, it has remained largely unaltered since then. Visitors cross a dry moat and pass through the Elizabethan timber-framed gatehouse to find themselves in a grassy courtyard, with pleasant views over the wall. Though the courtyard was once cluttered with lesser buildings, only the residential block remains, which contains the Hall and Solar and its two defensive towers. The top floor of the picturesque North Tower is timbered, but the South Tower is built entirely of stone, a sturdy 5½ feet thick. The Hall lies between them, a great barn-like room where the lord, his family, guests and servants ate, and where the servants also slept; a high table stood out of range of draughts from the door, and the open stone hearth is still visible in the centre of the room where the timbers of the lofty roof are blackened by smoke. On the first floor of the adjoining solar block, the solar itself is the most interesting of Stokesay's rooms. Though embellished in the seventeenth century with a carved overmantle and panelling, it began as a simpler room open to the sun – a private apartment where the lord and his family could withdraw after meals.

Guide to opening: March to November. [T] Craven Arms (058 82) 2544 for details. EH

Acton Scott Working Farm Museum

Near Church Stretton, Shropshire

The 22 acres at Acton Scott are farmed just as they were in the pre-tractor age. Harnesses still jingle as Shire Horses and skilled hands demonstrate nineteenth-century arable techniques, using a four-

Anneka's balcony scene, The Feathers Hotel, Ludlow.

course rotation to produce crops which provide winter food for the livestock. This includes a mixture of animals: Tamworth pigs, Shropshire Sheep, Dorking Hens, Aylesbury Ducks and other breeds which were common between 1875 and the 1920s. The horses are usually at work each day, butter is made in the dairy throughout the season and in addition there is an extensive programme of craft demonstrations and special farming activities.

Guide to opening: March to October. [T] Marshbrook (06946) 306/7 for details.

TOURIST INFORMATION

Tourist Information Centre: Castle Street, **Ludlow** [T] (0584) 3857.

- **Hopton Castle.**
- **Ludlow Craft Centre.**
- **Ludlow Museum.**
- **Shipton Hall, Much Wenlock.**
- **The White House Museum of Buildings & Country Life, Munslow.**

Other Shropshire attractions nearby:
- **Acton Burnell Castle.**
- **Aerospace Museum, Cosford.**
- **Attingham Park, Shrewsbury.**
- **Benthall Hall, Broseley.**
- **Berrington Hall.**
- **Buildwas Abbey.**
- **Butterfly World, Yockleton, nr Shrewsbury.**
  - **Clive House Museum, Shrewsbury.**
- **Croft Castle.**
- **Ironbridge Gorge Museum, nr Telford.**
- **Midland Motor Museum, Bridgnorth.**
- **Much Wenlock Priory.**
- **Rowley's House Museum, Shrewsbury.**
- **Severn Valley Railway, nr Bridgnorth.**
- **Shrewsbury Castle.**
- **West Midlands Safari Park, Bewdley.**

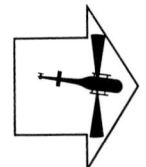

TREASURE HUNT 22

York

START POSITION NABURN LOCK

CLUE ONE At a Rocket base in Eboracum behold the fiery monster. The little red wheels will solve a Chinese puzzle.

Leads to **RAILWAY MUSEUM, YORK**   The train, 'Rocket', is on show at the museum in York, formerly Eboracum. Hanging on a red wheel in the cab of the Chinese locomotive is the clue.

CLUE TWO Murder will out, he wrote. Now he hangs – part of a capital picture show – beyond the Poppletons, beside a trusted bed. The next disclosure lies below the tester.

Leads to **BENINGBROUGH HALL**   The hall lies beyond the villages of Nether and Upper Poppleton. Among the paintings on loan from the National Portrait Gallery, is one of William Congreve, the writer. It hangs in a bedroom, and the clue is hidden under a pillow on the bed nearby.

CLUE THREE Currer Bell's brother sketched his lodgings in a Thorpe which was green and is now below the wood. The elm he drew harbours the clue.

Leads to **HOME FARM, THORPE UNDERWOOD** Branwell Brontë, brother of Charlotte (Currer Bell), sketched Home Farm, Thorp Green (now Thorpe Underwood) while he was a tutor there. The clue is in the elm tree that features in the picture.

CLUE FOUR A bear of very little brain is well and truly petrified by the Nidd.

Leads to **PETRIFYING WELL, KNARESBOROUGH** Pooh, the bear of very little brain, is one of the objects being petrified at the Petrifying WELL, by the River NIDD. The clue is hanging round his neck.

CLUE FIVE What Abbot Richard started, Marmaduke Huby finished; where the brothers washed before meals a Yorkshire rose lies hidden.

Leads to **FOUNTAINS ABBEY**   Abbot Richard started building the Abbey; Martin Hubey saw the completion of the work. The treasure, a white rose of York, lies hidden near the washbasins in the cloister.

CLUE SIX When Cromwell's bullets hit the gatehouse, the situation must have been close to Bedlam. Which family survived the attack and lives on in this village with a mildly continental air?

CLUE SEVEN Don't stray too far for this central sward on which, near a little bridge, you will find something round and stony. Do you chew it well or merely take a drink? Name the round and stony object.

York Minster – view from beyond the city walls.

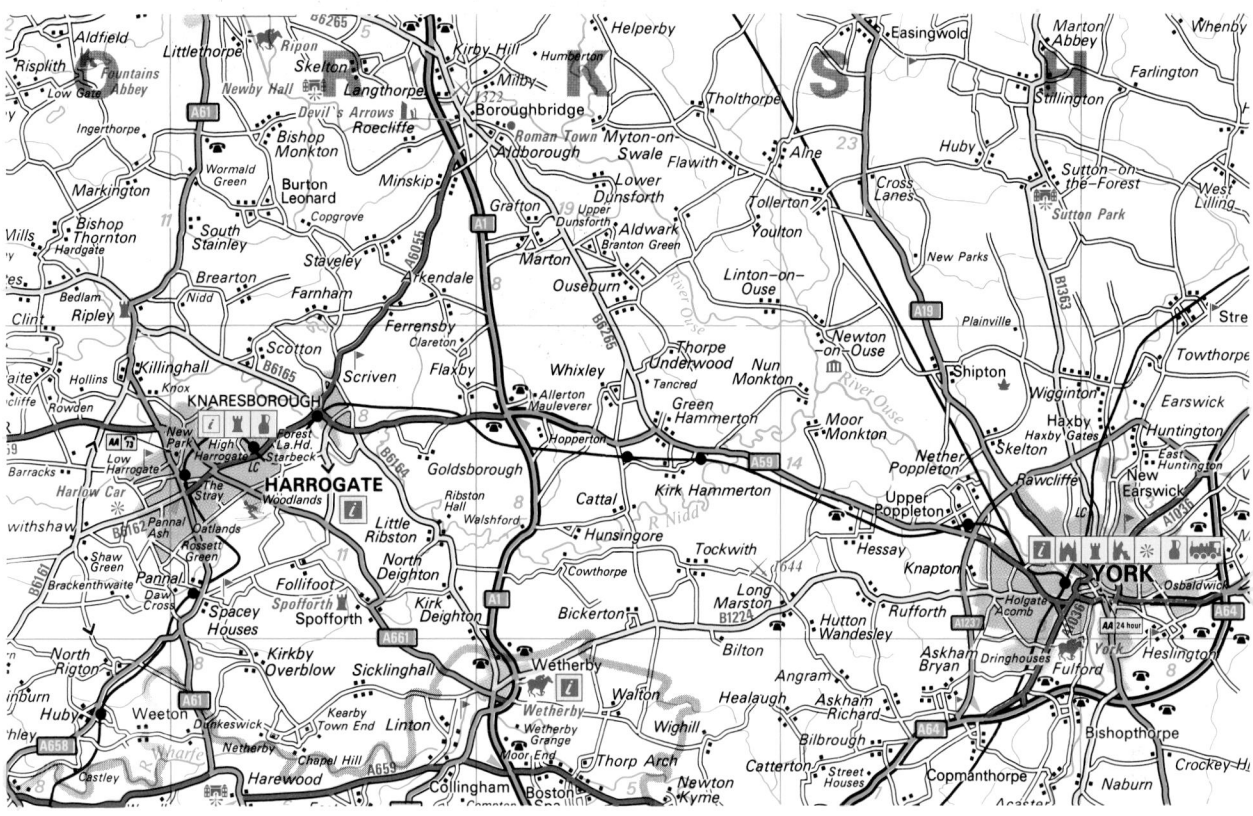

York

North Yorkshire

Known as one of the 'treasure houses' of England for the historic buildings it contains, York has been an important city for over 2,000 years. The Romans built the city and military base of Eboracum here, followed in turn by Viking Jorvik. The Normans founded York's first castle, and 1220 saw the commencement of the Minster, still the city's pride and joy. In the same century York was enclosed within protective walls, and narrow streets of timber-framed houses like the Shambles and Stonegate soon grew up within them.

National Railway Museum, Leeman Road. The Museum houses the finest examples of Britain's railway heritage from the earliest horse-drawn vehicles to the prototype of the InterCity 125. Full-size rolling stock of diesel, electric and steam locomotives are arranged around two original turntables in the Main Hall, once part of the depot which serviced steam locomotives operating from York. Besides the replica of the Rocket which held the *Treasure Hunt* clue, there are many genuine characters here with such diverse personalities as 'Coppernob' and 'Gladstone' or the famous 'Mallard', holder of the World Speed Record for steam locomotives.

Guide to opening: all the year. [T] York (0904) 21261 for details.

The Bar Convent, Blossom Street is England's oldest active post-reformation convent and one of the earliest girls' schools in the country. Now it is a museum offering a 'pilgrimage' of discovery through 300 turbulent years of Christian history in Northern England.

Guide to opening: all the year. [T] York (0904) 643238.

Clifford's Tower, York Castle, Tower Street is a thirteenth-century tower keep built by Henry III, which takes its name from Roger de Clifford who was executed here in the Wars of the Roses and hung in chains from the tower.

Guide to opening: all the year. [T] York (0904) 646940 for details. EH.

Fairfax House, Castlegate is a superb eighteenth-century town house described as a classic architectural masterpiece of its age.

Guide to opening: March to January. [T] York (0904) 655543 for details.

Jorvik Viking Centre, Coppergate. On the site of the Viking excavations, time-cars take visitors back 1000 years to an exact reconstruction of the Viking street.

Guide to opening: all the year. [T] York (0904) 643211 for details.

Merchant Adventurers' Hall, Fossgate is a superb fourteenth-century Great Hall of the York Merchants' Guild with an exhibition on the theme of merchant wealth and its influence on the history of York.

Guide to opening: all the year. [T] York (0904) 654818.

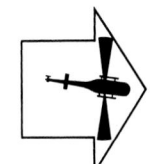

Treasurers' House, Minster Yard is a seventeenth/ eighteenth-century house on the site occupied by Treasurers of York Minster since medieval times.

Guide to opening: April to October. [T] York (0904) 624247 for details. NT.

York Castle Museum & York Story provides superb period displays including complete streets which recreate Victorian and Edwardian England.

Guide to opening: all the year. [T] York (0904) 653661 for details.

York City Art Gallery, Exhibition Square shows British and European paintings spanning seven centuries including the Lycett Green collection of Old Masters, and works by the York-born painter of the nude William Etty.

Guide to opening: all the year. [T] York (0904) 623839 for details.

York Minster is regarded as the finest gothic cathedral in Northern Europe.

Guide to opening: all the year. [T] York (0904) 624426

Yorkshire Museum displays some of the finest Roman, Anglo-Saxon, Viking and Medieval treasures ever found in Britain.

Guide to opening: all the year. [T] York (0904) 629745 for details.

Beningbrough Hall

Near York, North Yorkshire

The National Portrait Gallery and the National Trust share the credit for making Beningbrough Hall what it is today. An outstanding example of Baroque architecture, the house has altered little since it was completed in 1716. The interior features handsome panelled state rooms, some (like the Saloon) with fluted Corinthian pilasters, and most embellished with woodcarvings of the highest quality, which are the hallmark of the house. The work of William Thornton of York, the carving is at its finest in the Great Staircase and the Drawing Room, where it rivals the standard of Grinling Gibbons.

Guide to opening: April to November. [T] York (0904) 47066 for details. NT.

Old Mother Shipton's Cave and the Petrifying Well

Knaresborough, North Yorkshire

In 1488, an unmarried girl gave birth to her baby in this cave, after which she joined a convent leaving the child an orphan in the town. The young Ursula Sontheil was soon showing formidable powers of

Pooh is rescued from the Petrifying Well, Knaresborough.

prophesy, and when she married Tobias Shipton her fame as a Wise Woman earned her the title of 'Mother' Shipton. Her prophesies were first published in 1641 in cryptic couplet form worthy of any *Treasure Hunt* clue, and today they make fascinating reading for visitors to the cave. But such powers smacked of witchcraft, and Mother Shipton's death warrant was drawn up in York to await the signature of Cardinal Wolsey. Foreseeing that she was due to die, Mother Shipton predicted instead that although Wolsey would see the city, he would never reach it; sure enough, he was arrested for treason within sight of the Minster spire, and died on his way back to London.

The Petrifying Well beside the cave is another fascinating place. In Mother Shipton's time it was believed to be haunted by demons who turned people into stone, but by the seventeenth century people were paying to drink its waters to cure 'fluxes of the belly' and 'hot and choloric humours'. Rich in calcium sulphates, the spring which drips over the face of the rock can indeed coat things with stone, and a parasol and hat, left here in 1853 and now embedded in the rock, measures how dramatically this constant coating of minerals can grow. In 1923 Queen Mary left a shoe here to be petrified, and visitors still follow her example, donating items and reclaiming them when petrified, which may be anything from six weeks to two years later.

Guide to opening: March to October. [T] Harrogate (0423) 864600.

Fountains Abbey and Studley Royal Country Park

Studley Royal, North Yorkshire

The graceful ruins of Fountains Abbey form one of the loveliest and best known tourist attractions in Britain. It was among the first of the Cistercian abbeys, founded by 'breakaway' monks from the Benedictine Order who chose a 'lonely and forbidding spot' in the valley of the River Skell for their site. In the early years poverty reduced the community here to eating gruel made of elm leaves, but fortune smiled on Fountains when the Dean of York retired here with his riches, and as the reputation of the abbey spread, further gifts came flooding in. By the time of the Dissolution of the Monasteries, Fountains was the wealthiest of them all; Henry VIII was quick to seize so rich a prize, and stripped of its glory, the abbey was left in ruins. These are still a majestic sight, with the remains of the chapter house, refectory, infirmary and other monastery buildings springing from the south side of the imposing abbey church.

Guide to opening: all the year. [T] Sawley (076 586) 333 for details. NT.

TOURIST INFORMATION

Tourist Information Centres: Chapel Lane, **Easingwold** [T] (0347) 21530. Royal Baths Assembly Rooms, Crescent Road, **Harrogate** [T] (0423) 525666. Fishergate, **Boroughbridge** [T] (0423) 323373. Market Place, **Knaresborough** [T] (0423) 866886. Wakeman's House, **Ripon** [T] (0765) 4625. De Grey Rooms, Exhibition Square, **York** [T] (0904) 85595.

- **Aldeborough Roman Town.**
- **Friargate Wax Museum, York.**
- **Harewood House & Bird Garden.**
- **Harlow Car Gardens, nr Harrogate.**
- **Knaresborough Castle.**
- **Knaresborough Old Court House Museum.**
- **Newby Hall, nr Ripon.**
- **Norton Conyers, nr Ripon.**
- **Ripley Castle.**
- **Ripon Cathedral.**
- **Ripon Prison & Police Museum.**
- **Royal Baths Assembly Rooms & Royal Pump Room Museum, Harrogate.**
- **Rudding Park, nr Harrogate.**
- **Spofforth Castle.**
- **Sutton Park, Sutton-on-the-Forest.**
- **York Dungeon.**
- **Yorkshire Air Museum, nr York.**
- **Yorkshire Farming Museum, nr York.**

Fountains Abbey – 'a lonely and forbidding spot'.

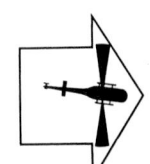

TREASURE HUNT 23 & 24

Yorkshire Dales/ West Yorkshire

HUNT 23 (YORKSHIRE DALES)

START POSITION HAWKSWICK

CLUE ONE **They're laiking by the gramineous woods where a latter-day Rhodes will deliver the goods.**

Leads to **GRASSINGTON CRICKET GROUND**   Local teams are playing (laiking) by Grass (gramineous) Wood. The bowler, an all-rounder like Rhodes, has the clue.

CLUE TWO **Something's up by old Amerdale's foot. Step inside to get the drift, Montgolfier fashion.**

Leads to **KILNSEY CRAG**   Amerdale is the old name of Littondale, and at its foot is Kilnsey Crag. The Montgolfier brothers were hot-air balloonists and in the basket of a balloon by the Crag is the clue.

CLUE THREE **Downstream, terpsichorean folk have discovered Scotland's national poet and letters from his birthplace. Best skirt round the Barguest of Trollers Gill!**

Leads to **BURNSALL**   Robert BURNS was born in ALLoway. At Burnsall, Morris dancers are performing. One of them portrays the Barguest of Trollers Gill; the clue is hidden under his skirt.

CLUE FOUR **Past the place where the Romille boy came to grief, and opposite his mother's memorial, take steps into the mesial current.**

Leads to **BOLTON ABBEY**   The Bolton community was founded by Alice de Romille, whose son came to grief at The Strid. The clue is secured to a stepping stone across the river.

CLUE FIVE **In Sheeptown's castle, Clifford's pride, Seek out the archers' tree inside.**

Leads to **SKIPTON CASTLE**   Sheeptown is the old name for Skipton, whose castle was built by Lord Clifford. In a yew tree, whose wood is used for making arrows, is the treasure – an arrow.

Take-off point for the Montgolfiers – Kilnsey Crag.

CLUE SIX Grand larch leaves pall? Carry out remedial work to correct the situation and you will find that things thrive in this lovely setting to the north east. Where is it?

CLUE SEVEN This may stump you and make you cross, so why not go underground? While you take a rest in the Cradle, who will be keeping watch nearby?

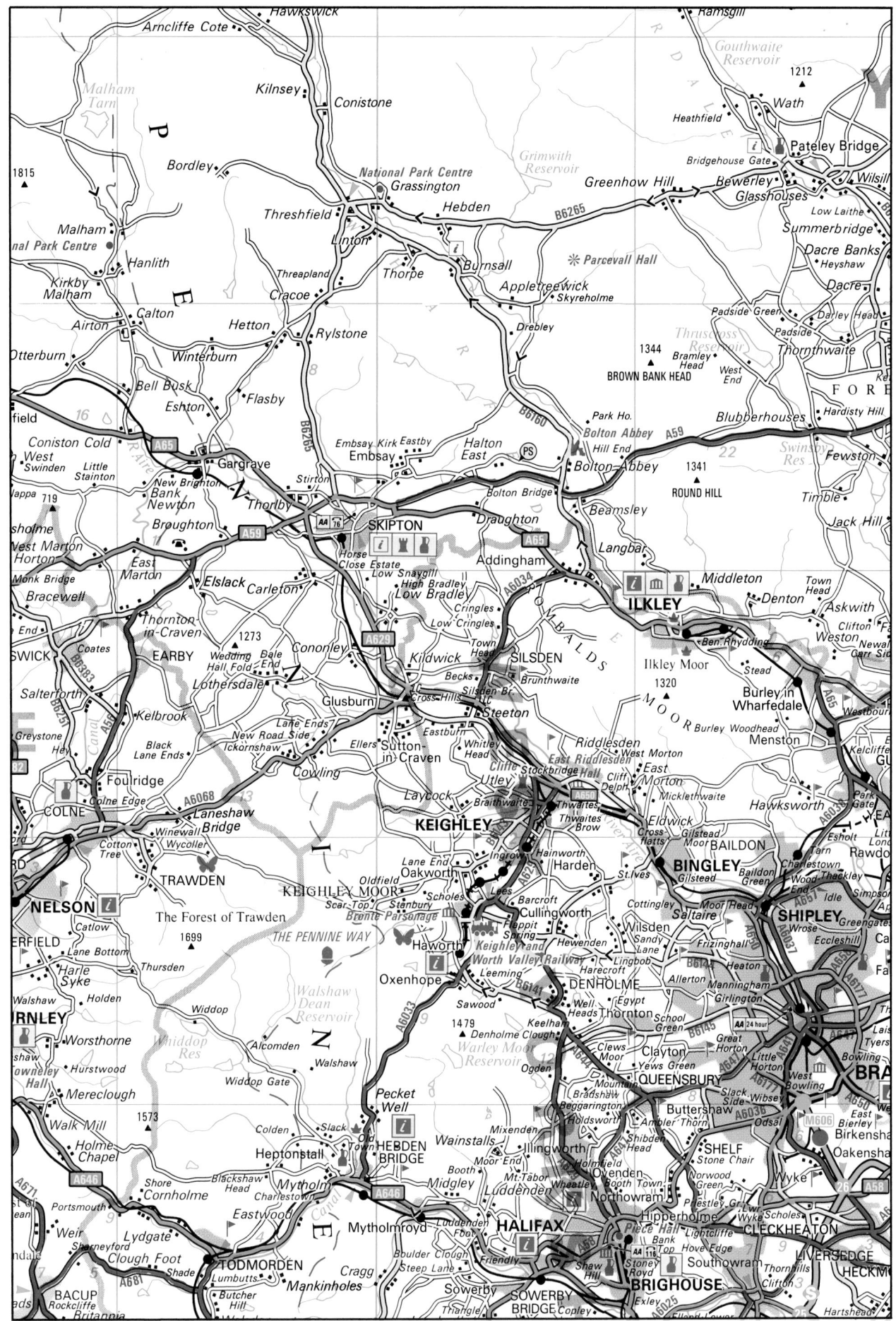

Wharfedale

North Yorkshire

This *Treasure Hunt* went to the heart of the Yorkshire Dales National Park, an area of spectacular Pennine scenery with bare, silent fells and the dramatic rock formations that only limestone can produce. Grassington, Kilnsey, Burnsall, Bolton Abbey and other delightful places shown on the screen are all in the green valley of the River Wharfe, renowned for its picturesque villages of grey Dales stone.

From Bolton Abbey, the country road winds through Barden Moor, a rearing ground for red grouse, and on to 'Bonny' Burnsall with its seventeenth-century grammar school and manor house, and handsome Perpendicular church. Next comes Grassington, the principal village in Upper Wharfedale and home of the National Park Centre, a mine of information on the Dales in general and on the opportunities for walking, birdwatching and all the other outdoor pursuits so popular here. The Wharfe here is spanned by a stone bridge built in 1603, from which a steep lane climbs to a cobbled square with lots of interesting little shops, and narrow 'folds' and passageways running from either side.

Travelling north again, the tiny village of Kilnsey is dwarfed by its towering limestone crag, a famous landmark which provides a tricky challenge to climbers. From here the River Skirfare lures visitors into wooded Littondale, which provided much of the inspiration for *The Water Babies*.

Bolton Abbey

North Yorkshire

This tiny village took its name from the abbey here, now a picturesque ruin in an idyllic riverside setting. The 'Abbey' was, in fact, an Augustinian Priory, built in 1154 on land granted by Alice de Romille. The 'black canons' of Bolton (so called because of their dress) led a life of devotion serving local churches and providing alms and hospitality, whilst also trading extensively in lead, iron and wool. Though often harrassed by marauding Scots, still the priory thrived, until it supported over 200 workers – free servants who were paid, and the 'unfree' who were not. Building was steady and spectacular, and some was still in progress when Prior Moone and his 14 brethren signed the Deed of Surrender by which Henry VIII suppressed the Priory in 1539. Although the Prior was paid a pension of £40 and the canons received between £4 and £6.13s.4d each, the buildings fared less well; only part of the church and the gatehouse were spared, and the rest were stripped of their lead and left to fall into decay. The church now consists of a nave and north aisle behind a superb thirteenth-century west front, and still serves the parish today; the gatehouse became a residence in 1720 and, like Bolton Hall, is used privately by the Duke of Devonshire, owner of the Bolton Estate.

The abbey setting repays exploration too: the 'Hole-in-the-Wall' permits a fine view of the remains; stepping stones lead out across the Wharfe, and a pleasant riverside walk leads to the memorial to Lord Frederick Cavendish. Beyond that is the Strid – a narrow neck of rushing water, thought to take its name from the Old English for 'turmoil'. Alice de Romille's son (Wordsworth's Boy of Egremond) is said to have drowned here whilst rashly trying to cross the gap.

Guide to opening: all the year. [T] Bolton Abbey (075 671) 227.

Skipton Castle

Skipton, North Yorkshire

Standing guard over the gateway to the Dales, this great Clifford stronghold is one of the most complete and well-preserved medieval castles in England. The first castle was founded here by Robert de Romille around 1090, but the strongest parts of the castle seen today were built in 1310 by the first Clifford Lord of Skipton. The Cliffords entered the Wars of the Roses on the Lancastrian side, and their estates were confiscated by the Yorkists on the death of the ninth Lord, whereupon his widow sent her young son to tend sheep in the Cumbrian fells, out of harm's way. When he and his castle were reunited the 'Shepherd Lord' built himself a Tudor home within its walls, and in 1536 Henry, the 11th Lord, added the Tudor Wing in anticipation of his son's marriage to Henry VIII's niece.

As a Royalist stronghold in the Civil War the castle withstood a three-year seige, but ultimately it gave in and was ordered to be slighted; as the officer in charge complained that the labourers came late, left early, and 'stood idle while they were there', this was clearly no easy task. Although fairly extensive damage was done, by 1657, Lady Anne Clifford had obtained permission to make it good, though with walls less sturdy than before. On completion of her thorough work she planted the famous yew tree in the Conduit Court (which held the fifth *Treasure Hunt* clue) and, still fully-roofed and floored, Skipton's warren of empty rooms remain very much as she left them.

Guide to opening: all the year. [T] Skipton (0756) 2442 for details.

TOURIST INFORMATION

Tourist Information Centres: Southlands Car Park, **Pateley Bridge** [T] (0423) 711147. 8 Victoria Square, **Skipton** [T] (0756) 2809.

- **Barden Tower, nr Bolton Abbey.**
- **Broughton Hall, nr Skipton.**
- **Craven Museum, Skipton.**
- **Parcevall Hall Gardens, Skyreholme.**
- **Stump Cross Caverns, Pateley Bridge.**
- **Upper Wharfedale Folk Museum, Grassington.**
- **Yorkshire Dales Railway, Embsay.**

HUNT 24 (WEST YORKSHIRE)

START POSITION STOODLEY PIKE

CLUE ONE **West of the town with the fabulous start, Walkleys live up to their first syllable by going Dutch. The sidecutter is your sole guide!**

Leads to **HEBDEN BRIDGE** West of MYTHolmroyd and near to Hebden Bridge is the Walkley Clog factory. By the sidecutting machine, the clue is hidden in a box of soles.

CLUE TWO **In the home of the literary Bells, look where Mrs Nicholls left her spectacles.**

Leads to **BRONTË PARSONAGE, HAWORTH** This was the home of the Brontë family. Charlotte, whose pen name was Currer Bell, married Arthur Bell Nicholls. The clue is hidden on Charlotte's desk.

CLUE THREE **Worth huffing and puffing downtown for – a cab ride to where Mr Cribbins held sway. There a penny in the slot will see you on your way.**

Leads to **OAKWORTH STATION** A ride in the cab of a train takes Anneka to OakWORTH station. *The Railway Children*, starring Bernard Cribbins, was filmed on this line. The ticket machine produces a ticket on which the next clue is printed.

CLUE FOUR **To terrier town and the staircase from Leeds. Unlock the puzzle at the 26th gate.**

Leads to **BINGLEY FIVE RISE LOCKS** The Airedale, or Bingley, terrier points to Bingley, and the staircase to the Rise on the Leeds and Liverpool Canal. The clue is waiting to be 'unlocked' at the 26th gate.

CLUE FIVE **Above the modern Olicana, take your hat off to Yorkshire grit and get to grips with the bovine mother.**

Leads to **ILKLEY – COW AND CALF ROCKS** Just south of Ilkley, the modern Olicana, on the Moor baht'at, tackle the climb up the Cow (bovine mother) of the Cow and Calf Rocks. The clue is on a ledge.

CLUE SIX **It may have a large medieval tithe barn, but there's no room for the Cow and Calf in this traditional seventeenth-century manor house. Which is it?**

CLUE SEVEN **Where Sir Titus built his riverside model, seek out the 'new' building with the unusual topping. After what is the topping fashioned?**

High aove Ilkley, Skyrunner on top of the 'Cow'.

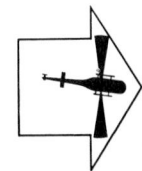

Hebden Bridge

Hebden Bridge takes its name from the Old Pack-horse Bridge built around 1510, which was later the site of a brisk battle in the Civil War. With its neighbour Heptonstall, the town illustrates the story of the Industrial Revolution in the dramatic Pennine valley of the River Calder. Heptonstall retains many of the old stone cottages where weavers worked at their hand-looms making 'pieces' for their Cloth Hall in Townsgate, one of the oldest such halls in the country. With the coming of steam power, mills were established beside the river in Hebden Bridge. Bridge Mill and nineteenth-century Nutclough Mill survive today, together with the unusual 'top and bottom' houses built for the mill workers.

P. Walkley (Clogs) Ltd is the only surviving clog mill in the country. This unique working attraction demonstrates how clogs of every kind are made. Clog soles and uppers are now machine made, but the final task of attaching the uppers to the soles is still performed by craftsmen using traditional methods and skills.

Guide to opening: all the year. [T] Halifax (0422) 842061

The Brontë Parsonage Museum

Haworth

Patrick Brontë was vicar of Haworth from 1820–1861, and here at the Parsonage his famous family lived, worked — and died. All the rooms are now decorated and furnished very much as they were then. Visitors can see a lock of Anne's hair, Emily's piano, Charlotte's tiny dresses and shoes — such intimate items as these form a very moving display. One large room is also set aside for the Bonnell Collection of Brontë drawings, books, letters and manuscripts, ranging from dramatic paintings to the incredible miniature books which the sisters wrote when they were young.

But the Brontë story leads beyond the Parsonage walls: to the Black Bull inn where Branwell drank, to the bleak slopes of the 'wuthering' moors, and finally to the church, and the family vault.

Guide to opening: all the year, excluding part of February. [T] Haworth (0535) 42323 for details.

Keighley and Worth Valley Railway

Steam trains arriving at Haworth Station provide a stylish introduction to Brontë Country. Haworth is one of six stops on the Keighley and Worth Valley line, which runs from the station shared with British Rail at Keighley up onto the South Pennine moors at Oxenhope. The steep gradient on the 5-mile trip

Haworth Parsonage, home of the Brontës.

means hard work for the locomotives, characters like 'City of Wells' which once pulled the Golden Arrow, or 'Bellerophon', one of the oldest working engines in the country. In all there are over 30 steam locomotives and 5 diesels in the collection here, and between them they operate an extensive service of scenic rides, with passengers enjoying the view from old-fashioned compartment coaches, most with a buffet on board. Locomotives and coaches are on display in the Goods Yard adjacent to Haworth Station, and the museum at Oxenhope contains more engines and carriages, together with smaller items of railway memorabilia. Oakworth station (the fourth stop on the line) was the hiding place of the third *Treasure Hunt* clue.

Guide to opening: all the year. [T] Haworth (0535) 45214.

Bingley Five Rise Locks

Bingley

'This joyful and much wished for event was welcomed with the ringing of Bingley church bells, a band of music, and firing of guns by the neighbouring militia, the shouts of the spectators and all the marks of satisfaction so important an event merits.' The official opening of Bingley Five Rise Locks was something to shout about, as it celebrated a dramatic feat of engineering – a staircase of five locks, raising the Leeds & Liverpool Canal by 60 feet. Built in the 1770s to the design of John Longbotham of Halifax, the locks have changed little since then. Each measures 62 feet × 14 feet 4 inches and, as the top gates of one lock forms the bottom gates of the lock above, each must be set with great care to avoid flooding, or leaving boats high and dry. Passage through all five takes half an hour, and in the heyday of the canals delays here were frequent as boats were unable to pass in the locks.

Ample car parking near Bingley Station serves visitors wishing to view the locks, or to follow towpath walks leading into the Pennines around Skipton, or to nearby Saltaire.

Ilkley

Ilkley's most famous landmarks, the Cow and Calf Rocks, lie on the edge of the moor just a pleasant walk from the town centre. According to tradition, it was whilst picnicking here beneath the 50 foot 'Cow' and its smaller 'Calf' that a church choir from Halifax composed the Yorkshire national anthem 'On Ilkley Moor Baht'at', and today this immortal spot is still popular for walking, climbing and other outdoor activities. Rocks curiously carved in prehistoric times bear witness to early settlements on the moor and in AD 79 the Romans built their fort of Olicana on the site of the town itself, although most of Ilkley dates from Victorian times. The Heather Spa sprung up around the health hydros built to take advantage of 'the waters' here and, though the fashion for health hydros waned, the original baths erected at White Wells in 1756 remain as a museum.

Other interesting features of the town include Saxon crosses in the Parish Church, the Manor House (now a museum) dating from the sixteenth century, the picturesque Old Bridge (start of the Ilkley-Cumbria Dales Way) and the Victorian Arcade which houses several of the town's high-class shops.

Bingley Five Rise Locks. A triumph of eighteenth-century engineering.

TOURIST INFORMATION

Tourist Information Centres: City Hall, Channing Way, **Bradford** [T] (0274) 753678. Bank House, Albert Road, **Colne** [T] (0282) 864721. 2/4 West Lane, **Haworth** [T] (0535) 42329. 1 Bridge Gate, **Hebden Bridge** [T] (0422) 843831. Station Road, **Ilkley** [T] (0943) 602319.

- British in India Museum, Colne.
- Cliffe Castle, Museum & Gallery, Keighley.
- Colne Heritage Centre.
- East Riddlesden Hall, nr Keighley.
- Haworth Museum of Childhood.
- Manor House Museum, Ilkley.
- Museum of Mining, Earby.
- Reed Organ & Harmonium Museum, Saltaire.
- White Wells Baths Museum, Ilkley.
- Bradford Attractions: Bolling Hall; Cartwright Hall Gallery; Colour Museum; Industrial Museum; National Museum of Photography, Film & Television.
- Halifax Attractions: Bankfield Museum; Calderdale Industrial Museum; National Museum of the Working Horse; Piece Hall; Piece Hall Pre-Industrial Museum; West Yorkshire Folk Museum, Shibden Hall.

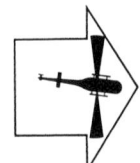

TREASURE HUNT 25 & 26

Cumbria

HUNT 25

START POSITION CALDBECK

CLUE ONE Don't fly – for here sleeps the man who wore a coat so gray and woke the fox from his lair in the mornings, with your clue near his head.

Leads to **JOHN PEEL'S GRAVE, CALDBECK**   Because this treasure hunt started in Caldbeck, Anneka doesn't need the helicopter to reach the churchyard where the great huntsman is buried. The clue is hidden by the headstone of the grave.

CLUE TWO Find Jimmy Glaister on the east side of the A591 near Binsey. His hounds will show you the way; but you'll have to fly to keep up with them and find a collar in the whin.

Leads to **BEWALDETH – HOUND TRAIL**   East of the A591, at Bewaldeth, are Jimmy Glaister and his hounds. Once on the trail, the helicopter keeps the hounds in sight. They point to a gorse bush (whin) in which a dog's collar has been hidden.

CLUE THREE There are islands in the Derwent in the toothless jaws of Borrowdale. Look beneath the voussoirs for the clue.

Leads to **BRIDGE IN JAWS OF BORROWDALE**   The voussoirs are the wedge-like stones that form the arches of the bridge. The clue is stuck under an arch.

CLUE FOUR The man who wrote: 'Spade! with which Wilkinson hath tilled his lands', made a garden here and there's a spade in the Drawing Room.

Leads to **RYDAL MOUNT**   William Wordsworth lived here and landscaped the garden. An Ace of Spades is hidden in the Drawing Room.

CLUE FIVE Turn slightly left at the round house on Belle Isle and at one of two houses with fourteenth-century Pele Towers there is a bird in a bush which is a bird.

Leads to **LEVENS HALL**   Make for the round house on Belle Isle, but then head south east, past Sizergh Castle (which has a Pele Tower) to Levens Hall. The treasure, a toy bird, is hidden in a 'bird' in the topiary garden.

CLUE SIX Once you've cottoned on to this clue, you'll soon get it wound up, so let a park for the cloven-hooved guide you to an old industrial scene. What is its name?

CLUE SEVEN While in the forest, look out for 'The Hunter' and 'Shootin' Moose' or you may end up in a hot spot. One of Frost's grainy characters, (numbered 22) is there already! What is he?

The steam yacht 'Gondola' on Coniston Water.

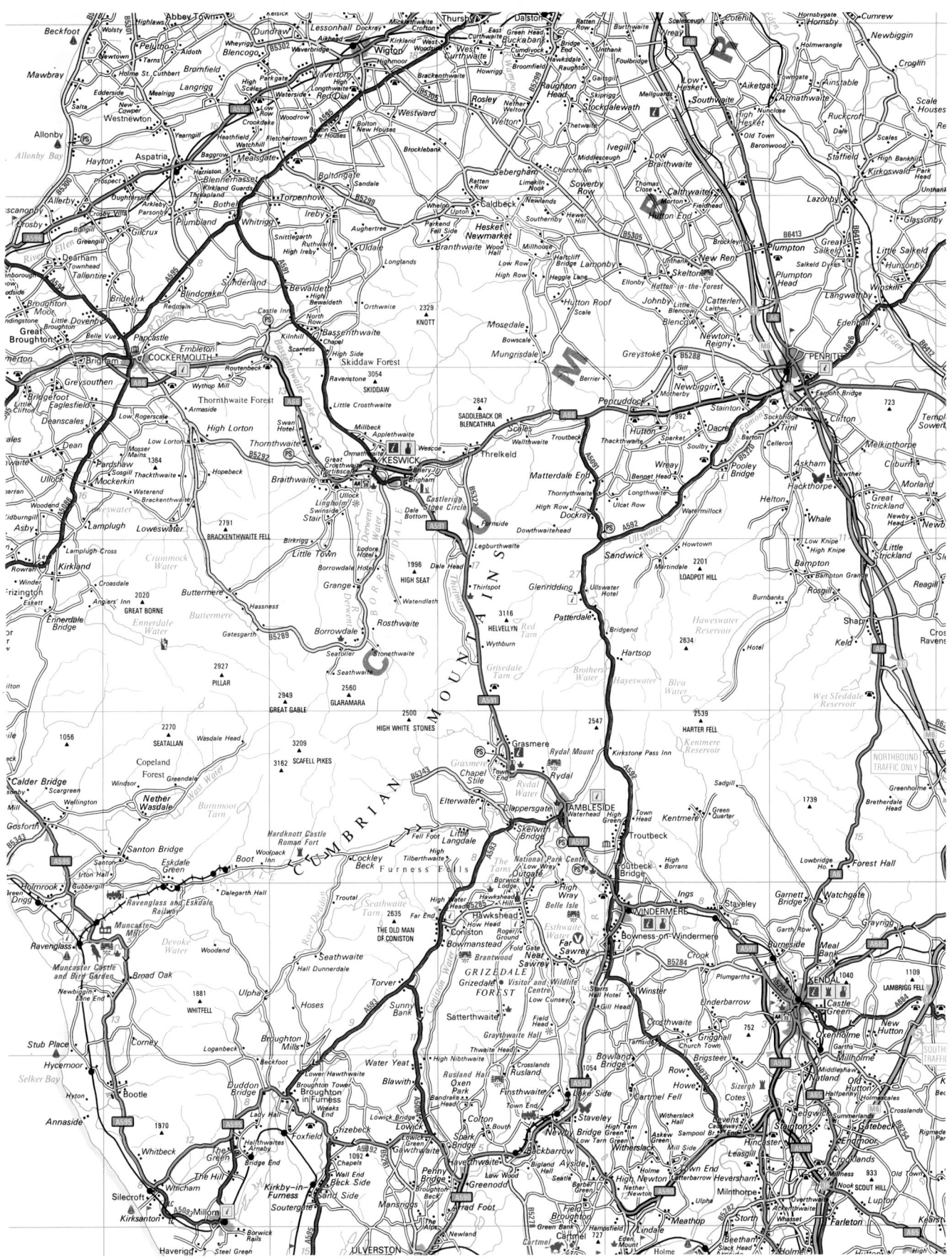

John Peel's Grave

Caldbeck

D'ye ken John Peel?

No one would, had it not been for the friend who immortalised him in verses which he then set to the tune of a traditional Cumbrian folk song. John Peel is certainly known to have kept his own pack of hounds so that he could indulge his passion for hunting, and as this regularly took him out at 'the break of day' he probably made quite a nuisance of himself in the process. Things are peaceful enough now; John Peel died in 1854, and is buried with the rest of his family in the churchyard at Caldbeck.

Cockermouth

During the summer months the traditional Cumbrian sport of hound trailing draws visitors to the fells above this pleasant old market town. Trails are usually some 10 miles long, and are laid by a cloth soaked in aniseed and paraffin being dragged across the fells. Hounds follow the trail to the encouraging cries of their owners, and meetings are further enlivened by some brisk betting as to who will be first home. The most outstanding features of Cockermouth itself are the ruins of its fourteenth/fifteenth-century castle, and its wide, tree-lined Main Street which still retains an eighteenth-century atmosphere. The highlight of this street for most visitors is the house where Wordsworth was born.

Borrowdale

Borrowdale has been called the 'loveliest valley in England', and certainly it is difficult to imagine scenery to surpass it. Motorists following the road which winds along the edge of Derwentwater are treated to some of its finest views, and a steep lane branching off to Watendlath adds its own special viewpoint at Ashness Bridge, framed by the magnificent backdrop of Derwentwater and Bassenthwaite Lake with the towering bulk of Skiddaw beyond. Back beside the lake, the road leads on to the Lodore Falls and nearby Shepherd's Crag, which provides climbers with many challenging routes. Beyond the village of Grange, the valley narrows suddenly to form the 'Jaws of Borrowdale', now National Trust Property. As shown on *Treasure Hunt,* the gap here is guarded by conical Castle Crag, and from here it is only a short walk to the 2,000 ton Bowder Stone. At 62 feet long and 36 feet high, it is the largest boulder in the Lake District; it is fitted with its own ladder, and is lodged in such a way that people can join hands beneath it.

Seatoller marks the start of a Nature Trail, and the National Park Information Centre here is also the starting point for guided walks. Back again at Grange, a road branches to the left to run along the other side of Derwentwater to Lingholm Gardens, noted for their rhododendrons and azaleas. Beatrix Potter often stayed at Lingholm with her father, and it was here that she wrote *Squirrel Nutkin* and found many of the

The 'loveliest valley in England', Borrowdale.

models for her beautiful woodland and nature sketches.

Rydal Mount

Ambleside

Rydal Mount was Wordsworth's home from 1813 until he died here (on the stroke of midnight) in 1850. The house lies in the heart of the Lake District commanding wonderful views of Lake Windermere and the surrounding fells, and Wordsworth, his wife Mary, sister Dorothy and his daughter Dora all loved it. They received a steady stream of visitors – famous poets, novelists and eminent people of every kind, and yet the years they spent here brought unhappy memories too. Dora, her father's constant and devoted companion, finally married and spent some years away from home, but returned to Rydal Mount to die; Wordsworth was at first inconsolable, but found some relief in caring for Dorothy, who in her turn suffered a long and distressing mental illness. Now the rooms which were occupied by the family are open to the public.

The Wordsworths' bedroom displays the portraits of Victoria and Albert presented to him by the Queen on his appointment as Poet Laureate in 1843; Wordsworth first declined the honour pleading his age (74), but relented when it was promised that 'nothing should be required of him.' Dora and Dorothy's bedrooms are also on view, together with the study which Wordsworth later built on to the house. 4½ acres of informal gardens make a delightful setting for this family home. Keen gardeners, the Wordsworths created sloping terraces, flowerbeds and lawns in complete harmony with the Lakeland countryside.

Guide to opening: all the year. [T] Ambleside (05394) 33002 for details.

Levens Hall

Near Kendal

The Elizabethan home of the Bagot family, Levens Hall makes a splendid contribution to Britain's heritage. The house is divided into three main periods: 1250–1300, when the original pele tower and hall were built; 1570–90, when these were converted into a gentleman's residence, and the late-seventeenth/early-eighteenth centuries when the house was furnished much as we see it today. With its superb panelling, decorative plasterwork and leaded windows inset with stained glass, this gem of a house is authentic through and through. A tour of the house includes the Great Hall, Dining Room, Drawing Rooms, Library and bedrooms, all still in use as the family home. Each contains a fascinating display of treasures, which include a portrait by Rubens, a marvellous set of Charles II chairs and a Sèvres coffee set once destined for Napoleon's mother, but appropriated instead by the Duke of Wellington and given to his niece, Mary Bagot.

The house also boasts: the earliest English-made pistols and patchwork in the country; one of the bowls reputedly used by Sir Francis Drake on Plymouth Hoe; and the Duke of Wellington's gloves, taken off his hands when he entered Paris in triumph after Waterloo. A display of very old glassware includes the Levens Constables from which visitors drank staggeringly powerful Moroccan beer before taking up the challenge of crossing the bowling green in a straight line. The famous topiary garden at Levens Hall is unique; designed by James II's gardener who trained at Versailles, it still features its original designs and many of the original trees, with magnificent specimens of yew and box clipped into fanciful shapes. There are also vast beech hedges and borders, together with one of the oldest ha-has in the country.

Guide to opening: Easter to October. [T] Kendal (05395) 60321.

TOURIST INFORMATION

Tourist Information Centres: Old Court House, Church Street, **Ambleside** [T] (05394) 32582. Market Square, **Cockermouth** [T] (0900) 822634. Main Car Park, **Glenridding** [T] (08532) 414. Red Bank Road, **Grasmere** [T] (09665) 245. Town Hall, Highgate, **Kendal** [T] (0539) 25758. Moot Hall, Market Square, **Keswick** [T] (07687) 72645. Robinson's School, Middlegate, **Penrith** [T] (0768) 67466. The Square, **Pooley Bridge** [T] (08536) 530. The Car Park, **Waterhead** [T] (05394) 32729.

- **Abbot Hall Art Gallery, Kendal.**
- **Acorn Bank Garden, nr Penrith.**
- **Dalemain, nr Penrith.**
- **Doll & Toy Museum, Cockermouth.**
- **Dove Cottage, Grasmere.**
- **Hall House Historic Collection, nr Kendal.**
- **Kendal Museum of Natural History & Archaeology.**
- **Lingholm Gardens, Kendal.**
- **Mirehouse, nr Kendal.**
- **Museum of Lakeland Life & Industry, Kendal.**
- **Penrith Steam Museum.**
- **Sizergh Castle, nr Kendal.**
- **Stagshaw Garden, Ambleside.**

A view across the grounds of Levens Hall.

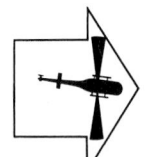

HUNT 26

START POSITION LANGDALE BLEA TARN

CLUE ONE Rock around the Old Man? Mr Wainwright will guide you to the Pudding Stone for a touch of the Whympers.

Leads to PUDDING STONE, CONISTON OLD MAN   Wainwright does, indeed, guide Anneka to this prominent boulder where a climb (Edward Whymper was an early climber) is necessary to reach the clue.

CLUE TWO Bluebird country near a likely Swallows and Amazons island, and a Venetian craft with a first-class recommendation.

Leads to STEAM YACHT GONDOLA, CONISTON WATER   Sir Donald Campbell's speedboat, 'Bluebird', and Peel Island, the setting for Arthur Ransome's *Swallows and Amazons*   lead to Coniston Water where the Gondola is about to set sail. The clue is in the first-class saloon.

CLUE THREE Follow the daffodil-gazer home from school and check up on his landlady's climbers.

Leads to ANN TYSON'S COTTAGE, HAWKESHEAD William Wordsworth lodged here when he was attending the Grammar School. The clue is concealed in the climbing rose round the front door.

CLUE FOUR Badger's set on Gaddum's place and an alfresco meal with the Ursa family. Who'll choose marmalade?

Leads to BROCKHOLE, WINDERMERE Brock(badger)hole, built for William Gaddum, stages teddy bears' picnics. The clue is tied to Paddington Bear who does, of course, choose marmalade.

CLUE FIVE Set out on the £25 trail near the old limekilns on the way to the Roman High Street. And discover a girl's best friend.

Leads to LIMEFITT PARK   Near some old limekilns, on the way to the Roman Road that runs on top of the fells, is this caravan and camping site. Riders are just setting off from the stables on a pony (£25) trail. A pony called 'Diamond' carries the treasure – a horseshoe.

CLUE SIX On your tiny feet, stride out along the edge, heading for a high spot. If you tire before reaching the summit, you may be tempted to rest by a colourful reviver below. What is it?

CLUE SEVEN Let's be blunt about it – if you don't get the point of this clue and propel yourself in the right direction, you won't find the place in which the world's very first of these everyday objects was made. Where is it?

Blea Tarn and the Langdale Pikes.

Coniston Old Man

Near Coniston

The huge fell which looms over Coniston village is the southern tip of the range of mountains known as the Furness Fells. The Old Man acts as a magnet to walkers, rewarding their two-hour climb with spectacular views of the lakes and surrounding countryside. Coppermines Valley, on the Old Man's side, still bears the scars of what was once a thriving industry here. Untouched for 50 years or more, spoil heaps, tunnels and shafts of old quarries and mines now provide pitfalls for the unwary, and a source of interest for enquiring minds.

Coniston Old Man boasts another distinctive feature in Boulder Valley, a shelf on the fellside which is littered with boulders fallen from the crags above. Several of the rocks here are big enough to prove a challenge to climbers, but the biggest and most taxing of them all is the massive Pudding Stone. Twenty-five feet high and 'as big as a house', this one rock alone offers a dozen routes which defeat all but the most determined assault.

Anne Tyson's cottage, Hawkshead.

Coniston Water

Near Coniston

The Steam Yacht 'Gondola', which featured on *Treasure Hunt*, first went into service on Coniston Water in 1859 when she was described by the *Illustrated London News* as 'a perfect combination of the Venetian Gondola and the English Steam Yacht.' Her working life came to an end in 1937; her boiler was sold to power a saw mill while her hull became a houseboat. But in 1977 the National Trust recognised 'Gondola' as a unique and graceful part of Coniston's history, and undertook the task of restoring her former glory. She was relaunched in 1980, and since then this stylish vessel with its opulent, upholstered saloons has provided a regular service between Coniston Pier and Brantwood, John Ruskin's lakeside home.

Guide to sailings: March to October. [T] Coniston (05394) 41288 for details. NT

Brantwood has the finest lake and mountain views in England. It still contains a large collection of Ruskin's drawings and watercolours, and visitors may also see his boat 'Jumping Jenny', his coach and various other personal mementoes. The grounds here are Ruskin's work too; he laid out a network of paths on the hillside above the house, and planted hundreds of daffodils, rhododendrons and azaleas to form a wonderful woodland garden which became his own lakeland paradise. Other attractions here include: Wainwright at Brantwood, an exhibition devoted to the great lakeland writer, artist and fellwalker; the 3-mile Lakeland Discovery Trail; the Lakeland Guild Craft Gallery and the Jumping Jenny restaurant and tea-room.

Guide to opening: all the year. [T] Coniston (05394) 41396 for details.

Hawkeshead

Although Anne Tyson's cottage (which was shown on *Treasure Hunt*) is not open to the public, visitors to Hawkeshead need not be disappointed. 1988 saw the opening of the Beatrix Potter Gallery here, in the building which was once the office of her husband, solicitor William Heelis. The gallery displays illustrations from her most famous books, together with lesser-known drawings and watercolours which faithfully reflect many lakeland landscapes. Another display tells the story of Beatrix Potter's life, and explains something of the character of this remarkable woman who was not only an artist, author and farmer, but also a national benefactress who did much to preserve the Cumbrian countryside that she loved.

Guide to opening: Easter to October. [T] Hawkeshead (09666) 355 for details. NT

Hill Top (Near Sawrey, Hawkeshead) is a little seventeenth-century farmhouse which once was Beatrix Potter's home. She described it as 'as near perfect a place as I ever lived in'. The house still contains her furniture, china and pictures, and her workroom — where she wrote the Peter Rabbit series — has been fully restored. She left Hill Top to the National Trust at her death, together with over 4,000 acres of land which include about half the village of Near Sawrey.

Guide to opening: April to October. [T] Hawkeshead (09666) 269 for details. NT

The Lake District National Park Centre

Brockhole, Windermere

Besides being an information and interpretive centre for the Lake District National Park, Brockhole is itself one of the most popular attractions in Cumbria. The house is set in lovely formal gardens with panoramic

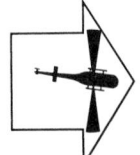

The Lake District National Park Centre, Brockhole.

views over Windermere and Langdale Pikes, and its extensive grounds reach down to the water's edge. The house is devoted to exhibitions and displays which aim to broaden visitors' enjoyment of England's largest National Park. 'Living Lakeland' is a walk-through audio-visual exhibition telling the story of Lakeland from prehistoric times to the present, and tape-slide shows illustrate specific topics such as wildlife and natural history, literary associations and human history. 'The World of Beatrix Potter' recreates scenes from the pen of the local author who enchants adults and children alike.

The calendar includes a variety of day courses and illustrated talks on an anything from 'Enjoying the hills in Safety' to a talk introducing live owls. Visitors can watch demonstrations of falconry or hound trailing, dry-stone walling or lacemaking, take a launch trip on the lake, join guided tours of the gardens, or venture further on organised walks based on heritage, map reading and other themes. Children have a marvellous choice here too; they are treated to juggling displays and Teddy Bears' Picnics, taken birdwatching and tree-hugging, and generally taught to be 'nature conscious'. Brockhole also provides a bookshop and cafeteria – plus plenty of information on the rest of the National Park!

Guide to opening: April to November. [T] Windermere (096 62) 6601 for details.

TOURIST INFORMATION

Tourist Information Centres: The Glebe, **Bowness** [T] (09662) 2895. 16 Yewdale Road, **Coniston** [T] (05394) 41533. Near Car Park, **Hawkeshead** [T] (09666) 525. The Gateway Centre, Victoria Street, **Windermere** [T] (09662) 6499.

- **Cartmel Priory.**
- **Graythwaite Hall, Hawkeshead.**
- **Lakeland Motor Museum, Holker Hall, Cark-in-Cartmel.**
- **Lakeside & Haverthwaite Railway, nr Newby Bridge.**
- **Lake Windermere Aquarium, Bowness.**
- **Muncaster Castle, nr Ravenglass.**
- **Ravenglass & Eskdale Railway, Ravenglass.**
- **Rusland Hall, nr Newby Bridge.**
- **Stott Park Bobbin Mill, Newby Bridge.**
- **Troutbeck Yeoman Farmers House, nr Windermere.**
- **Windermere Steamboat.**

TREASURE HUNT 27

Cheshire

START POSITION NETHER ALDERLEY

CLUE ONE Here's scope for a star performance. Take your cue from the dishy model. The azimuth's OK; but the elevation's wrong.

Leads to **JODRELL BANK**   The stars are studied here with the help of a radio telescope. Having altered its elevation, the clue is revealed hanging from a replica telescope.

CLUE TWO South east of Mrs Gaskell's Cranford a champion strongman opens a hall. Talk of the devil – look who's dropping in!

Leads to **CAPESTHORNE HALL**   Geoff CAPES is the champion strong man who opens this hall, south east of Knutsford, which is playing host to the Red Devils. One of the display team lands with the clue.

CLUE THREE Bollin banks at the priest's town. Who banks at the priest's house? Better ask for a statement.

Leads to **PRESTBURY**   The River Bollin flows through Prestbury. The Priest's House is now the National Westminster Bank, and the clue is written on a statement.

The team arrive at Capesthorne Hall, Macclesfield.

CLUE FOUR Trust Greg's to be no run-of-the mill place. Weave a way to the tackler – could his job be folding?

Leads to **QUARRY BANK MILL**   This model mill was built by Greg. The clue is in the weaving room with the tackler, who is folding material.

CLUE FIVE In the old hundred of Bochelau, the Egertons' home is a showplace. Find 'Our Cheshire Countryside', and take the bull by the horns.

Leads to **CHESHIRE SHOW, TATTON PARK**   Tatton Hall (in Bucklow Rural District), built by the Egerton Family, stages the Cheshire Show. Beside the 'Our Cheshire Countryside' exhibit is a highland bull, the treasure tied to one of his horns.

CLUE SIX South east now to a mossy place where Andy and Stephen found old Pete. There's no doubt he came to an untimely end here! Where is it?

CLUE SEVEN Once the home of a wayward maid and possible dark lady, and once quadrangular, this place became the subject of a famous duel. Where is it?

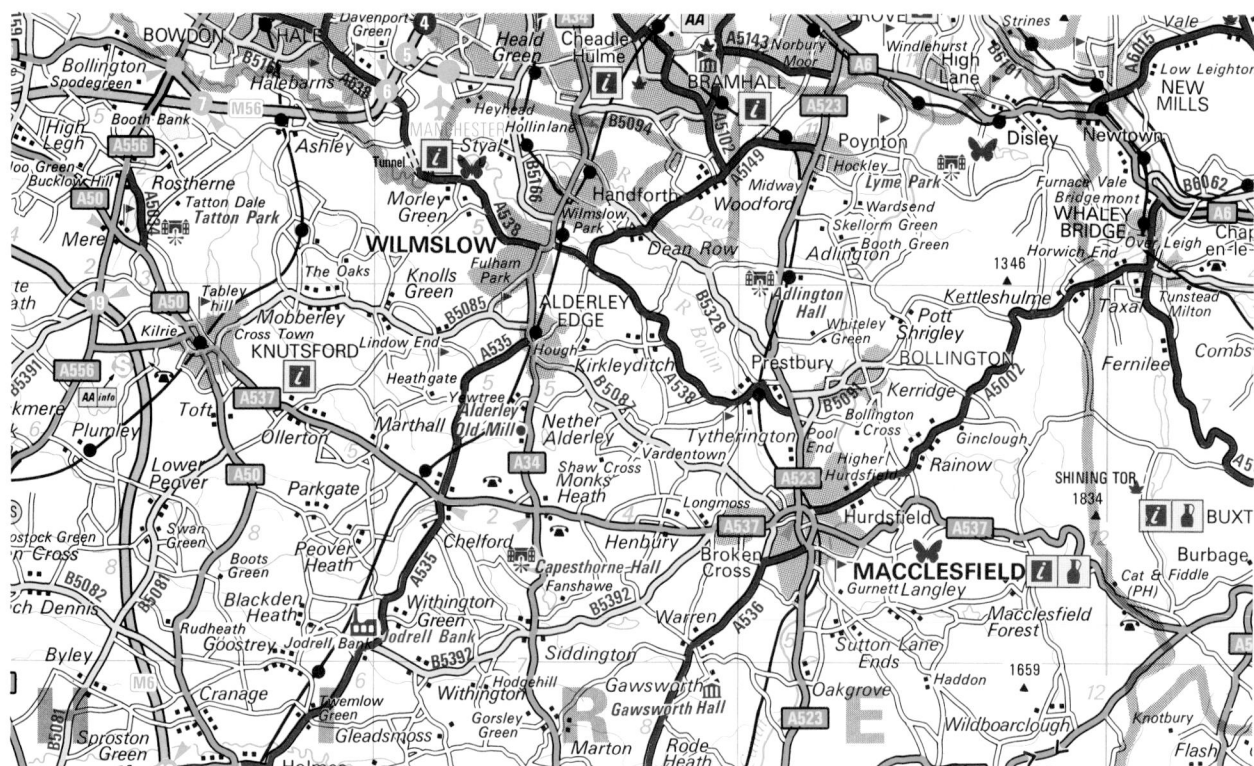

Nether Alderley Mill

Congleton Road, Alderley Edge

This overshot watermill dates from the fifteenth century, when it was built against the dam of the reservoir which had been created to supply the miller with enough water for the day's work. The mill is of sandstone, with a stone-tiled low-pitched roof broken by four dormer windows, and much of the woodwork inside is Elizabethan oak. The original wooden machinery has long since worn out, and the present machinery dates from the 1870s. It has now been restored to full working order, and grinds flour occasionally for demonstration.

Guide to opening: April to October. [T] Wilmslow (0625) 523012. NT

Jodrell Bank Science Centre & Tree Park

Near Macclesfield

The Lovell Radio Telescope forms the centrepiece of this exciting science complex. The largest and most famous exhibit is the 250-foot Radio Telescope itself, and this is complemented by a major exhibition presenting a historical survey of space from Galileo to the present day, and covering everything from satellites to astronomy. More recent additions to the Centre include the 'talking head' of Sir Isaac Newton, together with a 'hands on' science area where visitors can sit on the gyro chair, explore the gravity hollow, and operate the model telescope. The Planetarium Star Theatre provides the highlight of every visit;

presentations here take travellers on a whistle-stop tour of the Galaxy by means of the stunning three-dimensional 'voyage among the stars'.

A 35-acre Tree Park encourages everyone to get their feet back firmly on the ground; true to the Jodrell Bank theme, nature trails and tree trails here are laid out to represent a scale version of our solar system.

Guide to opening: all the year. [T] Macclesfield (0477) 71339.

Capesthorne Hall

Macclesfield

Capesthorne is the home of the Bromley-Davenport family, whose ancestors have owned the estate since the Norman Conquest. Theirs was the task of keeping law and order in the King's Forest of Macclesfield and Leek, at a time when the life of a man was less precious that the well-being of the royal deer. The family crest – a felon's head with a golden halter around its neck – reflects the Chief Forester's power to meet out life or death without trial or appeal. The Hall itself is a striking building, whose imposing façade is longer than that of Buckingham Palace. The house dates from 1719, but it was altered in 1837, and the central section we see today was remodelled following a disastrous fire in 1861. Inside, a series of elegant state rooms contain a great variety of sculptures, paintings and fine furniture, including a collection of American Colonial furnishings. Among the general splendour, many items of individual interest catch the eye; these range from the prodigious piece of needlework which kept Dorothy Davenport occupied for 26 years, to striking portraits of Jean Jacques

Rousseau, clad in the Armenian attire in which he roamed the hills of Derbyshire, to the utter astonishment of villagers there.

The Hall is set in colourful gardens, with an extensive park featuring a chain of man-made lakes. Attractions in the grounds include a nature trail, arboretum and adventure playground, and the Mill Wood Walk. South of the house is a beautiful Georgian chapel dating from 1720, and a stable wing of the Hall was been converted into a theatre, which stages productions throughout the season.

Guide to opening: April to September. [T] Chelford (0625) 861439.

Quarry Bank Mill

Styal

Founded in 1784, Quarry Bank Mill was one of the first generation of water powered cotton mills, and a pioneer site of the factory system. Restored by the National Trust, it now runs as a working museum. But Quarry Bank offers much more than machinery: visitors here can actually experience the noise, smells and working conditions so familiar to the original workers, many of whom were apprentice children. Work goes on in the mule room, cotton cloth is still woven in the historic weaving shed (where machines are often powered by the giant Victorian iron waterwheel) and there are further demonstrations of other textile processes. New displays also explain the role of water power and show the lives of the mill owner, mill workers and pauper apprentices. The village is now part of the Styal Country Park, where miles of woodland and riverside walks produce the beautiful surroundings so typical of early rural mills.

Guide to opening: all the year. [T] Wilmslow (0625) 527468. NT

Tatton Park

Knutsford

Tatton Park is a complete country estate, with so many historic attractions that one visit is hardly enough to get round them all. The focal point of the estate is a magnificent Georgian mansion designed by Samuel and Lewis Wyatt. The seat of the late Lord Egerton of Tatton, and a family home for two centuries, the mansion still has its original furnishings, including Gillow furniture, fine porcelain and paintings by Canaletto and Van Dyke. Now the cellars have been opened too, showing how and where the servants worked, and completing the contrast between life upstairs and downstairs in a Victorian country house. Another major attraction is the restored fifteenth-century Old Hall; this offers another taste of the past with its Medieval Great Hall, Jacobean bedrooms, cruck barn and Victorian gamekeeper's cottage.

Virtually untouched since 1938, Home Farm is also a period piece; it is stocked with original breeds of animals, and its livestock yards, mill, workshops,

Quarry Bank Mill, Styal.

stores and offices demonstrate the complex but fascinating operations needed to sustain the mansion and its estate. Tatton's grounds are a very impressive part of that estate. The extensive gardens include a Japanese Garden, a maze and a glorious display of rhododendrons and azaleas; beyond them there are a further 2,000 acres of deer park to explore, and a mile-long mere for fishing, sailing, picnicking or enjoying the view. The grounds play host to a wide range of special events such as country shows, car and caravan rallies, antique and craft fairs, music and drama. The biggest of them all is the Cheshire Country Show, held in June.

Guide to opening: Mansion, Old Hall and Farm, April to October; Park and Gardens, all the year. [T] Knutsford (0565) 54822 for details. NT

TOURIST INFORMATION

Tourist Information Centres: Council Offices, Toft Road, **Knutsford** [T] (0565) 2611. Town Hall, Market Place, **Macclesfield** [T] (0625) 21955.

- **Adlington Hall, nr Prestbury.**
- **Alderley Edge & Visitor Centre.**
- **Arley Hall, nr Northwich.**
- **Gawsworth Hall, nr Macclesfield.**
- **Hare Hill, Over Alderly.**
- **Lyme Hall & Park, Disley.**
- **Macclesfield Heritage Centre.**
- **Paradise Mill Working Silk Museum, Macclesfield.**
- **Peaks & Plains Discovery Centre, Bollington.**
- **Peover Hall, Knutsford.**
- **Silk Museum, Macclesfield.**
- **Teggs Nose Country Park, Macclesfield.**
- **West Park Museum, Macclesfield.**

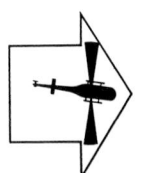

TREASURE HUNT 28

Lancashire

START POSITION LEYLAND

CLUE ONE Towards the Rovers, find the link between Good Queen Bess's successor and a Sunday roast, and try the dining table for the *carte du jour*.

Leads to HOGHTON TOWER   From the start point at Leyland Motors, head towards Blackburn (Rovers). *En route* is Hoghton Tower, where James I, successor to Elizabeth I, knighted a loin of beef. The clue *(carte du jour)* is on the sword used in the reenactment of the dubbing scene.

CLUE TWO An everyday story of Southworth folk, quivering before the quatrefoils, waiting for Annie to take a bow.

Leads to SAMLESBURY HALL   The hall, with its decorative quatrefoils, was once the home of the Southworth family. Archers (the everyday story) are practising in the grounds; the clue is on one of their targets.

CLUE THREE After the Romans, do's and don'ts in the Loyola tradition: pass Grammar, deny yourself a Good Do, but get into Campion's historic good books.

Leads to STONYHURST COLLEGE   Beyond Ribchester, a Roman fort, is this Jesuit College. Loyola founded the Jesuits. Pass by the Grammar room and the 'Do's' room to enter the Campion Room (library). A history lesson is taking place in a side room; a pupil has the clue.

CLUE FOUR Where Oliver made a hole, there are grounds for celebrating Merrie England – and for facing the music with a sovereign.

Leads to CLITHEROE CASTLE GROUNDS   Oliver Cromwell attacked the castle, making a large hole in the wall. In the castle grounds, a production of Merrie England is in progress. Elizabeth I has the clue.

CLUE FIVE To the haunt of secret, black, and midnight hags and a race round a water-filled clough for a spellbinding finish.

Leads to PENDLE HILL   This hill is famous for its witches. A fun run round a reservoir (clough) is taking place, and a participating 'witch' has the treasure.

CLUE SIX The Pilgrimage of Grace may have been responsible for the demise of its Abbey, but this village's Parish Church survives. Chief among the treasures it preserves are the choir stalls that once were used in the Abbey Church. Where is it?

CLUE SEVEN It's beyond Stidd, and is said to be the first brick-built domestic building in the country, but just how 'homely' can this most haunted house in Britain be? Which house is it?

Anneka sharpens up her archery at Samlesbury Hall.

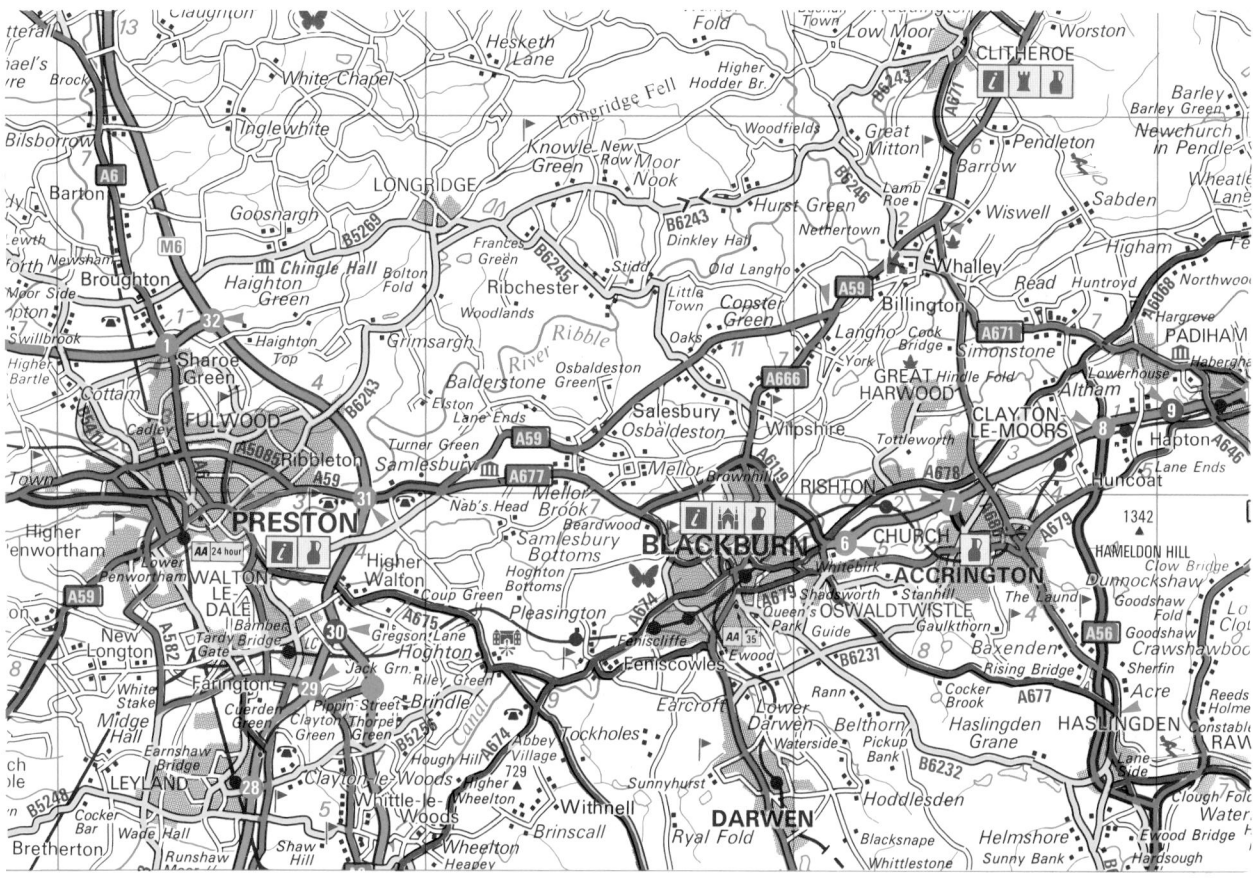

Hoghton Tower

Near Preston

The ancestral home of the Hoghton family is a sixteenth-century fortified manor built on a dramatic hilltop site. In 1671, Sir Richard Hoghton played host here to King James I, together with the Duke of Buckingham and a large retinue of nobles. To welcome the King, the steep ascent to the Tower is said to have been entirely carpeted with red velvet, and the rest of the visit was an equally splendid affair. Feasting was on a gargantuan scale, and it was here in the magnificent Banqueting Hall that the King showed his appreciation by knighting a loin of beef, known ever since as 'Sir Loin'.

The King's Bedchamber, Audience Chamber, Ballroom and other state rooms used by the party have escaped alteration, and have now been restored. Visitors may also see the Tudor Well House with its horse-drawn pump and oaken windlass; the underground passages with their tableaux of the Lancashire Witches; and the dungeons, wine cellar and stone cells which were once used to confine local malefactors and cattle thieves.

The Tower enjoys a lovely setting amongst lawns, walled gardens and an Old English Rose Garden, and walks through these hilltop grounds give wonderful views of the sea and moorlands, the Lakeland hills and the mountains of Wales.

Guide to opening: Easter to October. [T] Hoghton (0254 85) 2986.

Samlesbury Hall

Near Preston

Samlesbury Hall is a picturesque black and white timbered manor house dating from the fourteenth century, which has an interesting modern story to tell. It was modified and partly rebuilt in the sixteenth century and many further alterations followed, but by the nineteenth century it had fallen into disrepair and was saved from near ruin by timely restoration in 1835. For some time after that it was a girls' boarding school, and in 1911 it was even rumoured that the whole house might be dismantled and sent to America; but a local trust was formed and, further restored, Samlesbury became a popular place with tourists.

Many of its historic rooms survive, such as the Great Hall with its high roof and massive fireplace – but these are not the only attractions here. Faced with the daunting prospect of raising funds, the Trust allocated many of the non-historic rooms to the purpose of displaying and selling antiques on behalf of private individuals, and the varied and ever-changing stock of collectors items now helps to bring in over 1500 visitors a week. Other rooms are devoted to special 'selling exhibitions' featuring anything from sculpture to cigarette cards, and 'At Work at Samlesbury' gives craft workers the chance to show off their skills and sell their work.

Guide to opening: all the year. [T] Mellor (0254 81) 2010.

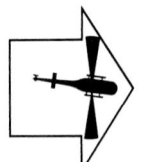

Clitheroe Castle

Clitheroe

One of the main touring centres of the lovely Ribble Valley, Clitheroe is dominated by its Norman castle, a landmark for miles around. Like so many others the castle has the stories of centuries to tell, but the final chapter here is different from them all. After the First World War a public subscription list has opened, and the residents of Clitheroe bought their castle, and turned it into a War Memorial. Now the cenotaph stands beneath the shadow of the Keep in a beautiful garden of remembrance, and the grounds have been landscaped to include a rose garden and terrace, a band stand, bowling greens and other leisure facilities. Visitors to the castle keep will notice a large hole in its east wall; one legend insists it was the work of a cannon ball fired when Oliver Cromwell attacked the castle, but another calls it the work of the devil, who threw a rock at the Keep from Pendle Hill.

Clitheroe Castle Museum is located in Castle House, adjacent to the castle. The displays include archaeological finds from the Ribble Valley, and a variety of objects, plans and photographs illustrating the history of the ancient Borough of Clitheroe. A range of household objects in a fire-side setting shows domestic life here as it used to be, while reconstructed cloggers' and printers' workshops, (fully-equipped with tools) bring traditional skills to life.

Guide to opening: March to October. [T] Clitheroe (0200) 24365 for details.

Pendle Hill

'Some folk say Pendle wants grandeur and sublimity, but themselves must be wanting in taste. Its broad, round, smooth mass is better than the roughest, shaggiest, most sharply splintered mountain of them all.' Thus local Squire Nicholas Assheton described Pendle Hill, the lofty, 7-mile ridge which rises majestically on the eastern side of Clitheroe. Visible

Anneka makes a guest appearance in 'Merrie England' at Clitheroe Castle.

for miles, Pendle once formed a link in the chain of beacons lit to summon the men of Ribblesdale to arms or to celebrate great national events, but now the flat-topped summit itself provides walkers with panoramic views.

Pendle Heritage Centre (Burrowford, near Nelson) occupies an historic seventeenth-century house some 4 miles from Pendle Hill. Various study courses are held here, and a variety of changing exhibitions on local themes set out to explore Pendle's heritage through its people and buildings, farming and other industries.

Guide to opening: Easter to November. [T] Nelson (0282) 695366.

TOURIST INFORMATION

Tourist Information: Town Hall, **Blackburn** [T] (0254) 53277/55201. Council Offices, Church Walk, **Clitheroe** [T] (0200) 25566. The Guildhall, Lancaster Road, **Preston** [T] (0772) 53731. 41/45 Kay Street, **Rawtenstall** [T] (0706) 217777.

- **British Commercial Vehicle Museum, Leyland.**
- **Browsholme Hall, nr Clitheroe.**
- **Duke of Lancaster's Own Yeomanry Museum, Preston.**
- **Gawthorpe Hall, Padiham.**
- **Harris Museum & Art Gallery, Preston.**
- **Haworth Gallery, Accrington.**

- **Helmshore Textile Museum.**
- **Lewis Textile Museum, Burnley.**
- **Museum of Childhood, Ribchester.**
- **Museum of Lancashire Textile Industry, Helmshore.**
- **Pendle Photographic Gallery.**
- **Queen Street Mill Working Museum, nr Burnley.**
- **Rossendale Museum, Rawtenstall.**
- **Towneley Hall Art Gallery & Museum, Burnley.**
- **Ribchester Roman Museum.**
- **Weavers' Triange and Visitor Centre, Burnley.**
- **West Lancashire Light Railway, Preston.**

TREASURE HUNT 29 & 30

Northumberland/ Durham

Hunt 29 (Northumberland)

START POSITION ALNMOUTH BAY

CLUE ONE **Home for Hotspur, with a lantern-lit hearth up in the donjon beyond the Grey Mare's Tail.**

Leads to **WARKWORTH CASTLE**   Hotspur was born here. Beyond the Grey Mare's Tail tower, and in the central keep (donjon), the clue is hidden in the hearth in the Great Hall, which is lit by the lantern.

CLUE TWO **Where the tenants said *merci* to Percy, there's a fair chance Annie's in the market for a punishing time — awaiting her sentence!**

Leads to **ALNWICK**   The Percy tenantry column, erected by Percy's grateful tenants, leads to Alnwick where a re-enactment of a fair from the Middle Ages is taking place in the market square. Annie is pilloried before being given her sentence (clue).

CLUE THREE **Go Wee Willie Winkie-like to the site of de Vesci's motte, and study, *pianissimo*, the Venetian view of the situation.**

Leads to **ALNWICK CASTLE**   A run through the town, now, like Wee Willie Winkie, to the Castle which was built by the de Vesci family. In the music room, behind Canaletto's view of the castle, is hidden the clue.

CLUE FOUR **East of the teatime Earl's home, and after discovering the Show Boat man, test the waves for a message from the crew.**

Leads to **THE NORTH SEA!**   East of Earl Grey's Howick Hall and Rumbling (Jerome) Kern, the Show Boat man, Anneka has to jump into the sea (test the waves). She is winched to safety by a handy Air-Sea Rescue helicopter; the pilot has the clue.

CLUE FIVE **Gaunt remains ahead, fishy preparations below. Where's the Spirit of Adventure? Hang on, your wires are crossed.**

Leads to **CRASTER**   Head towards the gaunt remains of Dunstanburgh Castle to reach the adventure school, Spirit of Adventure. Hanging from the Tyrolean traverse, which crosses a ravine, is the treasure.

CLUE SIX The only way to go is down, but unless you want to get the bird, you had better ignore this nature reserve and make a round trip. Around what have you circled?

CLUE SEVEN On a loop of the river stand the remains of William de Bertram's housing project. Some say that, as a result of a premature celebration, its bells remain too — hidden in a river pool. What was the project?

A Northumbrian sea-scape, Craster.

Warkworth Castle and Hermitage

Warkworth, Northumberland

Set high on a hill above a bend in the River Coquet, the fifteenth-century keep of Warkworth Castle looms over the well-preserved medieval village below. The castle was begun in the twelfth century, and the great keep, built in the shape of a cross, was added in the fourteenth century by the Percy family who owned the castle for 600 years. Like their stronghold at Alnwick, Warkworth saw plenty of fighting; in 1399, the third Lord Percy and his son Harry Hotspur (hero of the Battles of Otterburn and Hamildon Hill) were instrumental in putting Henry IV on the throne, and three scenes from Shakespeare's *Henry IV Part I* are set at the castle here. The keep was partially restored in the nineteenth century and is the dominant feature of the castle today.

The hermitage and Chapel of Holy Trinity lies half a mile above the castle in a wooded spot on the opposite banks of the Coquet, accessible either by boat or by footpath and ferry. This tiny fourteenth-century chapel, hewn out of the rock, accommodated the hermit who lived mainly on fish and on the produce of a little riverside garden. Legend insists that the hermitage began as a refuge for a knight who fought for the love of a lady, and killed his opponent before discovering it to be his own brother (the lady, too, was fatally wounded trying to intervene).

Guide to opening: Castle, all the year; Hermitage, April to September. [T] Alnwick (0665) 211423. EH

Opposite Warkworth Castle – from the air.

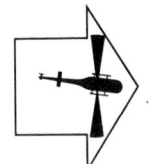

Alnwick Fair

Alnwick, Northumberland

As viewers of *Treasure Hunt* could see, this annual event is no ordinary fair; it is a strictly medieval occasion modelled on Alnwick's market fair of 1297, and everyone dresses accordingly. The Fair begins on the last Sunday in June, and to open the week of festivities a Herald leads the crowd in procession round the old gates of the town before things get underway with an ox roast, live entertainments and the opening of the Craft Fair. 'Offenders' are also brought to justice in the first of several 'courts' to be held in the Market Place. Market stalls stay open from Monday to Saturday, and trading is enlived by craft demonstrations, singing, dancing, and contributions from strolling minstrels. The fair ends with a flourish when the Alnwick Round Tables stages its popular jousting tournaments in the pastures of the castle.

The Tourist Information Centre at Alnwick [T] (0665) 603129 are happy to supply details of the festivities.

Alnwick Castle

Alnwick, Northumberland

Founded by the Normans, the magnificent border fortress of Alnwick stands sentinal over the eastern 'debatable lands' where the English and the Scots met and clashed in centuries of skirmish. The castle saw almost constant warfare as successive owners varied habitual hostilities against the Scots with occasional revolts against the Kings of England (besides fighting vigorously for the House of Lancaster in the Wars of the Roses and for Parliament in the Civil War). In all, the sieges, raids and laying waste of land that centred on Alnwick over the centuries must have reduced the local inhabitants to a wretched state.

Alnwick's story is bound up with that of the Percy family who acquired the castle in 1308 and whose descendant, the Duke of Northumberland, still owns it today. This powerful family produced some interesting characters. They include: Henry, son of the first Earl whose daring in battle at the age of 12 earned him the nickname 'Hotspur', later immortalised in Shakespeare's *Henry IV:* Henry 'The Magnificent' who loved finery, and was fittingly chosen to wait on the King of France on the Field of the Cloth of Gold; and the sixth Earl 'The Unthrifty' whose lifetime of bad luck included renouncing Anne Boleyn to Henry VIII only to find himself appointed by the King as one of her judges. But it was Hugh, first Duke of Northumberland (1750–86) whose interest in farming and forestry transformed the countryside around Alnwick. It was he who also restored the castle as a family residence, employing Robert Adam who adopted the style known as 'Gingerbread' or 'Strawberry Hill' Gothic with elaborate stucco work covering walls and ceilings.

Much of Adam's work was swept away by the fourth Duke (1847–1865) who fell in love with the fifteenth/sixteenth-century Italian style and commissioned Salvin to transform the interior in that way. As a result of his work, the Library, Music Room, Red Drawing Room, Dining Room and other apartments now provide sumptuous backgrounds for pictures of Titian, Canaletto, Van Dyke and other famous artists, together with fine pieces of furniture, china and treasures of many kinds.

Guide to opening: April to September. [T] Alnwick (0665) 602207 for details.

Spirit of Adventure Centre

Craster, Northumberland

The Spirit of Adventure Centre offers a choice of challenging leisure pursuits which take full advantage of Northumberland's unspoilt countryside. The centre is set on the coast in an Area of Outstanding Natural Beauty, and sailing, surfing, windsurfing and canoeing are popular both on the sea and on more sheltered inland waters. Sandstone outcrops and the Whin Sill sea cliffs provide excellent training and testing grounds for all aspects of climbing, and the rugged wilderness of the Cheviot Hills is ideal for practising 'hillcraft' (this involves campcraft, navigation and survival techniques). The centre offers residential courses based on one or many activities, and is open to non-residents too. All activities are supervised by qualified instructors and specialist equipment is provided.

Guide to opening: [T] Alnwick (0665) 76551 for details. For information on other activity centres both here in Northumberland and in other parts of the country, please contact the regional tourist boards listed on page 7.

TOURIST INFORMATION

Tourist Information Centres: The Shambles, Northumberland Hall, **Alnwick** [T] (0665) 603129. Council Office, Dilston Terrace, **Amble** [T] (0665) 712313. The Chantry, Bridge Street, **Morpeth** [T] (0670) 511323. **Newcastle Airport** [T] 091-271 1929.

- Dunstanburgh Castle, nr Craster.
- Edlingham Castle, nr Alnwick.

- House of Hardy Museum, nr Alnwick.
- Howick Hall Gardens, nr Alnwick.
- John Sinclair Railway Museum, Blyth.
- Morpeth Chantry Bagpipe Museum & Northumbria Craft Centre.
- Prudhoe Castle.
- L. Robson & Sons Ltd (kipper factory & shop) Craster.
- Seaton Delaval Hall, Seaton Sluice.

Alnwick Castle.

HUNT 30 (DURHAM)

START POSITION FINCHALE PRIORY

CLUE ONE Break the ice at the miners' gala place with a visit to the Wasps' nest. Find Robin Goodfellow hand-in-glove with the minder.

Leads to **DURHAM ICE RINK** The annual miners' gala is held in Durham, and the ice rink is the home of the Durham Wasps. Robin Goodfellow is another name for Puck, so it is the puck that Annie has to retrieve from the goal keeper (wearing gloves) in order to get the next clue.

CLUE TWO Use your pollex to reach Cuthbert's heritage, and visiting vellum from his holy isle.

Leads to **DURHAM CATHEDRAL** Annie has to thumb (pollex) a lift to the Cathedral, the shrine for the body of St Cuthbert, where a temporary exhibition of the Lindisfarne (his holy isle) Gospels is being staged. The clue is near one of the show cases.

Reposition **PENSHAW MONUMENT**

CLUE THREE Before the hexadic bridges where hopes are fostered and the terraces crammed, here's Annie's chance for a runaway victory.

Leads to **GATESHEAD STADIUM** Those heroes of the track, Brendan Foster and Steve Cram guide us to this stadium, which is on the way to Newcastle and its six bridges. Annie races against some local athletes; when she reaches the tape, the time-keeper hands over the clue.

CLUE FOUR To the Jabberwocky boy to buy posser, Bisto and liberty bodice – and collect the divi.

Leads to **BEAMISH NORTH OF ENGLAND OPEN AIR MUSEUM** 'And hast thou slain the Jabberwock? Come to my arms, my beamish boy!' These lines from *Through the Looking Glass* guide Annie to the Co-op at Beamish, and what wonderful value it is! Having done her shopping she still has change (divi) from a ten shilling note, not to mention the clue.

CLUE FIVE Just a few lines to reach the home of a type of shorthand. In a 90's sort of soap opera, Davy's alighted on a winner.

Leads to **PITMAN'S COTTAGE, BEAMISH** A short tram ride takes Annie to a PITMAN's cottage, where a miner is having a very soapy bath. The treasure is a miner's (Davy) lamp.

Durham Cathedral.

CLUE SIX Its designer had no confidence in it, but Stanley has good cause to be proud of this structure, the oldest of its kind. What is it called?

CLUE SEVEN The remains of St Cuthbert rested in a church here for over one hundred years while, against the wall of the present church's tower, there is evidence that hermits, too, came to rest here. Which town is it?

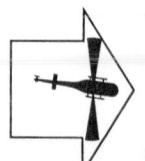

Finchale Priory

Near Durham, Co. Durham

The starting point of this *Treasure Hunt* had an interesting beginning itself. The site was first occupied by St Godric, one of the less conventional English saints. He is thought to have been born in East Anglia, and it is known that despite having made a pilgrimage to Rome, he became a pirate at the age of 20. He came to Finchale a reformed character, settled as a hermit and died in 1170 at the age of 107. His tomb became a place of pilgrimage, and in 1237 the hermitage became a Benedictine Priory attached to the monastery at Durham. Today, the majority of the riverside ruins here are from the thirteenth century, with later additions. The ruins of the church and the early fourteenth-century refectory with its vaulted undercroft are perhaps the finest of all the remains.

Guide to opening: all the year. [T] Durham 091-386 3828. EH

Durham Cathedral

Durham, Co. Durham

The history of this glorious building begins with the story of St Cuthbert, Bishop of Lindisfarne from 685–87 and the North Country's most famous saint. Ten years after his death, St Cuthbert's body was found to be perfectly preserved and the Lindisfarne monks placed it in a shrine, where it stayed for 200 years. But under the threat of Danish raids, the monks and the shrine left the island and began the wanderings which ended on a rocky piece of land almost surrounded by the River Wear – here, in what is now Durham, they built a church and monastery worthy of their saint.

The Saxon church was cleared away, and on the 11 August 1093 the first stone of Durham Cathedral was laid; by 1133, it was the finest Norman building in the land, and so it is today. Massive, yet beautifully proportioned, its mightly pillars, graceful stone vaulting and slender piers create a moving magnificence that cannot be captured in words. But one of its glories has been lost – the original shrine of St Cuthbert which was one of the most splendid monuments in England. In 1540 these riches were confiscated by the Crown, and the shrine itself was opened to reveal the body of the saint 'whole, incorrupt, with his face bare and his beard as it had been, a fortnight's growth, and all his vestments upon him.' The body was then buried under a marble slab where the shrine had stood and it remains there today.

A wealth of other precious things (including the Anglo-Saxon embroidered stole from St Cuthbert's coffin) are now on show in the Treasury, and other items of special interest are displayed in the fourteenth/fifteenth century Monks' Dormitory,

Guide to opening: all the year. [T] Durham 091-386 2367.

The Penshaw Monument

Penshaw, Tyne & Wear

Set on top of Penshaw Hill overlooking the River Wear, the monument to the first Earl of Durham is a startling sight. It was designed by John and Benjamin Green of Newcastle who modelled it on a Grecian temple, and when its foundation stone was laid in 1844 the ceremony attracted a crowd of over 10,000 people. Measuring 100 feet long, 53 feet wide and 73 feet high the finished monument is certainly very impressive, and is now owned by the National Trust. Its site is associated with the legend of the giant Lambton Worm who supposedly died wrapping its tail '10 times round Penshaw Hill'; undaunted, walkers still come here for the view, and to enjoy orchids and other wild flowers on the hillside. NT

Gateshead

Tyne & Wear

The town which held the solution of the fourth *Treasure Hunt* clue has put itself on the tourist map – in a big way. Gateshead's MetroCentre is the biggest out-of-town shopping centre in Europe. Every type of shop from major stores to market stalls rub shoulders in spacious malls bright with natural light and landscaped with plants and ornamental water. Besides a wide choice of restaurants, coffee houses and tea-rooms, there is a green and tranquil corner known as the Garden Court, a multi-screen cinema, and a Children's Village and Playground Creche. Newly opened in 1988, the fantasy fairytale Kingdom of King Wiz provides an indoor playground of fairground and rollercoaster rides.

Guide to opening: [T] 091 493 2040 for details of opening hours.

Beamish North of England Open Air Museum

Stanley, Co. Durham

The word 'museum' seems somehow inadequate for this award-winning site which is more an all-round 'living' experience. North-east England built its former wealth on the lead, coal and iron which produced ships and railways, and this in turn lead to the development of heavy engineering backed up by farming in the rural districts. As the visual remains of this heritage disappeared, Beamish set about saving what it could and presenting it to the public in an enjoyable way. An enormous variety of old buildings from all parts of the North East have been re-erected here equipped with the same kind of furniture and machinery they once held. More are added all the time and the collection now forms a wonderful illustration of the development of industry and the northern way of life.

The 200 acres of woodland and rolling countryside

Anneka sits in on a miner's ablutions, Beamish.

Advertising history, Beamish.

here are divided into different 'theme' areas joined by footpaths. The Town comprises a fine terrace of late-Georgian houses (complete with dental surgery and solicitor's office), the Sun Inn pub (with working stables), the Co-op, and a Victorian Park with bandstand. The pub serves Newcastle Ale, concerts are held in the bandstand, the co-op is fully stocked, trams run along the cobbled street and every building is perfect for its period. The Railway Station, with its passenger buildings, signal box, goods shed, coal and lime depot and weigh cabin shows the North Eastern Railway Company at work, while the more formal Transport Collection displays electric tramcars and horse-drawn and steam vehicles. The Pit Cottages and drift mine form part of the Colliery, with its steam winding engine, screens and boiler house. Finally, there is a Home Farm, which is a working farm laid out as it was in the 1790s, and still stocked with traditional local breeds.

Guide to opening: all the year. [T] Stanley (0207) 231811 for details.

TOURIST INFORMATION

Tourist Information Centres: Market Place, **Durham** [T] 091-384 3720. Central Library, Prince Consort Road, **Gateshead** [T] 091-477 3478. The Bede Monastery Museum, Jarrow Hall, **Jarrow** [T] 091-489 2106. Central Library, Princess Square, **Newcastle-upon-Tyne** [T] 091-261 5367. Ferry Terminal, **North Shields** [T] 091-257 9800. 20 Upper Chare, **Peterlee** [T] 091-586 4450. Ocean Road, **South Shields** [T] 091-454 6612. Crowtree Leisure Centre, **Sunderland** [T] 091-565 0960. Central Promenade, **Whitley Bay** 091-252 4494

- **Arbeia Roman Fort, South Shields.**
- **Bede Monastery Museum, Jarrow.**
- **Durham Castle.**
- **Durham University Oriental Museum.**
- **Durham University Museum of Archaeology.**
- **Laing Art Gallery, Newcastle-upon-Tyne.**
- **Lumley Castle.**
- **Monkwearmouth Railway Station.**
- **Museum of Science & Engineering, Newcastle-upon-Tyne.**
- **North East Aircraft Museum, Sunderland.**
- **St Mary's Lighthouse, Whitley Bay.**
- **Tynemouth Castle & Priory.**
- **University of Durham Botanical Gardens.**
- **Washington Old Hall.**
- **Washington Waterfowl Park.**

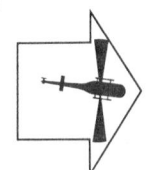

TREASURE HUNT 31

Speyside

START POSITION INNES HOUSE, FINDHORN BAY

CLUE ONE A famous naval signal, in a tower above the town where Banquo's ghost appeared, conceals or reveals your clue.

Leads to NELSON'S MONUMENT, FORRES   Standing high above the town is the tower erected as a monument to Lord Nelson. The clue is concealed behind Nelson's signal picture in the tower.

CLUE TWO 'This castle hath a pleasant seat, the air nimbly and sweetly recommends itself unto our gentle senses . . .' even though there is something smelly in the fish kettle.

Leads to CAWDOR CASTLE   Duncan's words from *Macbeth* lead to Cawdor Castle where, in the old kitchen, a salmon waits to be found in a fish kettle.

Reposition ROTHES GLEN

CLUE THREE Before there is whisky there has to be water, and a lot of it is confined in Glenlatterach. Your clue is on a door in the water.

Leads to GLENLATTERACH RESERVOIR   To the north west is this sizeable reservoir. The clue is pinned to the door of the tower.

CLUE FOUR If you can get into the new bit of No. 1 Warehouse at the Grant's place at Ballindalloch, the misplaced barrel is your goal.

Leads to GLENFARCLAS DISTILLERY   In bonded warehouse No. 1 at this distillery owned by J. & G. Grant, one of the barrels is out of place. A cheque is hidden beneath it.

CLUE FIVE To get up to the Glenlivet washbacks, enter under W.S.G. Smith's *initials*. **The bottle you want is labelled.**

Leads to GLENLIVET DISTILLERY   The washbacks, or fermentation vessels, are in the tun room. Over the door are the initials of Wm Smith-Grant. In a box of samples, the treasure is the one bottle that bears the 'The Glenlivet' label.

CLUE SIX Over the Spey, what once was the lair of the outlawed son of Robert II now stands in an isolated state of ruin. What was the lair?

CLUE SEVEN You may choose a fine old bridge, giving spectacular views, to lead you up to a detachment that will ring a bell. Where and what is the detachment?

Findhorn Bay.

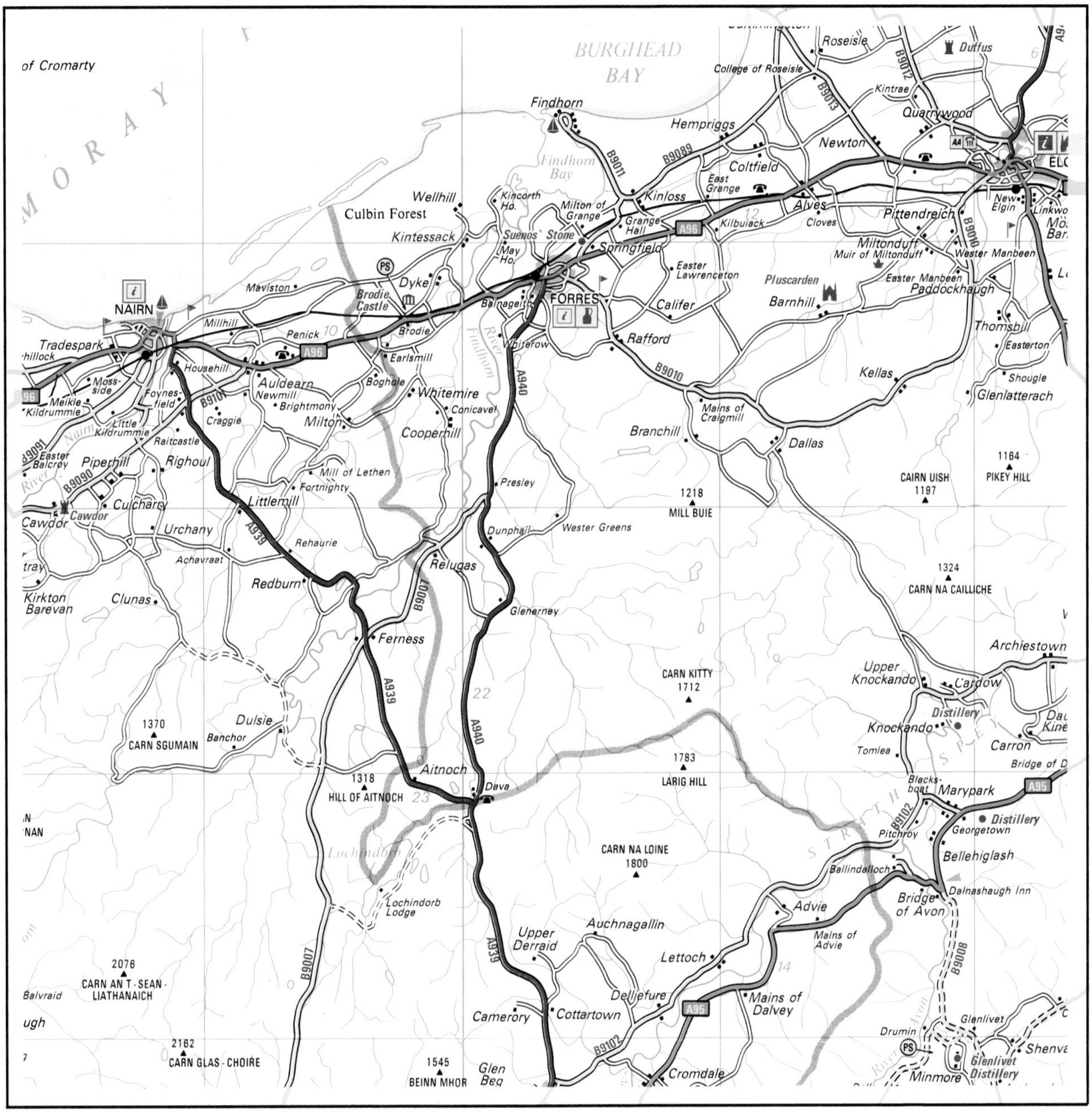

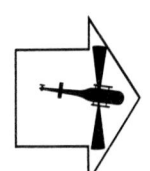

Forres

Moray, Morayshire

When shall we three meet again? In thunder,
   lightning or in rain?
When the hurlyburly's done, when the battle's lost
   and won.
That will be ere the set of the sun.
Where the place?
Upon the heath.
There to meet with Macbeth.

Shakespeare, *Macbeth*

In Shakespeare's *Macbeth,* the opening scene above
and the three which follow, are all set in and around
Forres, and there are several theories as to the exact
location of the 'blasted heath'. Contenders for the title
include Macbeth's Hillock, 5 miles to the west of the
town, and the Knock of Alves, 8 miles to the east.

Cawdor Castle

Nairn, Nairnshire

Although Cawdor owes its international fame to
Shakespeare's *Macbeth,* even the real Thanes of
Cawdor lived in a world where dark deeds were not
unusual. Within a space of 300 years, two Thanes
were murdered and several were killed in battle; the
ninth Thane slew his own brother-in-law 'under
silence of night' for having chained his sister naked to
a rock in the sea; the tenth Thane's niece and her
children were burned to death in their castle; the
thirteenth Thane died insane, and it is said that   his
brother-in-law died of laughter on hearing of the
restoration of Charles II. Still the home of Lord and
Lady Cawdor, the Thane's romantic castle is well
worthy of such a colourful past. Once across the
drawbridge, visitors can explore a series of rooms
which include the snug sitting room in the core of the
Tower, the dungeons, and the Old Kitchen with its

113

freshwater well. The room in the base of the tower is built around the trunk of a fourteenth-century thorn tree. Trees are also a magnificent feature of the castle grounds, which include three gardens, four nature trails, duck ponds, mini-golf and a putting green.

Guide to opening: May to October. [T] Cawdor (06677) 615 for details.

Glenfarclas Distillery

Ballindalloch, Banffshire

In 1836, tenant farmer John Grant built a small still on the land he rented for his cattle, and in 1865 bought the tenancy and the distillery for £511.19s.0d. At first, the distillery was rented out but in time the Grants took over the premises themselves and, on June 9 1870, John Grant's diary contained the momentous entry: 'Pumped first whisky at Glenfarclas, above 320 gallons.' Thus began the business which has spanned five generations of the Grant family to become one of few totally independent distilleries in the land. The Glenfarclas process uses pure water from the snow-flecked hills of Moray, and peat cut from Scottish hills, and after distillation the whisky is matured in old oak sherry casks which give it its distinctive hue. The result is a premium single malt whisky which, as they say, 'goes down singing hymns'. Visitors are welcome to tour the distillery, browse around the visitor centre, craft shop and exhibition and – of course – enjoy a 'wee dram'.

Guide to opening: all the year. [T] Ballindalloch (08072) 257 for details.

The Glenlivet Visitor Centre

Ballindalloch, Banffshire

In 1746, after the defeat of Bonnie Prince Charlie at Culloden, young Highlander John Gow fled with his family to Speyside where he Anglicised his name to John Smith and settled down to a new life. As a farmer he was soon distilling good but illicit malt whisky, and the fame of The Glenlivet spread far afield. In 1823 a new Act of Parliament made legal distilling a reasonable proposition, so John Smith's grandson George at last took out a license, and built The Glenlivet Distillery. The Glenlivet stayed in the family until 1978 when it became part of the Canadian company Seagram, under whose guidance it has become the leading malt whisky in the United States, and a well-known name in more than 100 other countries. As it is also the name of the glen, 'Glenlivet' appears on other labels too, but only this one distillery has the right to use the name by itself. The Glenlivet Visitor Centre is housed in the original maltings of the distillery. The Centre offers a 10-minute video presentation 'The Ballad of Glenlivet', together with tours of the distillery, and a taste of The Glenlivet itself.

A view of Cawdor through the poppies.

Guide to opening: April to October; other times by arrangement. [T] Glenlivet (08073) 427 for details.

The Malt Whisky Trail features seven distilleries which are open to visitors on a 70-mile, signposted route. A free leaflet outlining the route and giving brief details of the distilleries is available from: City of Aberdeen Tourist Board, St Nicholas House, Broad Street, Aberdeen, AB9 1DE. [T] Aberdeen (0224) 638727.

TOURIST INFORMATION

Tourist Information Centres: 17 High Street, **Elgin** [T] (0343) 3388. Falconer Museum, Tolbooth Street, **Forres** [T] (0309) 72938. 62 King Street, **Nairn** [T] (0667) 52753.

- Boath Doocot, Auldearn.
- Brodie Castle, Brodie.
- Darnaway Estate Visitor Centre, Brodie.
- Falconer Museum, Forres.
- Fishertown Museum, Nairn.
- Inshoch Castle, Penick.
- Kinloss Abbey, nr Findhorn.
- Lochnidorb Castle.
- Pluscarden Abbey.
- Rait Castle, nr Nairn.
- Viewfield Museum, Nairn.

TREASURE HUNT 32

Edinburgh

START POSITION LINLITHGOW PALACE

CLUE ONE General Tam Dalyell left his boots where his eponymous descendant now lives, under the royal plasterwork. The clue is in the right leg.

Leads to **HOUSE OF THE BINNS** Once the home of the General, this house is now occupied by Tam Dalyell MP. The General's boots are on display in a bedroom (with handsome plasterwork ceiling) and the clue is tucked into one of them.

CLUE TWO An inch below a bridge that spans the Forth will yield mugshots of the appropriate queen.

Leads to **INCH GARVIE** This island is connected by steps to the centre structure of the Forth Bridge. As Annie approaches the steps, she finds pinned to the railing a one penny coin minted in Queen Victoria's reign.

CLUE THREE The founder of the Rothschild/ Rosebery stud is visible from the air in the obvious place. He's got no shoes, so look for another boot.

Leads to **DALMENY HOUSE** A statue of King Tom, founder stallion of the stud, stands in the grounds of this home of the Earl of Rosebery. In a boot beside the statue, the clue is hidden.

CLUE FOUR There's an Ancient Monument embedded in the south eastern suburbs, and embedded in the fireplace in Queen Mary's room is a crown.

Leads to **CRAIGMILLAR CASTLE** Lying south east of Edinburgh is this well-fortified castle. The clue, a crown, is hidden in the fireplace in Queen Mary's room.

CLUE FIVE Uter Pendragon's son must have had a peculiar backside if this last site is any indication. What you seek was once very difficult to get hold of.

Linlithgow Palace.

Leads to **ARTHUR'S SEAT** Arthur, son of Uter Pendragon, leads to this extinct volcano. The treasure, reminding us of Arthurian legend, is a sword in a stone plinth on the summit.

CLUE SIX A salute was too much for Uncle Philip's impressive present to James II, and bang it went! Now restored, this magnificent gift dominates a castle vault. What is its name?

CLUE SEVEN Logarithms and Law each have their place in the history of this mansion, but it is the conditional bequest of Mr and Mrs Reid that has left a lasting impression of Edwardian times. What is the name of this mansion?

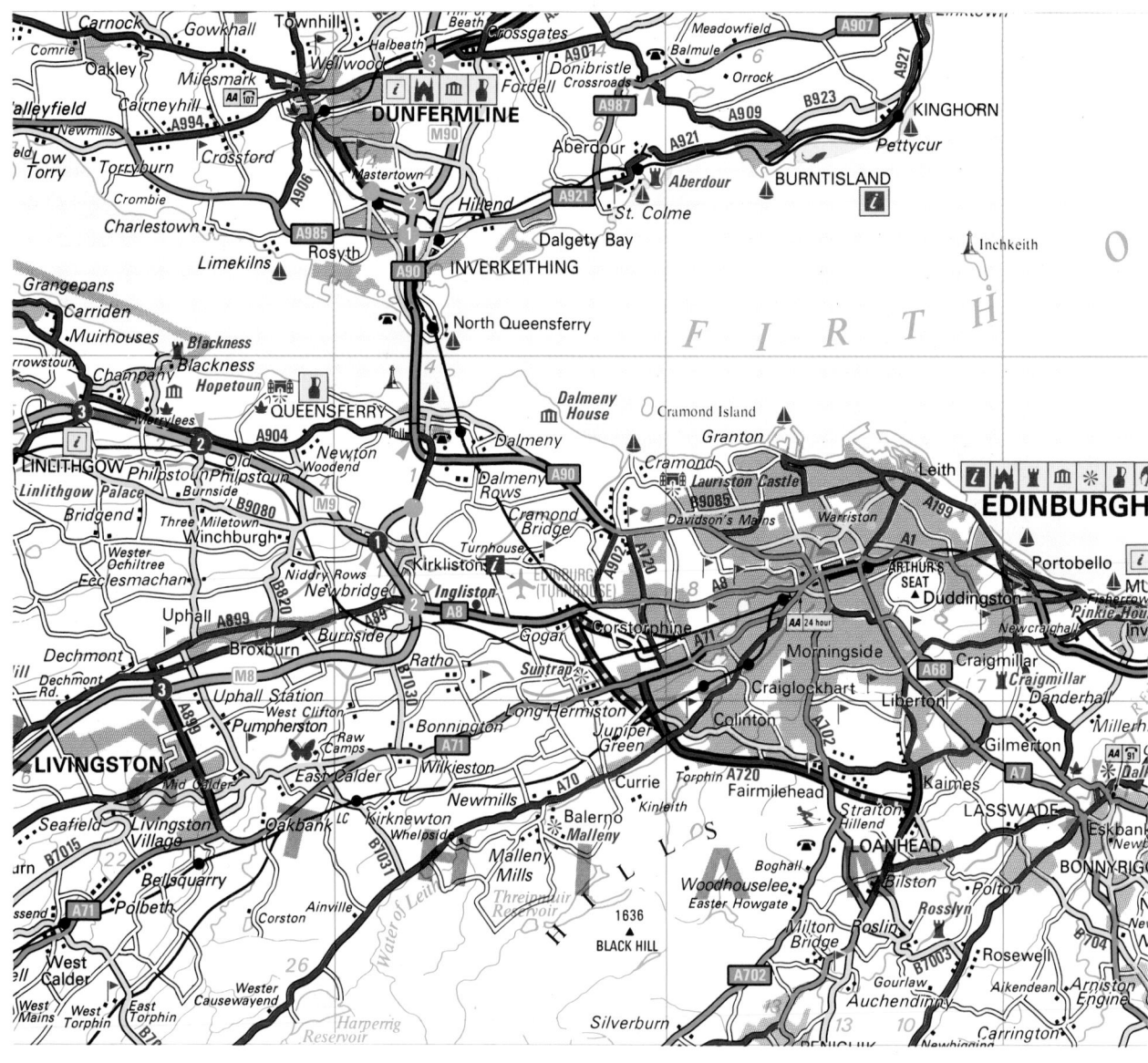

Linlithgow Palace

Linlithgow, Lothian

The magnificent ruins of this royal palace stand on a knoll jutting into the waters of the loch. Older palaces have stood here, but the present building was started by James I of Scotland in 1426 and additions continued intermittently for 100 years. Linlithgow saw the birth of James V of Scotland in 1512, and Mary Queen of Scots was born here on 8 December 1542; she became queen just one week later following her father's death (he supposedly died of a broken heart following the defeat of his army by the English at the Battle of Solway Moss). By this time the palace had achieved its present shape, and Mary's mother (Mary of Guise) declared she had never seen such a 'princely palace' but, following the transfer of the Scottish Court to London, Linlithgow soon fell into disrepair.

In 1745, Bonnie Prince Charlie landed in Scotland to try to regain the throne of Britain for his father, the son of the deposed James II, and he was entertained at Linlithgow on his way south. 1746 saw 'Butcher Cumberland' and his troops quartered here after the disastrous Battle of Culloden in which the half-starved and exhausted Highlands, led by the Bonnie Prince, lost over 1200 men. Cumberland's troops also set the seal on Linlithgow's fate: in 1746, a fire broke out, and the palace was destroyed leaving just the ruins which remain today.

Guide to opening: Easter to October. [T] Linlithgow (0506) 844600 for details.

House of the Binns

Linlithgow, Lothian

The historic home of the Dalyells sits aside twin hills known as 'binns' in old Scots. In 1612, it was bought by Thomas Dalyell who enlarged and altered the house thus setting a precedent which culminated in a complete refacing of the building in the nineteenth century. Outstanding features such as the exquisite seventeenth-century plaster moulded ceilings were retained along the way, and as a result this Regency style country mansion represents a broad mixture of architectural tastes. The Binns has gone down in legend as the home of General Tam Dalyell, the larger-than-life son of Sir Thomas. A staunch royalist in the Civil War, he was placed in charge of His Majesty's Forces in Scotland by Charles II and charged with the task of suppressing the Covenanters. The stern measures he used to achieve this earned him the title 'The bluidie Muscovite'. General Tam is certainly known more for his personality than for his profession. An eccentric, who married four times without the blessing of the church, he went down in legend as a brutal soldier who roasted his prisoners alive, and there are numerous stories of his 'trookings' with the Devil. One relates how the Devil lost his temper when losing at cards and threw the table at the General's head, which it missed and fell into the pond; an old table was found there in 1878 and is now on show in the house.

Guide to opening: Easter, April to September. [T] Philipstoun (050683) 4255.

Dalmeny House
South Queensferry, Edinburgh, Lothian

Dalmeny House has been the home of the Primrose family, Earls of Rosebery, for over 300 years. Set in beautiful parklands on the shores of the Firth of Forth, the present house was designed by William Watkins in 1815, and with its fantastic exterior decorations, fan vaulted corridors and hammerbeam hall it was Scotland's first Gothic Revival house. The contents of the house are as splendid as their setting, for Dalmeny boasts two famous collections of fine things. The first, the Rosebery Collection comprises early Scottish portraits, seventeenth-century furniture and Goya tapestries together with eighteenth-century political portraits by Reynolds, Gainsborough, Raeburn and Lawrence collected by the fifth Earl when he was the Liberal Prime Minister. The second is the Rothschild Collection which comprises superb French eighteenth-century tapestries and paintings, all of which came from Mentmore in Buckinghamshire. This collection features some exquisite pieces of Sèvres porcelain which was a particular favourite of Madame de Pompadour, mistress of Louis XV. To please her, the king rescued the Sèvres factory from bankruptcy, even conducting private sales of its wares in his dining room at Christmas. In contrast to such delicate displays, Lord Rosebery's Sitting Room is a very masculine place; it is sacred to mementos of racing and the world-famous Mentmore Stud, whose horses won the Derby seven times.

Guide to opening: May to September. [T] 031–331 1888 for details.

Dalmeny House, home of the Mentmore Stud.

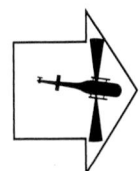

Edinburgh's extinct volcano – Arthur's Seat.

Craigmillar Castle

Craigmillar, near Edinburgh, Lothian

Craigmillar is best known for its association with Mary Queen of Scots, and the part it played in the death of her second husband, Lord Darnley. Mary came to the castle following a severe illness, and during her stay here she suffered from a deep depression which had its roots in the murder of her Italian secretary, Riccio, at Holyrood in 1566. Riccio had been dragged screaming from Mary's presence and stabbed by a group of nobles, abetted by Darnley whom she already held in contempt. The French Ambassador who attended her at Craigmillar reported that 'she is in the hands of the physicians, and not at all well. During her stay at the castle a group of nobles hatched a plot to be rid of Darnley and in 1567 he was murdered at Kirk o' Field. The suspicion that Mary had been involved later helped to feed the discontent which led to her abdication.

Though in ruins, Craigmillar is still a handsome structure, with fifteenth- and sixteenth-century curtain walls and courtyard buildings spreading from the base of a fourteenth-century tower house. The tower affords wide views over Edinburgh, 2½ miles away, and of Arthur's Seat, the final destination of this Hunt.

Guide to opening: all year. [T] Edinburgh 031-244 3101 for details.

Arthur's Seat

Holyrood Park, Edinburgh, Lothian

It is not every city that has an extinct volcano in its midst, but Edinburgh does, and no visitor can miss it. Arthur's Seat has nothing to do with the legendary king, but probably arrived at its present name through a corruption of Archers' Seat. Set right in the centre of Holyrood Park it is a dramatic sight, yet it is easily climbed, and its 823-foot summit gives the very best views of the capital. The cliffs on its western side are known as Salisbury Crags, and the 'Wells o' Wearie' at its base are said to have been named by people worn out after trudging out here to draw their water.

TOURIST INFORMATION

Tourist Information Centres: 4 Kirkgate, **Burntisland** [T] (0592) 872667. Glen Bridge, **Dunfermline** [T] (0383) 720999. Waverley Market, **Edinburgh** [T] 031-557 1700. **Forth Road Bridge** [T] (0383) 417759. Burgh Halls, **Linlithgow** [T] (0506) 844600.

Edinburgh attractions include:
Edinburgh Castle; Edinburgh Wax Museum; Edinburgh Zoo; John Knox House; Museum of Childhood; National Gallery of Scotland; Palace of Holyroodhouse; Royal Botanic Garden; Royal Museum of Scotland; Royal Scottish Academy;
St Giles Cathedral; Scott Monument; Scottish National Gallery of Modern Art; Scottish National Portrait Gallery.

Other Attractions:
- **Blackness Castle.**
- **Edinburgh Butterfly & Insect World, Lasswade.**
- **Hopetown House, South Queensferry.**
- **Inchholm Island & Abbey, Dalgety Bay.**
- **Livingston Mill Farm & Country Museum.**
- **Rosslyn Castle.**

TREASURE HUNT 33

Ayrshire

START POSITION LOCH FERGUS

***CLUE ONE* By the banks and braes o' bonnie Doon, where Tam O'Shanter fled, look above a keystone.**

Leads to **BRIG O'DOON, ALLOWAY** Tam O'Shanter fled from Alloway across the Bridge over the River Doon. The clue is on the keystone of the bridge.

***CLUE TWO* Between Brown Carrick and Blackburn, Redcoats are in the swim. See if they'll play ball.**

Leads to **BUTLINS HOLIDAY CAMP** Between Brown Carrick Hill and Blackburn is the holiday camp. In the paddling pool, Redcoats and children are playing with a ball on which the clue is stuck.

***CLUE THREE* In the towering home of the abbot who got a roasting in the Black Vault of Dunure, see what's left over the fireplace.**

Leads to **CROSSRAGUEL ABBEY** The Abbot of Crossraguel was roasted alive in the Black Vault of Dunure Castle. The clue hangs over the fireplace.

Thirteenth-century Crossraguel Abbey.

***CLUE FOUR* Find a link between Eisenhower and Kennedy and look behind Adam's colour scheme for a room in the round.**

Leads to **CULZEAN CASTLE** General Eisenhower was given a flat in the Castle, which is a former home of the Kennedy family. The castle was converted by Robert Adam; behind his drawing of the Circular Room's ceiling is hidden the clue.

***CLUE FIVE* Where others leave for Ailsa Craig, go in search of a life saver in the shape of Philip Vaux.**

Leads to **GIRVAN HARBOUR** Girvan, departure point for visitors to Ailsa Craig, is the home of the Philip Vaux Lifeboat. The boat is out, so Anneka tracks it down, and is then dropped by helicopter into the sea. She is rescued by the crew who have the treasure on board.

***CLUE SIX* In the village where Burns was set off at a tangent and John Davidson used to cobble shoes, a restored ale-house shelters some well-known figures. What is the name of the village?**

***CLUE SEVEN* It was horror tales of this kirk 'where ghaists and houlets nightly cry' that inspired 'Tam o' Shanter'. Which one was it?**

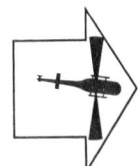

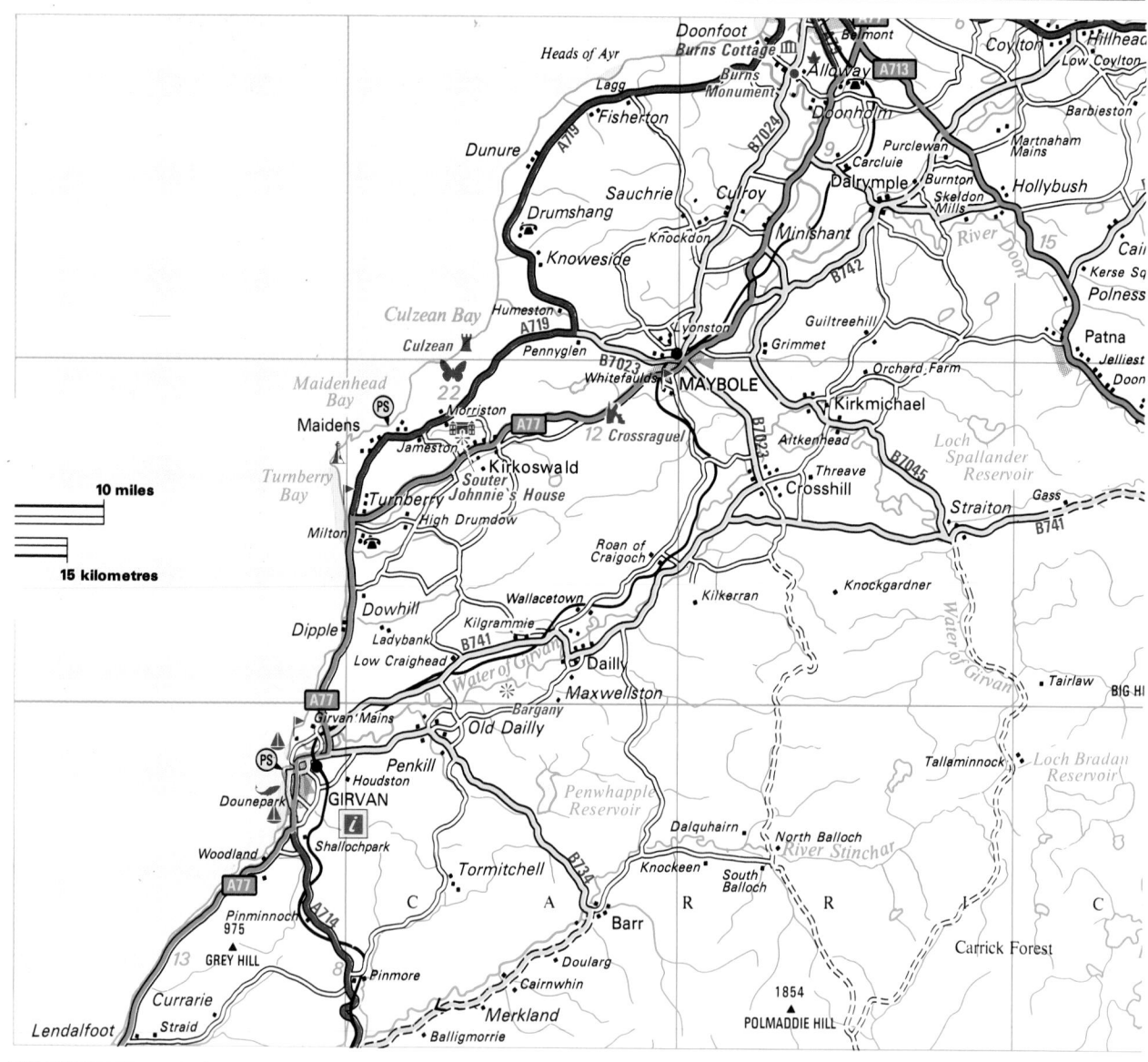

Alloway

The eldest son of a farmer, Robert Burns was born in Alloway and lived here for five years before moving to a small farm nearby. He grew up in a world of toil and poverty, yet despite this his father saw to it that his sons were well educated, and his mother taught him the many folk songs which she knew. He loved song and when he began to write at the age of 15 his poems took this form. He went on to become Scotland's greatest collector of folk songs. In 1785 he began writing satires and 'epistles' which won him local fame, and in 1786 the success of the first edition of his poems encouraged a move to Edinburgh, where he was lionised by society. Through his friends there he obtained a minor post in the Excise in Dumfreisshire, where he eked out his salary by continuing to farm. Promotion followed, and finally he was able to leave farming and moved into Dumfries where he died in 1796 at the age of only 37.

His popular poetry and colourful character have combined to make Burns a Scottish hero, and his birthplace is now one of the best known places on the tourist map. Yet Alloway was famous in the poet's own lifetime too; the ancient bridge (Brig o' Doon) and other local landmarks made a memorable appearance in the narrative poem 'Tam o' Shanter', the humorous story of witchcraft inspired by folk tales Burns remembered from his youth.

Land o' Burns Centre marks the start of the Burns Heritage Trail, which runs from Alloway to Dumfries and links the many places of interest associated with the poet. The centre itself presents an audio-visual introduction to the man and his life, together with an enticing preview of the trail.

Guide to opening: all the year. [T] Alloway (0292) 43700 for details. The Burns Heritage Trail brochure is available free from The Scottish Tourist Board, 23 Ravelston Terrace, Edinburgh EH4 3EU.

Burns Cottage is the birthplace of the poet which now includes a large museum, gift shop and tearoom.

Guide to opening: all the year. [T] Alloway (0292) 41215 for details.

Burns Monument & Gardens was erected in 1820. This handsome monument overlooks the famous Brig o' Doon, now landscaped with restful riverside gardens.

Guide to opening: April to October. [T] Alloway (0292) 41321 for details.

Crossraguel Abbey

Near Maybole

One of the few Cluniac houses in Scotland, Crossraguel was founded in the early thirteenth century by Duncan, Earl of Carrick. In 1404 it received a charter from Robert III confirming its extensive wealth and giving its abbot jurisdiction, thereby making him the most powerful person in Ayrshire. Yet just over one hundred years later, the end of the abbey was already in sight.

The abbey ruins which survive today reflect the former importance of Crossraguel, and are of high architectural distinction. The walls of the church and chapter house generally remain to eaves' level, and there are clear remains of all the other buildings here including: a lovely circular dovecot; the bakehouse (still with a large oven); the corrodiars' houses built for abbey 'pensioners'; and the abbot's house itself. It was William Kennedy who extended the house with a four-storey tower (probably to accommodate his ward, the third Earl of Cassillis), and who further dignified the abbey with the addition of an imposing Gatehouse, now rerolled and floored.

Guide to opening: all the year. [T] Edinburgh 031-244 3101 for details.

Culzean Castle and Country Park

Maybole

The flagship of the National Trust for Scotland, Culzean Castle is a triumphant blend of romance and restraint. It owes its present form to the instigation of the tenth Earl of Cassillis, who called in fellow Scotsman Robert Adam to transform a square fortified house into an imposing and comfortable residence. Work went on from 1777 to 1792, by which time Culzean had emerged as a romantic thing of towers and turrets, with a graceful and restrained interior which represents the classic perfection of Robert Adam's art. For the last 40 years or so the Trust has been busy restoring the castle to its former glory. The result is a series of memorable rooms, linked by a dramatic Oval Staircase with Corinthian columns, and crowned by the splendour of the Saloon. Eighteenth-century elegance within and untamed sea and mountains without, this is one of the finest of Robert Adam's many wonderful rooms.

In 1969, 560 acres of ground belonging to the castle became Scotland's first Country Park, offering long and solitary woodland walks, and 3 miles of coastline with rocky shore, sandy beaches and spectacular views over the Firth of Clyde. What was once the estate home farm is now the Visitor Centre, providing the focal point of many other attractions which include two gardens, a forestry exhibition, play areas, adventure playgrounds, a deer park, aviary, a regular programme of ranger guided walks, talks and film nights and numerous special events.

Guide to opening: Castle, April to October; Country park, all the year. [T] Kirkoswald (06556) 269 for details. NT

Girvan

Girvan is the leading resort on Scotland's south-west coast, and an ideal centre from which to visit the lovely locations shown on this Hunt. The town is spread around a bay of safe sandy beaches, facing out over the Firth of Clyde to a large island 10½ miles offshore. The harbour itself is still in use by fishing fleets, and is one of the town's most picturesque features. Other seafront attractions include the pier and promenade, entertainments Pavilion, children's fun fair, boating lake, amusement arcade, colourful gardens and all the facilities usual to a thriving family resort.

TOURIST INFORMATION

Tourist Information Centres: **Culzean Castle** [T] (0656) 293. Bridge Street, **Girvan** [T] (0465) 4950.

- **Carleton Castle, Lendalfoot.**
- **Electric Brae (optical illusion), nr Dunure.**
- **Fantasyland, Beach Pavilion, Girvan.**
- **Souter Johnnie's House, Kirkoswald.**
- **Turnberry Castle.**

Alloway, birthplace of Robert Burns.

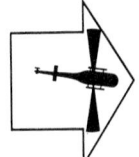

TREASURE HUNT 34

Stirlingshire

START POSITION STIRLING UNIVERSITY

CLUE ONE In Mary's crowning town, above Argyll's lodging and beyond the forework, there's a major opportunity to pick a pocket among the drones and chanters.

Leads to **STIRLING CASTLE**   Past the Argyll Lodging (town house of the Dukes of Argyll) and beyond the entrance (forework) to the castle, where Mary Queen of Scots was crowned, a pipe band is playing in the Lower Square. The clue is in the Drum Major's sporran.

CLUE TWO The real-life Orwell meets a bulldog at an animal farm. Ask for the leonine playgroup – and look out!

Leads to **BLAIR DRUMMOND SAFARI PARK**   Blair was the real name of George Orwell, author of *Animal Farm* and Bulldog Drummond is another literary hint. Inside the lion (leonine) and tiger cub enclosure, tied to a fallen log, is the clue.

CLUE THREE Up and Doune to Royce's Old Girl.

Leads to **DOUNE MOTOR MUSEUM**   North, now, to Doune! The clue is on a Rolls Royce called the 'Old Girl'.

CLUE FOUR Sounds like it's time to visit Tannochbrae. Check at the Spindle – it's got just what the doctor ordered.

Leads to **CALLANDER**   In the main street of this homonym of 'calendar' is a shop called 'The Spindle'. The clue is hidden in the (Doctor) Cameron tartan.

CLUE FIVE Prior knowledge would help on Scotland's only lake. Before you reach the aumbry, look for the ling on the lancets.

Leads to **INCHMAHOME PRIORY**   Lake Menteith and prior(y) knowledge lead to the priory where the treasure, a sprig of heather (ling), is hanging from a lancet-shaped window in the east gable. The aumbry is a recess ro church vessels.

Stirling Castle, scene of the coronation of Mary Queen of Scots.

CLUE SIX Above Abbey Craig, 246 steps will bring you to the point. Take a look around and, inside, identify a famous two-handed implement. What is it?

CLUE SEVEN He may have become James VI's Lieutenant for the Plantation of Nova Scotia, but it was here that life began for Sir William, as present day displays recall. Where was Sir William's birthplace?

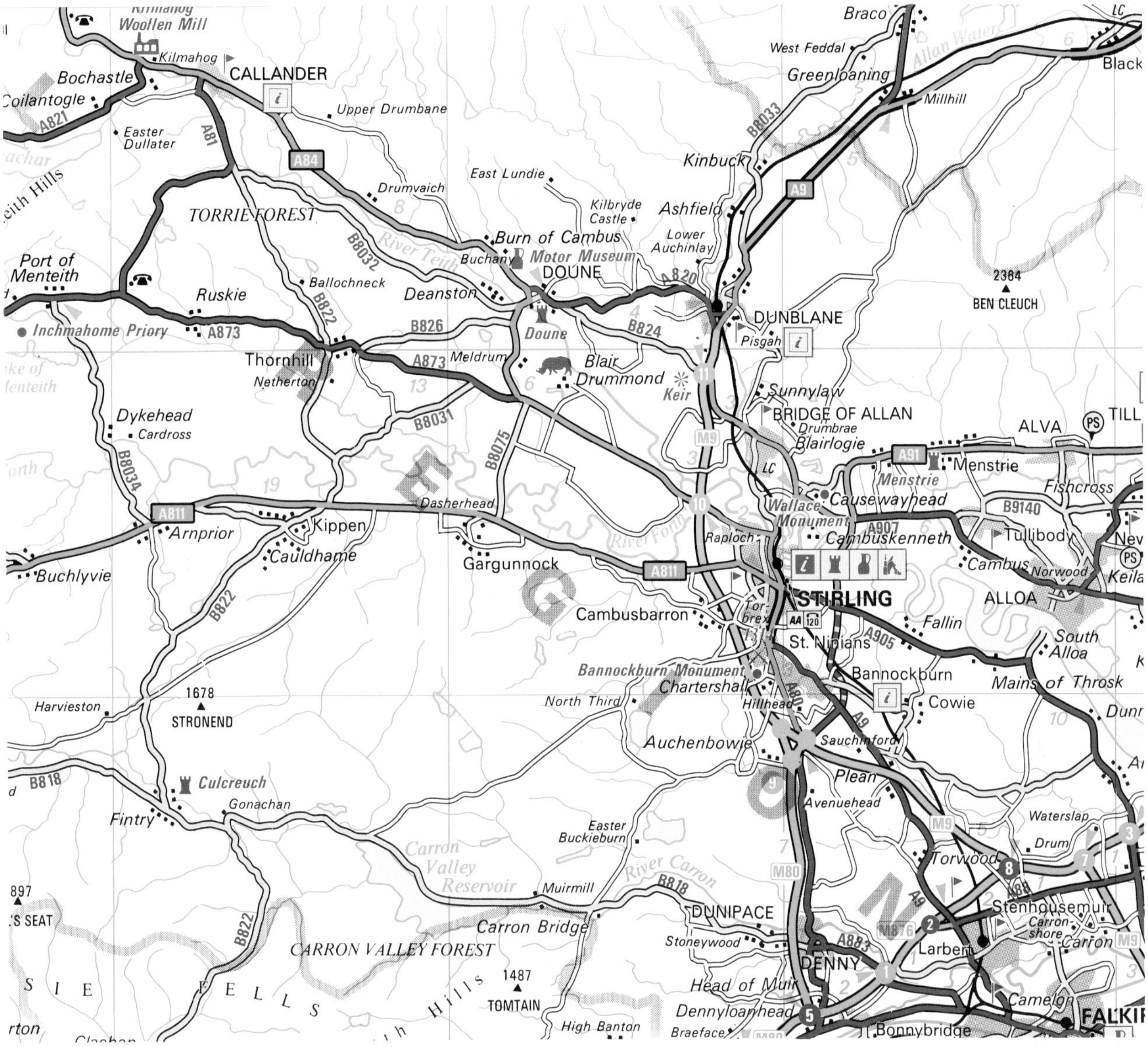

Stirling Castle

Stirling, Stirlingshire

As one of the most important castles in the kingdom, Stirling served not only as a military stronghold, but also as the favoured residence of successive Scottish kings. The twelfth-century castle was the home of the Canmore dynasty, and subsequent rulers continued to fortify this rocky site as it guarded the principal routes across Scotland. The stone castle which stood here by the late thirteenth century was to play a major part in the struggle against English overlordship, and to witness some notable events. In 1297 the Scots overthrew the English in a famous victory at Stirling Bridge, but by 1313 it was the English who held the castle, though under seige; their attempt to lift the seige gave Robert the Bruce his victory at the Battle of Bannockburn.

The sixteenth century again saw Stirling as a favoured royal residence; Mary Queen of Scots was crowned in the Chapel Royal in 1533, and her son the future James VI of Scotland and his son Henry were both baptised here, but when James went south to accept the English crown in 1603, Stirling lost much of its prestige. It was never to be re-established as a court for Stuart kings.

Today's visitors are able to explore the defences and see the main buildings of the Royal Residence, much restored. Chief among them are the Great Hall (mainly the work of James IV), the handsome Chapel Royal (reconstructed by James VI), and the Kings Old Building (now housing the Argyll and Sutherland Highlanders Regiment). The Old Palace which dates from the 1540s is of outstanding historic and architectural importance; its exterior represents one of the earliest British attempts at a classical façade, and its interior has been restored to show the original layout and function of the royal rooms. The castle now has a Visitor Centre, where an audio-visual presentation explains the full history and significance of the building.

Guide to opening: all the year. [T] Stirling (0786) 50000 for details.

123

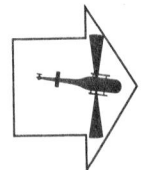

Blair Drummond Safari and Leisure Park

Near Stirling, Stirlingshire

Clue 2 lent a natural touch to this *Treasure Hunt* trail. Scotland's only safari and leisure park offers a family day out 'in the wild', where visitors come face to face with zebras and camels, elephants, lions, tigers and a variety of other animals all roaming free in drive-through reserves. The penguins have a big new pool to themselves, and visitors can take to the water too aboard the popular Chimp Island and Waterfowl Sanctuary Cruise. Children tend to make a bee-line for the Monkey House, home of Sam the baby chimpanzee, and for Pets' Farm where residents include donkeys, ponies, piglets, rabbits, wallabies, rheas, goats and peafowl. Other highlights here include an Adventure Playground, Amusement Arcade and Children's Rides, and 'Cinema 180' which presents a breathtaking rollercoaster ride or a bird's-eye view of the Grand Canyon, both in 3D vision. Anyone who works up an appetite will find plenty of refreshments in the park, together with a picnic area fully-equipped with barbecue facilities.

Guide to opening: March to October. [T] Stirling (0786) 841456 for details.

One of the residents at Blair Drummond.

Doune Motor Museum

Doune, Perthshire

In 1953 when the Earl of Moray (then Lord Doune) bought a 1934 Type 26 Hispano-Suiza for his own use, he unwittingly laid the foundation of what was to become a unique collection of vintage and non-vintage thoroughbred cars. In the early 1960s the Hispano was joined by a 1933 Invicta and Abbot Bentley, together with an SS 100 Jaguar and A CM Masarati to be used as Hill Climb competition cars. The idea of a museum was gradually taking shape, and following the opening of the Doune Hill Climb Course in 1968, the adjacent farm buildings were converted to house and display the cars. New purchases were made in the late 1960s, and several cars of special interest have since been loaned to the museum by private owners. Now some 40 cars are on display here ranging from a 1965 Ford GT 40 to the second oldest Rolls Royce in the world, yet despite its size the collection makes no claims to represent any particular motoring theme, remaining as it began, a personal and pleasing selection of attractive cars. The museum now provides an appropriate setting for vintage rallies and other motoring events, including Hill Climbs in April, June and September.

Guide to opening: April to October. [T] Doune (0786) 841203 for details.

Callander

Perthshire

As the 'Gateway to the Trossachs' Callander is one of Scotland's most popular holiday resorts, and it looks after its visitors well. Ceilidhs, open-air pipe band performances and Highland dancing displays give a taste of traditional entertainment at its best, and shops selling local crafts and quality Scottish goods stay open late to cater for holidaymakers taking an evening stroll. The little town is widely known as the Tannockbrae of *Dr Finlay's Casebook* and more recently as the setting for *The Country Diary of an Edwardian Lady* both of which showed something of its surroundings. Picturesque walks lead to beauty spots like the Falls of Leny or Bracklinn Falls (which Sir Walter Scott once crossed on horseback for a bet) and the heart of the Trossachs is just an easy drive away. This gives southerners their first taste of the Highlands, and most find the unique areas of mountains, glens and lochs a romantic sight. Wordsworth, Coleridge and Queen Victoria were among the earliest tourists to come here, fired by Sir Walter Scott's vivid descriptions of a landscape he found 'so wonderous wild the whole might seem The scenery of a fairy dream.' In particular, his 'Lady of the Lake' was inspired by Loch Katrine, and now tourists can admire the loch from a steamer which bears his name.

A leaflet entitled *The Trossachs Trail* guides motorists through the heart of this lovely area and is available free from The Loch Lomond, Stirling and Trossachs Tourist Board, 41 Dumbarton Road, Stirling or from local Tourist Information Centres.

Inchmahome Priory

Near Port of Menteith, Perthshire

Built on a secluded island in the Lake of Menteith, Inchmahome has one of the most attractive and romantic settings of any of Scotland's medieval religious houses. The priory was founded in the thirteenth century for a small community of Augustinian canons, but its greatest claim to fame is as the hiding place of the infant Mary Queen of Scots, who was brought here from Stirling for safe-keeping when an English army invaded the lowlands in 1547. Today, only parts of the church and claustral buildings remain, together with a little garden popularly known as 'Queen Mary's Bower'. The island may be reached by a regular boat service operating from the Port of Menteith.

Guide to opening: April to September. [T] Stirling (0786) 50000 for details.

TOURIST INFORMATION

Tourist Information Centres: Leny Road, **Callander** [T] (0877) 30342. Stirling Road, **Dunblane** [T] (0786) 824428. Dumbarton Road, **Stirling** [T] (0786) 75019.

- **Bannockburn Monument & Heritage Centre.**
- **Cambuskenneth Abbey, Stirling.**
- **Church of the Holy Rude, Stirling.**
- **Cowane's House, Stirling.**
- **Culcreuch Castle, Fintry.**
- **Dunblane Cathedral.**
- **Kilmahog Woollen Mill, Callander.**
- **Menstrie Castle.**
- **Smith Art Gallery & Museum, Stirling.**
- **Wallace Monument, Stirling.**

Inchmahome Priory–refuge for Mary Queen of Scots

Index

Solve
The Best of
Treasure Hunt
competition

and you could win the first prize of:

£1000

Also to be won –
10 runners-up prizes of ETB weekend breaks

Part One
Work out the answers to the two competition clues which accompany every hunt. Write out your answers. (You should have 68.)

Part Two
The 68 answers from Part One are also the solutions to the 68 cryptic clues below. Match each answer to its clue. This will provide the order in which the answers must be written into the grid on page 128. The answers should be written from left to right, one letter to a square, starting from the top left hand corner. Hyphens count as one square and there are no spaces between words. None of the answers include definite or indefinite articles, i.e. the, a, or an.

There are a total of 21 blocked-in squares. Ten are printed in the grid, the remaining 11 must be fitted in along with the answers. There is never more than one blocked-in square to a line.

When the answers and the 11 blocked in squares have been correctly arranged in the grid, a phrase, reading from bottom to top will appear in the question mark . . . it's what no successful treasure hunter should be without!

Cryptic Clues

1 Family blemish on aviary.
2 Beginner is fried in aching hell.
3 No love for the flying ace.
4 Bird calls in a northerly direction.
5 Girl in middle in Merchant's Harbour.
6 Sell a sandbank and go Scottish.
7 Five hundred lure bird when drunk with royal leader.
8 Nine piece suite?
9 Watch rebel collar old penny in fracas.
10 Drunken attempt almost blanches model Charlie.
11 The points have gone.
12 Mallet game almost played on Anglesey.
13 Europe was free before the Sun rose.
14 Prefer brisket?
15 Last male preserve adds year in anger overturned.
16 Illiterate Welshman ignites element before asking why.
17 Prevent ship having races with a poet and philosopher.
18 Boot around little Wesley.
19 The smell in 'ades we hear.
20 I crossed Milwall by Russia.
21 Did Mary live chez Ron?
22 Tea for Bee in murder site.
23 Participle wearing two thirds of a hat.
24 Exist on motorway span.
25 Fish carries weight – a long way to Lancashire town.
26 Confused, one carries germ and dines with British Rail.
27 Two-man dwelling?
28 Ancient Stoker quietly goes north.
29 Is Mercury sick with hydrogen?
30 Mister Banjo.
31 Mancunian range.
32 Lake is fashionable at 500; rook stands on globe.

33 Plover in best of health.
34 Singular Irish folk band.
35 Author, marshall and biologist.
36 Admiral's caravan.
37 Lobby, finally oriental sieve's lair.
38 Racket – alternatively trimmed candle.
39 Foil for fish.
40 Tipsy clown goes south for valuation.
41 Say, covered Eden.
42 Thorax hesitates before French highway.
43 Rex's interval.
44 Will ye trouble more?
45 Down is not central.
46 A cuckoo flew over his nest, royal included.
47 Home for wayward animals?
48 What is found in Will Tudor.
49 Regard Valhalla in turmoil with a policeman's lens.
50 A divine manor for the family.
51 Amusement reverses into pasture.
52 Lawrence surrounds lost cats about north.
53 Jimmy's giant?
54 Entreat beginner over house of cards.
55 . . . and effect short question before enemy.
56 Otherwise mouse litter tower.
57 Captain Mosley.
58 A cook mixes a promise.
59 Officer cracks cipher with first rule.
60 Is this a steeple?
61 Mad minstrel with bag nearly comes to tea.
62 Fool acts to scatter one of the pieces.
63 Mount Margaret.
64 Milky greeting?
65 This explosive can discolour.
66 Doctor cries in pain before racer.
67 Crusty as he turns out.
68 The hip fifties ring a bell in days gone by.

Tie-breaker

Complete the following phrase in no more than fifteen words:

Treasure Hunt is my favourite programme because

....

....

....

....

To Enter

Either fill in and cut out the grid on this page, or photocopy it. Send in the completed grid, along with your 68 clue solutions on a separate piece of paper and the completed tie-breaker.

Send your entry (only .the solutions please, not a detailed explanation of how they were arrived at) together with the price corner from the front jacket flap or other proof of purchase to:

> Treasure Hunt Competition,
> Boxtree Ltd,
> 36 Tavistock Street,
> London WC2E 7PB

Entries should arrive by 30 November, 1989.

RULES

1 Competition closes 30 November, 1989.
2 Employees and their families of Chatsworth Television, Channel 4 Television and Boxtree Limited and their agencies, participating bookshops and anyone connected with the competition are not eligible to enter.
3 Judges decision is final.
4 Winner will be notified and announced in the *TVTimes*.
5 Full rules available from above address. Please send a stamped addressed envelope with your request. After 6 January, 1990, winner's name and correct answers also available.

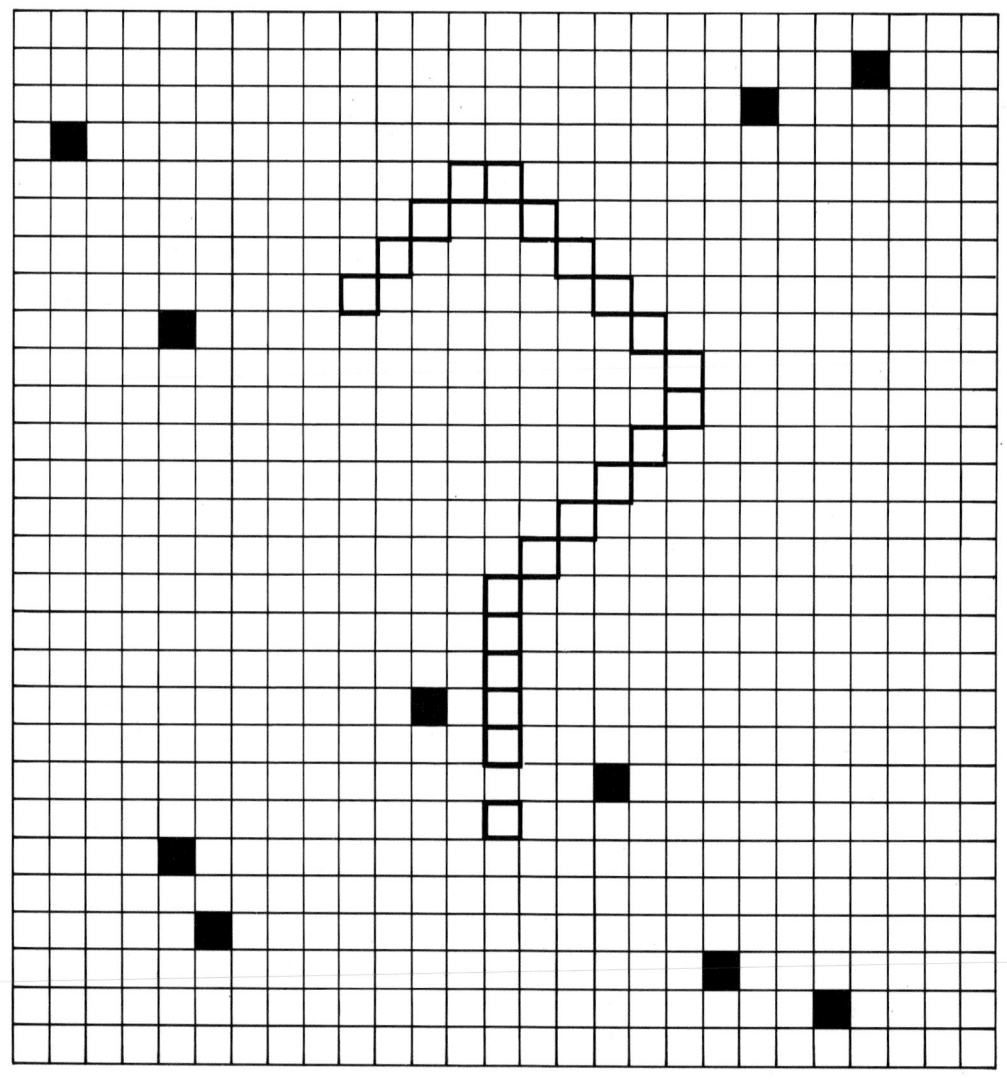